MW01154202

The Gardener's Palette

The Gardener's Palette

Creating Colour Harmony in the Garden

JO THOMPSON

TIMBER PRESS
Portland, OR

Photo and illustration credits appear on page 372.

Published by Timber Press, Inc., in association with The Royal Horticultural Society
The Haseltine Building
133 S.W. Second Avenue, Suite 450
Portland, Oregon 97204-3527
timberpress.com

Printed in China on paper from responsible sources
Text design by Rita Sowins

The colour palettes for each featured entry were inspired by the RHS Colour Chart, the standard reference used by horticulturists worldwide for recording plant colours. Resembling a paint chart, it has 920 colours which can be matched precisely to flowers, fruits and other plants in order to record and communicate colours accurately across the world. It is available to purchase online from the RHS.

ISBN 978-1-60469-959-3
Catalogue records for this book are available from the Library of Congress and the British Library.

Contents

Introduction

An enormous grace arises from the harmony of colours and lines.

—*from* Commentary on Plato's Symposium on Love, *Marsilio Ficino, 1484*

I wish you could see what I see out the windows—the earth pink and yellow cliffs to the north—the full pale moon about to go down in an early morning lavender sky behind a very long beautiful tree-covered mesa to the west—pink and purple hills in front and the scrubby fine dull green cedars—and a feeling of much space—It is a very beautiful world.

—Georgia O'Keeffe to Arthur Dove, 1942

Colour exists. It is an entity that scientists will say is the result of reflected light. For the purposes of this book, colour is very much a "thing," and each colour, each tone and hue, are real. To me, colour exists not only as an entity but also as a sentiment. Experiences, memories, all form associations with colour; one person's lilac is another one's mauve. I have never been quite sure what mauve is—I had it down as a purple, but others will confidently point towards a pinky blue.

And it's not just me. People have been wrestling with colour for a long time: how to define it in words, how to capture it in form, how to harness it in thought, how to apply it in our world. Is it subjective, is it objective? How can we see it as a whole when—although it may seem material and our experience of it physical—it is in fact simply sensory and cultural, according to our lived experience?

Theories on colour go back as far as Aristotle, with layers of meaning as many in number as the 346,000 to even 17 million colours that are thought to exist. From Dante and Leonardo da Vinci through to Goethe and Braque, artists, philosophers, scientists, and writers have all contributed to the investigation of colour, its theory, its psychology, its application in art, culture, and science. The first record of a colour chart to describe plants and animals dates from 1686, when Walter Charleton created a system of five primary colours (white, black, yellow, red, and blue) and five secondary (green, purple, grey, brown, and bay), with further subdivisions relating each to colours of the natural world—for example, "yellow like the yolk of an egg." Isaac Newton, he of the colour wheel, presented colours, seven in number, to fit in conveniently with the number of notes on a music scale and generally with the Classical notion of seven—although in Canto 29 of his *Purgatorio*, Dante had already preempted Newton by over 350 years: "I saw the flames advance, leaving the air behind them tinted, and they had the appearance of trailing banners, so that the air above remained coloured in seven bands, of the hues in which the sun creates his bow."

Specifically, this book concerns itself not just with colours in the garden but the meanings and effects created by them and their interactions. Once, a few miles outside the walls of Siena, I entered another walled city: a city of self-sown trees and brambles growing over the picturesque remains of a nineteenth-century park designed by Agostino Fantastici, now left to crumble. This garden, the secret garden that everyone dreams of finding, was marked by a rusty old gate that was easily pushed aside. I could just pick out the forms that shaped the garden and the routes around it; glades and grottoes were discernible by the shades and layers, and as I looked more closely, I realised that the greens and greys and browns were speckled with yellows and oranges, reds and pinks. But these weren't coming from flowers: they were the result of light and shadows as they played on different surfaces.

Moods changed from gentle to brooding as I explored further, moving from bright glades into darker areas; the atmosphere was sometimes still, sometimes full of a sense of what had gone before as leaves started to rustle and their colours flickered. What had clearly once been tamed lawns in one shade of emerald were now wild, in a thousand shades and hues of green. I wondered to myself, is it just colour which creates atmosphere? Or is it so tied up with other elements—location, light, climate, one's own cultural references—that one person's romantic is another person's tepid bore?

Colour is as much about perception and position as it is about light, whether in gardens or painting. The primary colours of light are red, blue, and green, but over the centuries, painters gradually reduced colour to three primaries, red, blue, and yellow, from which, it was thought, the whole range of colours could be generated by mixing—rather a daring approach, as it had long been thought that nature should not be interfered with by man. The Impressionists exploited light, and as for colour, Monet called it his "day-long obsession, joy, and torment." For Gauguin and van Gogh, colour could create both order and chaos, simultaneously, and Matisse believed its chief aim was "to serve expression."

When we observe and consider assemblies of plants in gardens, we are to a large extent considering colour. Looking at each creation featured in this book, it quickly became impossible for me not to reference the understanding of what artists have spent a lifetime developing. This is not to say in any way that any of the plantings here are a direct, or indirect, study of a certain painting; rather each is a demonstration of how colours work together and how different people see them and translate them in different ways.

Some gardens in this book have a piece of art referenced or shown. I haven't included a comparison for every planting; nor have I attempted to force an explanation for the reasoning behind the inclusion of each piece of art—for one reason or another the specific piece came to mind and I simply share a train of thought. You may be able to see the reference clearly or just get a sense of where a similarity may be. But I'm not going to push an issue. The combined warmth and coolness of the light, the perceived atmosphere, whether of garden or of art, is simply how I see it. It may not be how you see it. And from there, so many questions arise.

What is a specific colour? How to define the colour of a tree trunk that forms a key part of a planting combination: do we ignore it and work despite it, or do we embrace it and use it to inspire the colours around it? And then, how to combine them to create a picture which changes minute by minute depending on the weather, the season, the temperature, the light? The colour wheel, applied so frequently in our first lessons on the use of colour, may spring to mind here. But I have a confession to make. I have never understood the colour wheel. I understand the principles and I understand Newton's arrangement of colour, but as far as colour in the garden is concerned, I think it constrains us. Why, for example, can't we use "cool" and "warm" colours together, when they may work so well to create a certain effect?

Who am I to write about good and bad colour? I can only describe my own reaction, as I am not quite sure what you are seeing, and I don't have your bank of memories and experiences. For example, a favourite childhood dress of mine was, and remains, most definitely "peachy" in my mind, to the confusion (and even irritation) of others who saw it as brown. Looking back, I can safely say that I was viewing it and thus describing it in terms of its rather alarming 1970s velour texture, as fuzzy as the skin of a peach itself. But whatever we're thinking, let's embrace and celebrate words for colour; let's make new ones and use them alongside old, unfamiliar ones. Murrey. Isabelline. Tyrian. The lack of words restrains us; the ability to describe something specifically frees us. Let's use our words for colour: if we fall out of practice, we may lose them forever.

Which brings us neatly to a history of the gloriously specific RHS Colour Charts. J.H. Wanscher wrote in 1953, "In horticulture there is a natural need for exact, but also simple colour descriptions." The RHS Colour Chart is the standard reference used by horticulturists worldwide for recording plant colours. Since its first publication in 1966 it has been used extensively by the RHS, growers, registration authorities, and specialist growers to identify and describe plant colour with precision. As well as being widely used by horticulturists, it is also used in other industries such as food, cosmetics, pharmaceuticals, and fashion because its wide range of colours is based on the natural world. Resembling a paint chart, it has 920 colours which can be matched precisely to flowers, fruits, and other plant parts in order to record and communicate colours accurately across the world. Each colour has a unique number and letter code as well as a name.

There are so many different strands of colour—light and colour, perception of colour, colour psychology, how the eye works, colour in nature—too many to explore and examine here, but I urge you to go further if you're inspired. Whatever our intention is in the garden, we are creating an effect, an atmosphere, something pleasing, sometimes challenging, expected or unexpected. We can highlight one plant with a surprising background; we can highlight that same plant by choosing instead to paint a background that is more harmonious, or even understated. We can educate, inspire, and—the greatest thing about gardens—observe and *change*, moving along with Nature's own tweaks and shifts. One year our roses flower alongside the latest tulips, while the next, the tulips have already been and gone, and alliums have taken their place. One year the early leaves of the copper beech shine amber in the early light; in the same month of another year, the leaves are silhouettes against a grey sky. That's the joy, the excitement, the adventure.

So fasten your seatbelts; we're going on a journey through colour.

The Gardener's Palette

– 1 –

Strawberries and Cream, with a Drop of Wine

We know that looking more closely reveals more. This is frequently the case with plantings of a "wilder" nature: the flowers of the plants in these schemes tend to be smaller and daintier, revealing themselves and their colours only upon a slower investigation.

This colour scheme looks very similar to the scheme shown in "Wild Pastels." I have included both to show how the inclusion of one more hue can change a picture completely. The intention in this grouping was to bring about a sense almost of a reconstitution of light by the use of colour, and these little flowers are just the thing for creating a blurring-together of colours in this perennial and wildflower meadow mix. Against the white of *Achillea millefolium* and *Leucanthemum vulgare*, there are clumps of *Nepeta grandiflora* 'Dawn to Dusk' whose very pale purple tubular flowers, held in stronger purple calyxes, create the perfect background wash, picking up on the almost invisible pinks of wild carrot and the pale purples of *Daucus carota* 'Dara'.

The very slight silvery grey of the nepeta's bushy leaves tones with the stems of the true wildflowers here: it was important that the majority of plants should have muted, almost insignificant stems and leaves, all supporting the idea of non-attention-seeking foliage. A counterpoint was needed to set off the pale purple, so *Scabiosa atropurpurea* 'Fata Morgana' takes a bow with its pale yellow/light yellowish pink flowers moving through yellow-white ivory into orange-white buttercream, and then into blush. Its pincushion heads appear almost apricot against the pale purple and white background, and the younger button-like flowerheads in an acidic yellow-green link to the background of small-leaved foliage.

And then we need a contrast—this blurred, painterly planting is in need of a proper input of colour in order to draw the eye in, to alert us that the more we look, the more we will see. Foxgloves are happy in a wild environment, and the romantic dusky pink tones of *Digitalis* ×*mertonensis* were exactly what was needed to create those little pops of toning yet contrasting colour against the muted background, Krehbiel's ladies in pink dresses waiting by the window for whoever it is to come home. With the tones of crushed strawberry–old rose working so well with an element of copper, which in turn links with the apricot-peach-cream (whichever the individual bloom is deciding to be at the time) of the scabious—the digitalis sits happily just on the edges of this planting, which becomes shadier as it retreats.

One more element is needed to allow the strawberry rose colours to settle in comfortably against the whites and pale purple: taking the cue from the strong purplish red insides of the petals of the digitalis, taking up this hue and travelling with it through red-purples, we see that we can have another tiny counterpoint in the form of the deep dark crimson of *Knautia macedonica*, whose pincushion heads need ask no permission to sit alongside.

Opposite | Design: Jo Thompson for BBC Springwatch/RHS Hampton Court 2019

	NAME	TYPE	HEIGHT	SPREAD	SEASON	LIGHT	MOISTURE	HARDINESS	SOIL PH
A	*Digitalis ×mertonensis*	perennial	0.5-1 metre, 3-4 feet	0.1-0.5 metre, 1-2 feet	summer	full sun / partial shade / full shade	moist but well-drained / well-drained	very hardy, USDA 4-8	acid / alkaline / neutral
B	*Nepeta grandiflora* 'Dawn to Dusk'	perennial	0.5-1 metre, 2.5 feet	0.5-1 metre, 2.5 feet	summer	full sun / partial shade / full shade	moist but well-drained / well-drained	very hardy, USDA 4-9	alkaline / neutral
C	*Scabiosa atropurpurea* 'Fata Morgana'	annual	0.5-1 metre, 3 feet	0.1-0.5 metre, 1-2 feet	summer	full sun / partial shade / full shade	well-drained	very hardy, USDA 9-11	acid / alkaline / neutral
D	*Daucus carota* 'Dara'	biennial	0.5-1 metre, 3 feet	0.1-0.5 metre, 3 feet	summer	full sun	moist but well-drained / well-drained	very hardy, USDA 2-11	acid / alkaline / neutral
E	*Knautia macedonica*	perennial	0.5-1 metre, 1.5-2 feet	0.1-0.5 metre, 1.5-2 feet	summer	full sun	well-drained	very hardy, USDA 5-9	alkaline / neutral

– 2 –

Lemon and Peach

"I don't like yellow."

Yellow is a love/hate colour—people are very clear about their feelings on yellow, more so than any other colour. It's an uplifting colour, the colour of sunlight and gold and newborn chicks, yet the thought of a vivid yellow flower fills some people with horror. Move along to a pale greenish yellow—which is essentially lemon—and suddenly that person is happy again.

Yellow is highly visible, and perhaps this is why people are moved to feel so strongly. Once it is literally "toned down" to lemon, it is much more acceptable. Erring on the side of cream makes it even more appealing, and that's what is happening here with annual *Eschscholzia californica* 'Ivory Castle'. The pale lemon on large petals catches the light and holds on to it; somehow the brighter yellow centres seem restrained in comparison. The creaminess of this palette needs only a gentle contrast: the *Geum* 'Cosmopolitan' is the palest peach, its orange-yellow flowers ageing to a light yellowish pink, just right against the California poppy.

This *Geum* 'Cosmopolitan' is in the Cocktail Series, which includes geums with flowers in colours almost as drinkable as their names suggest: 'Mai Tai' and 'Banana Daiquiri' are also good as small highlights of lemon, pink, and apricot against larger blooms of any of these colours.

Here, the larger flower in the background provides bolder colour higher up—*Iris* 'Pink Charm' repeats the pink-yellow in the simplest of colour arrangements: a low band of peach, a middle section of lemon, and then the peach reintroduced.

To create more variety here, one could take the cue from the dark purple calyx of the geum and introduce another tall bearded iris: *Iris* 'Burgundy Party' replicates the shades of the geum almost perfectly and would add interest. Alternatively, the addition of copper beech domes would bring fabulous structure while still chiming with the simple tones of this planting.

A

B

C

	NAME	TYPE	HEIGHT	SPREAD	SEASON	LIGHT	MOISTURE	HARDINESS	SOIL PH
A	*Eschscholzia californica* 'Ivory Castle'	annual	0.1-0.5 metre, 1-1.5 feet	0.1-0.5 metre, 1-1.5 feet	summer	full sun	well-drained	half hardy, USDA 6-10	acid / alkaline / neutral
B	*Geum* 'Cosmopolitan'	perennial	0.5-1 metre, 1-2.5 feet	0.1-0.5 metre, 0.75-1.5 feet	spring / summer / autumn	full sun	moist but well-drained / well-drained	very hardy, USDA 4-9	acid / alkaline / neutral
C	*Iris* 'Pink Charm'	perennial	1 metre, 3 feet	0.5-1 metre, 2 feet	summer	full sun	well-drained	very hardy, USDA 4-9	acid / neutral

Opposite | Design: Jo Thompson

– 3 –

Coral and Light

Colour is bringing us happiness in huge quantities here. It's a friendly combination with just a hint of a Caribbean cocktail in these warm tones. Coral is one of those colours that we can't quite put our finger on. Is it orange, is it apricot—perhaps it's peach? Whichever the individual settles on, this colour is used to brilliant effect when the associations of gentleness and romance are celebrated.

Here at Wildside, the Devon garden of plantsman Keith Wiley and his late wife, Ros, the tiny kinked tubular flowers of *Kniphofia thomsonii* var. *snowdenii* display the effectiveness of coral against light. Rather than selecting another swathe of flower colour, the red hot pokers roam freely along, an unlikely veil, allowing us to see through to the grasses beyond. The smallest suggestion of yellow in their flowers is a subtle link with the buff-yellow of *Hemerocallis fulva* and *H.* 'Little Tawny'.

It's the selection of gentle tones with sunlight filtering through all which make this coral and yellow combination feel so easygoing. I'd love to experiment with this planting and to explore in my own garden how perhaps *Kniphofia* 'Apricot' and *Hemerocallis* 'Children's Festival' might work alongside these, although they're definitely more peachy than coral, less pink and more orange.

Crimson *Astrantia* 'Hadspen Blood' fades through a more muted deep pink purple. One of the attractions of astrantia is the colour change, depending on the age of the blooms and on how much light they get. *Pennisetum thunbergii* 'Red Buttons' introduces a deep rosy red to the scheme, the size and the form of the button flowers creating small dashes of colour and yet adding just the right amount of strength and structure to this breezy planting.

Opposite | Design: Keith Wiley

	NAME	TYPE	HEIGHT	SPREAD	SEASON	LIGHT	MOISTURE	HARDINESS	SOIL PH
A	*Kniphofia thomsonii* var. *snowdenii*	perennial	0.5-1 metre, 2-3 feet	0.5-1 metre, 1-2 feet	summer / autumn	full sun / partial shade	moist but well-drained	hardy, USDA 6-11	acid / alkaline / neutral
B	*Hemerocallis fulva*	perennial	0.5-1 metre, 2-2.5 feet	0.5-1 metre, 2-2.5 feet	summer	full sun / partial shade	moist but well-drained	very hardy, USDA 3-9	acid / alkaline / neutral
C	*Pennisetum thunbergii* 'Red Buttons'	grass	0.5-1 metre, 2-3 feet	0.5-1 metre, 2-3 feet	summer / autumn / winter	full sun	well-drained	half hardy, USDA 7-9	acid / alkaline / neutral
D	*Hemerocallis* 'Little Tawny'	perennial	0.5-1 metre, 1.5 feet	0.5-1 metre, 1.5 feet	summer	full sun / partial shade	moist but well-drained	very hardy, USDA 3-9	acid / alkaline / neutral
E	*Hemerocallis* 'Children's Festival'	perennial	0.5-1 metre, 2 feet	0.5-1 metre, 2 feet	summer	full sun	moist but well-drained	very hardy, USDA 4-11	acid / alkaline / neutral
F	*Astrantia* 'Hadspen Blood'	perennial	0.5-1 metre, 2 feet	0.1-0.5 metre, 1.5 feet	summer	full sun / partial shade	moist but well-drained / poorly drained	very hardy, USDA 5-7	acid / alkaline / neutral

– 4 –

Gentle Energy

André Derain, whose sunstreaked landscapes are backlit with warmth, described his mission to capture the buzz and the heat in them this way: "Colours became sticks of dynamite. They were expected to discharge light." I look at the palette in this planting and straight away, the bold contrasting colours suggest a wash of relaxed, understated energy, a scene polished by the sun. The colours bring light and strength while at the same time avoiding the punch of a bolder scheme.

Andrew Fisher Tomlin, the designer of this planting, chose the palette with the intention of bringing some strength to the scheme as well as a saturation of colours, a sense of working with hues just to one side of the primaries and letting the foliage "mix" the colours.

Derain's heated palette would probably have included cadmium or chrome yellow, lead white, vermilion, cobalt, Prussian blue, and viridian. *Rosa* The Poet's Wife = 'Auswhirl' has hints of chrome yellow in its rich yellow flowers, which provide proper pops of colour before fading softly to butter and white. The cobalt of the *Salvia* 'Amistad' in flower, together with its Prussian blue foliage, are excellent foils for the strong vermilion-to-minimum-minium of *Helenium* Mardi Gras = 'Helbro'. Against these more or less primary colours, the green and white foliage of *Calamagrostis* ×*acutiflora* 'Overdam' becomes blue-green viridian, and without even trying, there we have the Fauvist palette.

It isn't obvious when we first look at this that the primaries are in play; shuffled along a little, the shades and tones are much more refined than bold red, yellow, and blue. It's a clever exercise in achieving an effect by taking the obvious and gently moving away from it, at the same time referencing it in the subtlest way. A suggestion of confident strength and innate energy on a lazy day in the South of France, with no need to prove itself. It knows it's good.

Design: Andrew Fisher Tomlin

	NAME	TYPE	HEIGHT	SPREAD	SEASON	LIGHT	MOISTURE	HARDINESS	SOIL PH
A	*Rosa* The Poet's Wife = 'Auswhirl'	shrub	1-1.5 metres, 4 feet	1-1.5 metres, 4 feet	summer / autumn	full sun	moist but well-drained / well-drained	very hardy, USDA 4-11	acid / alkaline / neutral
B	*Salvia* 'Amistad'	perennial	1-1.5 metres, 3-4 feet	0.1-0.5 metre, 1.5 feet	summer / autumn	full sun	moist but well-drained / well-drained	hardy, USDA 1-13	acid / alkaline / neutral
C	*Helenium* Mardi Gras = 'Helbro'	perennial	0.5-1 metre, 2-3 feet	0.1-0.5 metre, 1-2 feet	summer / autumn	full sun	moist but well-drained	very hardy, USDA 4-8	acid / alkaline / neutral
D	*Calamagrostis ×acutiflora* 'Overdam'	grass	0.5-1 metre, 2.5-3 feet	0.1-0.5 metre, 1.5-2 feet	spring / summer / autumn	full sun / partial shade	moist but well-drained / well-drained	very hardy, USDA 4-8	acid / alkaline / neutral

– 5 –

Proud in Pink and Purple

There's a special garden in County Wicklow, Ireland, and within it there's a very special garden indeed. In Ashley's Garden, part of Hunting Brook Gardens, Jimi Blake has scooped up colour, run with it, rejoiced in it, and celebrated it. It's hard to know where one is: the bordering cool dappled woodlands suggest Ireland, but when you are then greeted by exuberant beds bursting with texture and colour, you're immediately transported to a more whimsical, wilder world of exotica.

Wine red and purple foliage anchor us in this exotic world. On the right, a large-leaved Abyssinian banana, *Ensete ventricosum* 'Maurelii', offers a seductive welcome as it throws open its leaves in a bold gesture which belies its tender nature. These Schiaparelli rose tones are scrumptious, as deliciously coloured as the *Roldana cristobalensis*, the beautifully formed purple leaves in the left corner, one of Jimi's favourite plants. There's still a hint of purple-red in *Itoa orientalis* towards the right at the rear. Together, they are the perfect purple triumvirate on which all else hangs.

I have been trying to pinpoint what it is that is just so wonderful and uplifting about these colours; looking at colour charts, it appears that it's the warmth of each shade that sparks these reactions. There's a pink present in the foliage which then radiates out of the fluffy, vivid light purple flowers of *Astilbe chinensis* var. *taquetii* 'Purpurlanze', and to a lesser but by no means less striking extent from the magenta of *Monarda* 'On Parade'. *Angelica sylvestris* provides fractal scatterings of deep burgundy as well as hazy fluffs of flowerplates, fluffs carried by the creamy white panicles of *Artemisia lactiflora* and the reddish-tufted brown leaves of *Chionochloa rubra*.

I've saved the best for last. Amongst all this warmth—this positively cheery singing-out of colours in a garden named after Jimi's late friend Ashley, who loved this garden so much—late-summer heat pours in through the sunshine of *Dahlia* 'Sunny Boy'. There's a lack of blue in this part of the garden which works in the orange-pink combination's favour, and there's only one yellow, from Sunny Boy himself. What happens when there's no blue, is that the yellow of the dahlia is able to drench itself in the surrounding rosiness, and the very-gently-redded tips of the dahlia's petals create a sense of being dipped in pink.

Colour expertise and texture combine in this planting to create a garden I want to leap into (don't worry, Jimi, I won't). So much hard work has gone into this garden, yet with the result of a feeling of complete relaxation, a garden that isn't a museum but a place to enjoy, to live in, to be lifted up by the sense of colour joy.

Above | Design: Jimi Blake
Right | Elsa Schiaparelli, *Cap with Morning Glories*, c. 1948–52

	NAME	TYPE	HEIGHT	SPREAD	SEASON	LIGHT	MOISTURE	HARDINESS	SOIL PH
A	*Dahlia* 'Sunny Boy'	perennial	0.9-1.2 metres, 3.5 feet	0.5-0.6 metre, 1.5 feet	summer / autumn	full sun	well-drained	half hardy, USDA 3-10	acid / neutral
B	*Astilbe chinensis* var. *taquetii* 'Purpurlanze'	perennial	1-1.5 metres, 2-4 feet	0.1-0.5 metre, 1.5-2 feet	summer / autumn	full sun / partial shade	moist but well-drained / poorly drained	very hardy, USDA 4-8	acid / alkaline / neutral
C	*Monarda* 'On Parade'	perennial	0.7 metre, 4 feet	to 0.7 metre, 3 feet	summer / autumn	full sun / partial shade	moist but well-drained	hardy, USDA 4-9	acid / alkaline / neutral
D	*Roldana cristobalensis*	shrub	2-3 metres, 6-10 feet	2-2.5 metres, 6-8 feet	spring	full sun / partial shade	moist but well-drained	half hardy, USDA 9-11	acid / alkaline / neutral
E	*Ensete ventricosum* 'Maurelii'	perennial	2.5-4 metres, 8-10 feet	2.5-4 metres, 6-8 feet	evergreen	full sun / partial shade	well-drained	tender, USDA 10-11	acid / alkaline / neutral
F	*Itoa orientalis*	tree	to 13 metres, 40 feet	3-4 metres, 10-12 feet	evergreen	full sun / partial shade	moist but well-drained	half hardy, USDA 9-11	acid / alkaline / neutral

– 6 –

Coppery Pink

One of my childhood memories is of a certain sofa, covered in chintz. I can't place where it was, but its swirling florals—ranging from dusty oranges and peach intertwined with the deepest crimson hues—were mesmerising. I felt that the colours, if they could have spoken, would ask me to come and sit down and just sink into them, which is precisely what I used to do.

I'm sure one of those colours was the coppery pink of *Verbascum* (Cotswold Group) 'Cotswold Beauty', inviting us in to this planting, come-hithering us as we marvel at her quietly seductive shades, which sashay into the peaches, just swerve the oranges, and shimmer back into pink. Some way lighter than what we might think of as burnt sienna, these colours have a connection to the earth, and always surprise us in spring and summer, accustomed as we are to these shades showing themselves in autumn. The colour wheel as we are used to it would suggest a blue as an efficient, tidy, satisfying combination, but we're beyond the colour wheel in this instance.

Here's where examining the centre of the flower really helps; the purple stamens have a touch of Bordeaux wine about them, which offers a more layered suggestion for a colour combination. *Rosa* Chianti = 'Auswine' here has those wine colours in abundance; there's also a layer of cochineal and a touch of vermilion in there, the earthiness of which circles back to the verbascum's earthy tones. It's a restful combination; it feels different but not over-complicated, lightened by the small hint of blue from the mullein's leaves, which in turn are held up by the silver-blue of artemisia foliage.

If you haven't ever come across the work of Hilma af Klint, do take a look. In particular, this one: *The Swan, No. 11, Group IX/SUW*. Possibly not one of the most romantic, evocative names for a painting; more a technical record of a lifetime of colour experimentation in summoning up the very essence of the soul. We look at this extraordinary piece, which could have been created yesterday but in fact was painted in 1914–15, and we are absolutely enveloped and at the same time almost lifted up and away into a pinwheel of pinks and peaches with a shaft of lilac-blue. I'm not trying to impose an artificial comparison; both painting and planting appear to me to work in the same way. There's a hint of flamboyant rebellion in a combination that has a contradictory calming effect, vibrant and consoling at the same time. The peach feels nurturing; the deep scarlet carries with it wisdom.

On a practical level, *Rosa* Chianti = 'Auswine' flowers only once in a season, but if you have room for many, many roses then by all means dedicate some space to it and its blooms, which fade to an elegant purple as they age. *Rosa* Munstead Wood = 'Ausbernard' will give you a longer season of colour, but be prepared for its ballgown blooms to steal the show. Admittedly, I'm always happy for this to happen; I anticipate the scene-stealing by partnering it with *R.* The Lark Ascending = 'Ausursula', with its equally improbable peach, mother-of-pearl, pink, and apricot shades. The wild carrot *Daucus carota* 'Dara' would bring in a perfect burgundy here, with a little silver-blue from artemisia foliage to calm it all down.

	NAME	TYPE	HEIGHT	SPREAD	SEASON	LIGHT	MOISTURE	HARDINESS	SOIL PH
A	*Verbascum* (Cotswold Group) 'Cotswold Beauty'	perennial	1-1.5 metres, 3-4 feet	0.1-0.5 metre, 1-2 feet	summer	full sun	well-drained	hardy, USDA 7-10	alkaline
B	*Rosa* Chianti = 'Auswine'	shrub	1.5-2.5 metres, to 6 feet	1.5-2.5 metres, 5 feet	summer / autumn	full sun	moist but well-drained / well-drained	very hardy, USDA 5-11	acid / alkaline / neutral
C	*Rosa* Munstead Wood = 'Ausbernard'	shrub	1.5-2.5 metres, 4-6 feet	1.5-2.5 metres, 4-6 feet	summer / autumn	full sun / partial shade	moist but well-drained / well-drained	very hardy, USDA 5-9	acid / alkaline / neutral
D	*Rosa* The Lark Ascending = 'Ausursula'	shrub	1-1.5 metres, 5.5 feet	1-1.5 metres, 5.5 feet	summer / autumn	full sun	moist but well-drained / well-drained	very hardy, USDA 4-11	acid / alkaline / neutral

Opposite | Jo Thompson for M&G Garden/RHS Chelsea 2015

- 7 -

Jewels

We talk of jewel tones in planting combinations: of rubies, sapphires, and emeralds. This is one of the most sumptuous palettes to work with, and I have to admit that I do get very over-excited at its seemingly endless possibilities. A combination of these colours transports me in a heartbeat to an apartment I lived in as a student in Venice, the piano nobile of a 15th-century palazzo with windows, frescoes, and furnishings in colours so extraordinary that memories of these have stayed with me for life. I can return to visit to see the colours for themselves, but from far away I can also conjure up the same atmosphere with plants.

In this garden designed for M&G at the RHS Chelsea Flower Show, the focal point, the jewel in the crown if you like, is the deep rich purplish red of two roses: *Rosa* Chianti = 'Auswine' with its velvety, petal-filled flowers of the richest wine red, and *R.* 'Tuscany Superb'. The latter has gloriously dark (murrey-purple says Graham Stuart Thomas) semi-double flowers with a gold coronet of stamens nestling inside the petals. This rose can sometimes touch on the ceremonious when planted in large groups; a gentle quelling of its spirit is achieved

Design: Jo Thompson for M&G Garden/RHS Chelsea 2015

by looking for a colour that still has some purple in it, but which goes off into the pinks. *Rosa* 'Louise Odier' achieves this beautifully: it isn't in a hue that takes quite all the attention away, but once we notice it, we would probably admit that it is equally attention-grabbing; the warm pink flowers with hints of lilac echo the size and form of the red flowers which sit in front, just shifting slightly along the colour wheel to achieve a harmonious effect.

The gemstone theme continues with the strong purple spires of *Salvia nemorosa* 'Caradonna'. The contrast in form needs no explanation, nor does the colour combination, which can sometimes seem a touch mannered, so to temper it all, alongside the pale blue amsonia forming the mat of background colour along with the fresh green foliage of the bulk of the other plants, the odd splash of *Verbascum* (Cotswold Group) 'Cotswold Beauty' is dotted around. It isn't immediately obvious, but once spotted, you understand its necessity. Its apricots and peaches are a clear and confident contrast, its violet centres a subtle link to the blue tones in the foreground.

Nepeta racemosa 'Walker's Low' continues the lilac-blue and drifts along the amsonia, giving the latter's somewhat weedy stems a bit of bulk. The rich deep colour of the catmint provides the opportunity for more silver, so *Artemisia absinthium* 'Lambrook Mist' is a useful choice as a foliage plant behind.

Echoes are essential, both for succession and for underlining your aim: the plume thistle *Cirsium rivulare* 'Atropurpureum' nods to the red roses, and its blue tones are vital against the deep purple stems of the salvia, as well as against its petals. *Digitalis purpurea* 'Sutton's Apricot' is a subtle suggestion of the peachy tones of the verbascum in the background; happy in full sun to full shade, foxgloves are fabulous for linking palettes through the garden, their hooded bells of flowers creating vertical streaks up and down, along and away.

D

E

F

	NAME	TYPE	HEIGHT	SPREAD	SEASON	LIGHT	MOISTURE	HARDINESS	SOIL PH
A	*Rosa* 'Louise Odier'	shrub	1-1.5 metres, to 5 feet	1-1.5 metres, 4 feet	summer	full sun / partial shade / full shade	well-drained	very hardy, USDA 5-11	acid / alkaline / neutral
B	*Rosa* Chianti = 'Auswine'	shrub	1.5-2.5 metres, to 6 feet	1.5-2.5 metres, 5 feet	summer / autumn	full sun	moist but well-drained / well-drained	very hardy, USDA 5-11	acid / alkaline / neutral
C	*Verbascum* (Cotswold Group) 'Cotswold Beauty'	perennial	1-1.5 metres, 3-4 feet	0.1-0.5 metre, 1-2 feet	summer	full sun	well-drained	hardy, USDA 7-10	alkaline
D	*Digitalis purpurea* 'Sutton's Apricot'	biennial	1-1.5 metres, 3-4 feet	0.1-0.5 metre, 1-1.5 feet	summer	full sun / partial shade / full shade	moist but well-drained / well-drained	very hardy, USDA 4-8	acid / alkaline / neutral
E	*Salvia nemorosa* 'Caradonna'	perennial	0.1-0.5 metre, 1-2 feet	0.1-0.5 metre, 1-2 feet	summer	full sun / partial shade	moist but well-drained	very hardy, USDA 4-8	acid / alkaline / neutral
F	*Nepeta racemosa* 'Walker's Low'	perennial	0.1-0.5 metre, 2-2.5 feet	0.1-0.5 metre, 2.5-3 feet	spring / summer	full sun / partial shade / full shade	well-drained	very hardy, USDA 4-8	acid / alkaline / neutral

– 8 –

Rich Red and Blue

Red and blue—or so it seems. This most elegant of colour schemes by Luciano Giubbilei uses a restrained yet sumptuous palette for very early summer. The deep crimson of *Paeonia* 'Buckeye Belle' contains the same red tones as *Astrantia* 'Hadspen Blood'; the deeper wine of the outer petals of the peony's bowl-shaped semi-double blooms and the stems and buds of *Salvia nemorosa* 'Caradonna' are matched beautifully. The misty giant that is *Foeniculum vulgare* creates clouds that set off the handsome blue-green foliage of the peony. Here we have highly saturated colours that contrast each other yet at the same time all work together to create a feeling of light and movement, colours so difficult to capture and reproduce. Even El Greco, considered a master of colour intensity, believed that the greatest difficulty in art was "the imitation of colour"—the rich reds and blues here suggest a heavenly world in contrast to the brown, more muted colours of the earthly world.

We may have been stopped in our tracks by the peony; there's another wow of a moment when the eye falls upon *Iris* 'Superstition'. Slightly waved purple-black flowers are gorgeous enough, but then black velvety falls are something else. The whole palette is a tasteful tapestry—it would not be that long-lived in a garden, and although the heart might sink at the request for "year-round colour," in a smaller space it's helpful if a border can give a couple of seasons. Further perennials might overcrowd, but a few specimens of *Rosa* Munstead Wood = 'Ausbernard' or *R.* 'Tuscany Superb' would continue the deep red nicely through the summer, still supplying a few blooms here and there until early October. But the best bet in a planting like this would be to introduce early colour with tulips: *Tulipa* 'Ronaldo', *T.* 'Black Parrot', and *T.* 'Red Georgette' would bring along shades of crimson and plum, offering a foretaste of things to come.

We shouldn't take for granted the job that the astrantia does here. In a lovely shade of plum, it is a fabulous plant which works as well in all but the deepest shade as it does in the sun. Its little starry flowers are a pure delight, bringing light to this palette.

Plum in general is a very satisfying colour in the border: if you did want to vary this scheme a little, I would err on the side of caution and continue the restrained selection of hues: *Papaver* (Oriental Group) 'Patty's Plum' and *Geranium phaeum* var. *phaeum* 'Samobor' would both look at home here.

Design: Luciano Giubbilei for Laurent-Perrier/RHS Chelsea 2009

A
B
C
D
E
F
G
H
I

J

K

L

	NAME	TYPE	HEIGHT	SPREAD	SEASON	LIGHT	MOISTURE	HARDINESS	SOIL PH
A	*Paeonia* 'Buckeye Belle'	perennial	0.5-1 metre, 1.5-2 feet	0.5-1 metre, 2-3 feet	spring / summer	full sun / partial shade	moist but well-drained	very hardy, USDA 4-8	acid / alkaline / neutral
B	*Astrantia* 'Hadspen Blood'	perennial	0.5-1 metre, 2 feet	0.1-0.5 metre, 1.5 feet	summer	full sun / partial shade	moist but well-drained / poorly drained	very hardy, USDA 5-7	acid / alkaline / neutral
C	*Salvia nemorosa* 'Caradonna'	perennial	0.1-0.5 metre, 1-2 feet	0.1-0.5 metre, 1-2 feet	summer	full sun / partial shade	moist but well-drained	very hardy, USDA 4-8	acid / alkaline / neutral
D	*Foeniculum vulgare*	biennial or short-lived perennial	1.5-2.5 metres, 3-5 feet	0.5-1 metre, 2-3 feet	spring / summer	full sun / partial shade	moist but well-drained	very hardy, USDA 4-9	acid / alkaline / neutral
E	*Iris* 'Superstition'	perennial	0.5-1 metre, 3 feet	0.1-0.5 metre, 1.5-2 feet	spring	full sun	well-drained	very hardy, USDA 3-7	alkaline / neutral
F	*Rosa* Munstead Wood = 'Ausbernard'	shrub	1.5-2.5 metres, 4-6 feet	1.5-2.5 metres, 4-6 feet	summer / autumn	full sun / partial shade	moist but well-drained / well-drained	very hardy, USDA 5-9	acid / alkaline / neutral
G	*Rosa* Falstaff = 'Ausverse'	shrub	1-1.5 metres, 4 feet	0.5-1 metre, 3.5 feet	summer / autumn	full sun / partial shade	moist but well-drained / well-drained	very hardy, USDA 5-11	acid / alkaline / neutral
H	*Tulipa* 'Ronaldo'	bulb	0.1-0.5 metre, 1.5-1.75 feet	0.1-0.5 metre, 0.25 foot	spring	full sun	well-drained	very hardy, USDA 3-8	acid / alkaline / neutral
I	*Tulipa* 'Black Parrot'	bulb	0.5-1 metre, 1.5-1.75 feet	0.1-0.5 metre, 0.25 foot	spring	full sun	well-drained	very hardy, USDA 4-7	acid / alkaline / neutral
J	*Tulipa* 'Red Georgette'	bulb	0.1-0.5 metre, 1.5 feet	0.1-0.5 metre, 0.25 foot	spring	full sun	well-drained	very hardy, USDA 4-7	acid / alkaline / neutral
K	*Papaver* (Oriental Group) 'Patty's Plum'	perennial	0.5-1 metre, 2-2.5 feet	0.5-1 metre, 1.5-2 feet	spring / summer	full sun	well-drained	very hardy, USDA 3-7	acid / alkaline / neutral
L	*Geranium phaeum* var. *phaeum* 'Samobor'	perennial	0.5-1 metre, 1.5-1.75 feet	0.1-0.5 metre, 1 foot	spring / summer / autumn	full sun / partial shade / full shade	moist but well-drained / well-drained	very hardy, USDA 4-9	acid / alkaline / neutral

– 9 –

Grey-Lilac and Deep Red

Imagine having a botanical garden of your very own, one with extraordinary forms in restrained shades that come together to create a welcoming feeling of being in your own space and yet, simultaneously, transport you into a world of restful shades of green.

It's actually not all green here in this seaside garden designed by Eric Brandon Gomez. The background clouds of hazy and transparent strong yellow-green—provided by *Bambusa oldhamii* (giant timber bamboo) and *Otatea acuminata* subsp. *aztecorum* (Mexican weeping bamboo)—blend seamlessly with the landscape beyond: the colour is an inspired choice as it's a shade of green that is expected, which doesn't seize our attention and instead lures us into feeling that this garden goes on and on and on, even though we can see the wall snaking along through the planting. We don't "see" the dark grey of this structure; instead we are drawn to the dramatic shapes that scatter through this space. Highlights, still in the same palette of green, come from the tall *Euphorbia ammak* (African candelabra) and the darker green *Aloe vaombe* (Malagasy tree aloe).

Design: Eric Brandon Gomez

A thoughtful choice of colour is important when using succulents. Here Gomez has taken *Agave americana* and celebrated it by allowing this century plant to take centre stage, its leaves creating an explosion of pale blue-green. These silvery blue-greens are then picked up by the mat of the grey *Curio talinoides* subsp. *mandraliscae*; ricocheting off these blue-greys is the silver-leaved blue-flowered *Salvia clevelandii* (Cleveland sage).

An effective pale grey-green base has been created by these plants; against these, deep red sits elegantly and perfectly. The red grass tree, *Cordyline* 'Red Star', echoes the radiating leaves of the agave, bursts of dark red and dark greyish purple with a hint of blue-grey in the leaves—this hint explains why the whole thing works together so effectively.

The subtlest placement is *Euphorbia* Blackbird = 'Nothowlee'; this ground-hugging sub-shrub sits as a ripple of deep red at the foot of this colour palette, in front of the rest of the planting. This colour scheme is restrained and dramatic at the same time, a masterclass in well-considered selection of shades and tones. We are aware that we could be by the sea, but we could just as well be in another world completely. Wherever we think we are, it all feels just right.

	NAME	TYPE	HEIGHT	SPREAD	SEASON	LIGHT	MOISTURE	HARDINESS	SOIL PH
A	*Salvia clevelandii*	perennial	1-1.5 metres, 3-4.5 feet	1-2.5 metres, to 8 feet	summer	full sun	moist but well-drained	tender, USDA 8-11	acid / alkaline / neutral
B	*Curio talinoides* subsp. *mandraliscae*	perennial	0.5-1 metre, 1-3 feet	0.5-1 metre, 2-3 feet	summer	full sun / partial shade	moist but well-drained	tender, USDA 9-11	acid / alkaline / neutral
C	*Euphorbia ammak*	perennial	8-12 metres, to 33 feet	to 0.1 metre, 0.5 foot	evergreen	full sun	well-drained	tender, USDA 9-11	acid / alkaline / neutral
D	*Euphorbia* Blackbird = 'Nothowlee'	sub-shrub	0.1-0.5 metre, 1-2 feet	0.1-0.5 metre, 1-2 feet	spring	full sun	well-drained	hardy, USDA 6-9	acid / alkaline / neutral
E	*Agave americana*	perennial	1-1.5 metres, 3-6 feet	2-3 metres, 6-10 feet	summer	full sun	well-drained	tender, USDA 8-10	acid / neutral
F	*Aloe vaombe*	perennial	2.5-4 metres, 8-12 feet	1-1.5 metres, 4-5 feet	winter	full sun	well-drained	tender, USDA 9-10	acid / alkaline / neutral
G	*Otatea acuminata* subsp. *aztecorum*	grass	4-8 metres, 15-20 feet	4-8 metres, 15-20 feet	evergreen	full sun / partial shade	moist but well-drained	hardy, USDA 9-11	acid / alkaline / neutral

- 10 -

Clarets and Creams

Oehme, van Sweden's garden at Cornerstone Sonoma is a lesson in less-is-more simplicity. What looks at first sight a virtual monoculture, reveals itself to be an absorbing layering of tones, demonstrating that meadow landscapes don't have to be rendered in varying shades of faded yellow-brown.

There's a foundation of light brown throughout. The *Stipa tenuissima* forms the anchor to this planting: almost as you would paint a wall in a neutral colour and then use paintings and furnishings to bring it alive, so have OvS done here with plants. This neutral

Right | Design: Oehme, van Sweden
Below | Paul Cézanne, *Banks of the Seine at Médan*, c. 1885–90

background is cleverly punctuated with the glaucous green of chunky aloes, counter-intuitive to the tall thin stems that a New Perennial planting might offer. The aloes are a masterstroke, not planted throughout but just here and there, their yellow-green tones tying the eye to the ground while their blue tones link to the sky, which is seen through a veil of gunmetal grey olive stems. The glamorously sweeping trunks of these olives, harnessed neatly by Grace Knowlton's sculptural sphere (again in tones of grey), kick into life the dryness of the grass, but not before being sliced by a strip of blue-green rosemary. It is as if the designer has taken that magical landscaping rule of no more than three hard materials in one place and applied it to the plant material. Grey, blue, and green are the positives, the masses in this scheme, while the paler yellow serves as the splendid neutral.

Seasonal uplifts are important in capturing the simplicity of this planting scheme: the light yellow of the stipa needs a counterpoint, and eschscholzia and *Allium sphaerocephalon* do the job perfectly. The vivid yellow-orange of the California poppy finds a suitable companion in the form of the red-violet drumstick heads of the allium. Both are dots, pointillist highlights scattered happily through the meadow in this Garden of Contrasts.

The stipa is a great choice of a neutral—early on it's a pale green background, a carpet for the year-round aloes. As they grow, the green stems of this grass are invaluable for what they bring in terms of texture, movement, and light; as they age, they provide a different neutral backdrop, a different colour completely as they turn from pale green to the palest yellow-brown, and, as they dry and die, they add yet another colour to this scheme.

It's very easy when creating a new colour scheme, to want to include something of everything. The call is often for "year-round interest," and this is often interpreted as year-round colour. The temptation is to think seasonally: this is a logical approach, but we should always try to remember to look at what can link all those seasons rather than having four disjointed pictures. What OvS have done is to take the simplest idea—the neutral with counterpoints—and created a landscape of colour which is both easy on the eye and exquisite at the same time.

Cézanne's sunlit *Banks of the Seine at Médan* captures the visual sensations of nature in much the same way, examining the relationship between colour and light. The dots of canvas just showing through are to me OvS's stipa and its light-catching qualities, its verticals echoing Cézanne's short parallel brushstrokes which form so much of the foliage. A bright palette of predominantly yellows and grey to greens unifies the composition, with the smallest hint of deep red to burgundy. I'm not suggesting that the planting was inspired by the painting; I'm saying that this planting too is truly an inspired use of colour and light.

A

B

C

D

	NAME	TYPE	HEIGHT	SPREAD	SEASON	LIGHT	MOISTURE	HARDINESS	SOIL PH
A	*Eschscholzia californica*	annual	0.1-0.5 metre, 1-1.5 feet	0.1-0.5 metre, 1-1.5 feet	summer	full sun	well-drained	half hardy, USDA 6-10	acid / alkaline / neutral
B	*Allium sphaerocephalon*	bulb	0.5-1 metre, 2-3 feet	0.1-0.5 metre, 1-1.5 feet	summer	full sun	moist but well-drained / well-drained	very hardy, USDA 4-8	acid / alkaline / neutral
C	*Agave americana*	perennial	1-1.5 metres, 3-6 feet	2-3 metres, 6-10 feet	summer	full sun	well-drained	tender, USDA 8-10	acid / neutral
D	*Stipa tenuissima*	grass	0.5-1 metre, 1-2 feet	0.1-0.5 metre, 1-2 feet	spring / summer / autumn	full sun	moist but well-drained / well-drained	hardy, USDA 7-10	acid / alkaline / neutral

– 11 –

Silver Light

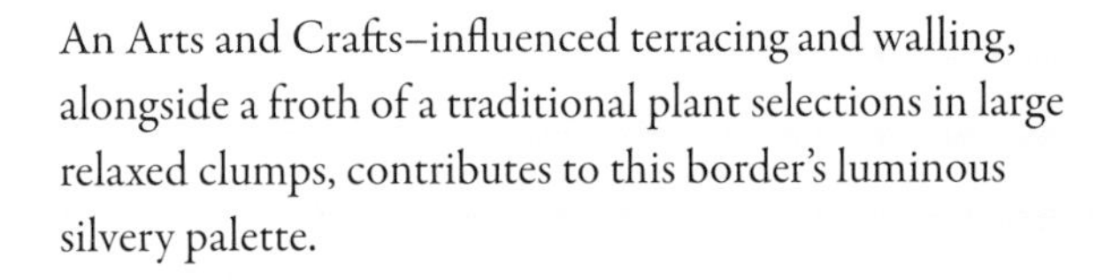

An Arts and Crafts–influenced terracing and walling, alongside a froth of a traditional plant selections in large relaxed clumps, contributes to this border's luminous silvery palette.

This area of the garden of Jade and Julian Dunkerton's Cotswolds home was planted for particular interest in the early summer, with multi-stemmed amelanchier and multiple vintage tulips and bulbs amid a mass of strong foliage plants such as hostas and alchemilla.

Designers Lulu Urquhart and Adam Hunt are modern-day alchemists, turning light into silver and gold. In later summer this planting reaches its crescendo of light, without being an obvious "white" border. The early structural plants burst into a display of gold and silvers all designed to catch the western sun. *Molinia caerulea* subsp. *arundinacea* 'Transparent' starts the grass suggestion, while *Deschampsia cespitosa* 'Bronzeschleier' is an exceptional ornamental grass, perfectly suited for the intention here, its plumes tall and light, firework sprays over the whiter-than-white flowers of *Anemone* ×*hybrida* 'Honorine Jobert'.

Euphorbia characias subsp. *wulfenii* is both chunky in mass yet delicately and unseasonally frosted in colour,

Design: Urquhart & Hunt

Silver

Silver-leaved plants are so useful in the garden, but what is silver? In trying to describe this colour, I turn to my trusty *Chroma* by Derek Jarman, which didn't leave my side as I wrote this book. Was silver grey, he wondered? What separated silver and gold from other colours—was it their lustre or their value? In the case of silver, both, I believe.

Silver can bring light to a planting; it also brings with it a sense of the special, of something worth having, its sheen shapeshifting the atmosphere of a space.

Silver *is* essentially grey, multiple shades of grey, with highlights of white on the surface which create a sheen.

Imagine silver with black and orange irises: that would grab the attention, spark curiosity. Yet move the orange along to a peach, and the atmosphere moves into a dreamier zone. Silver evokes a magical feeling when mixed with black purple and palest blue; combine it instead with a redder purple and add pink, and everything becomes a little bit more romantic.

starred with late *Cosmos bipinnatus* Sonata Pink = 'Pas1787' and proper pink *Persicaria bistorta* 'Superba'. All is light and brightness back and forth across this planting, with the light-absorbing and light-reflecting textures and forms thought through as carefully as the colours of the flowers themselves.

The walls are not to be forgotten. The beige-grey of York sandstone both absorbs and reflects light; the designers have celebrated the neutral tones and made them part of the palette. Silvering *Nepeta racemosa* 'Walker's Low' has been commandeered here; by now looking past its best in most gardens, here the catmint's faded grandeur teams up with *Lavandula angustifolia* to overflow onto the Yorkstone edging.

The steep rear bank behind the wall is, in the daylight sun, a mass of *Ceanothus griseus* var. *horizontalis* 'Yankee Point', which blooms lilac-blue from spring into summer; it is underplanted with strong purple-blue *Geranium* 'Orion' in order to create Bee Heaven. The bright caerulean blue of the California lilac may have finished for now, but we can quickly understand the intention: in this space its glossy leaves form an important dark band of a backdrop. It's a brilliant lesson in enlisting every element to form a palette, including the intangibles and variables of light and where it will fall. The dazzling blue of the ceanothus flowers has given way to a "negative," a dark mass which is as flattering to plants as the painted black background of an auricula theatre. Below this naturally formed black—which isn't actually black, more an obsidian with an iridescent sheen—the selection of plants brings the sky to the ground.

Clever. Romantic. Brilliant. Magic.

	NAME	TYPE	HEIGHT	SPREAD	SEASON	LIGHT	MOISTURE	HARDINESS	SOIL PH
A	*Anemone ×hybrida* 'Honorine Jobert'	perennial	1-1.5 metres, 3-4 feet	0.5-1 metre, 1.5-2 feet	summer	full sun / partial shade	moist but well-drained	very hardy, USDA 4-8	acid / alkaline / neutral
B	*Cosmos bipinnatus* Sonata Pink = 'Pas1787'	perennial	0.1-0.5 metre, 1-2 feet	0.1-0.5 metre, 1-2 feet	summer	full sun	moist but well-drained	half hardy, USDA 2-11	acid / alkaline / neutral
C	*Ceanothus griseus* var. *horizontalis* 'Yankee Point'	shrub	0.5-1 metre, 2-3 feet	2.5-4 metres, 8-10 feet	spring / summer	full sun	well-drained	half hardy, USDA 8-11	acid / alkaline / neutral
D	*Euphorbia characias* subsp. *wulfenii*	perennial	1-1.5 metres, 2-3 feet	1-1.5 metres, 1.5-2 feet	spring / summer	full sun	well-drained	very hardy, USDA 6-8	acid / alkaline / neutral
E	*Deschampsia cespitosa* 'Bronzeschleier'	grass	0.5-1 metre, 3 feet	0.5-1 metre, 3 feet	summer	full sun / partial shade	moist but well-drained / well-drained	very hardy, USDA 5-9	acid / neutral

– 12 –

White with a Dash of Lemon

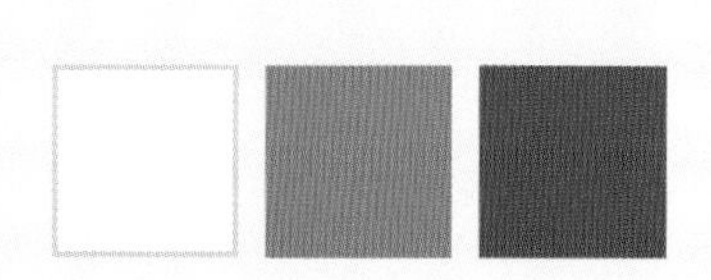

Not all white gardens are white. From a distance, this area of the Cool Garden at RHS Rosemoor in south-west UK appears to be a planting of white flowers, but on approaching, we realise that it's so much more than that. It's an example of how important it is to consider foliage—both background foliage and foliage within the planting—and to get it right. The whites and silvers and greys and greens are soft and relaxing, while the light-speckles in the foreground turn out not to be white at all, but instead the pale lemon of the elegant *Nepeta govaniana*.

You can be as relaxed as you want to be with a colour scheme—a white garden will of course be predominantly filled with white-flowering plants, but a few interlopers here and there create both unexpected interest and also a feeling that as much as you care, you are not controlling this palette to within an inch of its life. The plants are happy, the colours breathe out, the feeling is mellow.

Buddleia has had terrible PR, its associations with freestyle self-seeding on railway embankments and derelict buildings leading too many to fear its unruly plentifulness. Let me take the opportunity to reassure you—even if they do cast themselves around a little, you won't regret a buddleia for the late-summer bulk of colour as well for the butterflies it continues to bring to the garden. Just make sure you prune twice and deadhead during the flowering season.

Buddleja davidii 'Darent Valley', found as a chance seedling in the 1980s, has become a favourite buddleia. It produces many sweetly scented, orange-throated white flowers and is an excellent addition to a white garden with perhaps a looser, slightly less restrained feel. The dots—rather than blocks—of flowers are clustered together, each panicle a Sheringham glass candlestick; the horizontal layers find their perfect foil in the verticals of *Miscanthus sinensis* 'Morning Light', whose creamy-white-edged leaves shine from a distance in a silvery haze against the dark green "blackground" of the yew hedge.

The buddleia, nepeta, and miscanthus do inevitably grab all the attention, alongside the globes of the echinops, which seem to be photobombing this planting, but there's also an invaluable wallflower here. *Artemisia lactiflora*'s stiff yellow-green stems are good value through the season, but oh my goodness, when the fluff of creamy white flowers appears in early autumn, you understand why you included it. Look again and you can see this artemisia bridging the gap and uniting the buddleia and the grass.

Opposite | Design: Jo Thompson

	NAME	TYPE	HEIGHT	SPREAD	SEASON	LIGHT	MOISTURE	HARDINESS	SOIL PH
A	*Buddleja davidii* 'Darent Valley'	shrub	1.5-2.5 metres, 5-6 feet	1.5-2.5 metres, 5-6 feet	summer / autumn	full sun / partial shade	moist but well-drained / well-drained	very hardy, USDA 5-9	acid / alkaline / neutral
B	*Miscanthus sinensis* 'Morning Light'	grass	1.5-2 metres, 4-6 feet	0.5-1 metre, 2.5-4 feet	autumn	full sun	moist but well-drained / well-drained	very hardy, USDA 5-9	acid / alkaline / neutral
C	*Artemisia lactiflora*	perennial	1-1.5 metres, 4-5 feet	1-1.5 metres, 2-3 feet	summer / autumn	full sun	moist but well-drained	very hardy, USDA 3-8	acid / alkaline / neutral

– 13 –

Purplish Red and White

Some joyous colour combinations reveal their mysteries slowly. On first acquaintance, it's hard to pin down why they are actually a little bit exciting, why what could have nearly become a boring old pastel arrangement is instead rather cheering, with a bit of zing and a ton of pizzazz.

That's not happening here, I hear you say—but stop, wait a minute, and look. Clusters of tiny white flowers of *Anthriscus sylvestris* form a lacy veiled backdrop, the pale dots little highlighted pinpricks. Denser clouds of the palest pinkish white, the heads of *Valeriana officinalis*, gather up the cow parsley's white dots and make a statement, a punctuation, an ending of white. The blue-green foliage (let's not forget the foliage) is in total harmony with the foliage of *Astrantia major* 'Rubra', whose purple bracts tone tastefully with its companions.

This planting could all be very lovely and muted and understated, to the extent that it could be completely missed as one views the border. But there is one plant which ties everything together and turns the mundane into the eye-catching.

That literally most regal of plants, *Osmunda regalis* (royal fern), saves the day. This upstanding giant has the most beautiful bipinnate fronds, in the freshest of greens, which blouse out and over its neighbours without swamping them. Young furled fronds in a coppery bronze stand out against the greens and white, making a connection with the astrantia flowers.

I love *Osmunda regalis*. It's an incredibly useful plant, being one of the few ferns which doesn't mind sun. While you wouldn't want it to dry out and you most definitely wouldn't plant it in a rock garden, it can take a bit of heat, which means I'll often repeat it around in a garden to give a sense of unity. It is a proud plant, its crown needing exposure: the height gives it that sense of majesty from which it takes its name.

Design: Jo Thompson

	NAME	TYPE	HEIGHT	SPREAD	SEASON	LIGHT	MOISTURE	HARDINESS	SOIL PH
A	*Astrantia major* 'Rubra'	perennial	0.5-1 metre, 1.5-2.5 feet	0.5-1 metre, 1-1.5 feet	spring / summer / autumn	full sun / partial shade	moist but well-drained / poorly drained	very hardy, USDA 4-7	acid / alkaline / neutral
B	*Anthriscus sylvestris*	perennial	1-1.5 metres, 3 feet	0.1-0.5 metre, 2 feet	spring / summer	full sun / partial shade	moist but well-drained / well-drained	very hardy, USDA 7-10	acid / alkaline / neutral
C	*Valeriana officinalis*	perennial	1-1.5 metres, 3-5 feet	0.5-1 metre, 2-4 feet	summer	full sun / partial shade	moist but well-drained	very hardy, USDA 4-7	acid / alkaline / neutral
D	*Osmunda regalis*	fern	1.5-2 metres, 2-3 feet	0.5-1 metre, 2-3 feet	autumn	full sun / partial shade / full shade	moist but well-drained / poorly drained	very hardy, USDA 3-9	acid / alkaline / neutral

– 14 –

Wine, Peach, and Coral

What colours stand out to you in this planting? Foliage of green predominates with the very slightest hints of blue in the leaves of the iris and astrantia, but it is the coral and buff of the peonies and roses which take centre stage.

I derive most colour schemes from the close study of one single flower. I take the bloom and note everything: the colour of the stamen, how the shades change as the colour washes along a petal, how the colour of each petal changes depending on its position, and how all these interweave and work together. This provides me with the starting point for my palette, and from then on it's more a question of who is going to harmonise with what, and what is going to contrast with whom.

Paeonia 'Pink Hawaiian Coral', the flower that appears the least in this planting, is the showstopper in this scene. She gets the attention because she is the only plant in this scheme with the whole palette amongst her petals. Her name sums her up—corals and pinks sit so neatly together, creating that gorgeous uplifting effect that makes us just so happy when we see a particularly

Design: Jo Thompson

	NAME	TYPE	HEIGHT	SPREAD	SEASON	LIGHT	MOISTURE	HARDINESS	SOIL PH
A	*Astrantia major* 'Rubra'	perennial	0.5-1 metre, 1.5-2.5 feet	0.5-1 metre, 1-1.5 feet	spring / summer / autumn	full sun / partial shade	moist but well-drained / poorly drained	very hardy, USDA 4-7	acid / alkaline / neutral
B	*Paeonia* 'Pink Hawaiian Coral'	perennial	0.5-1 metre, 2.5-3 feet	0.5-1 metre, 2.5-3 feet	spring / summer	full sun / partial shade	moist but well-drained	very hardy, USDA 3-8	acid / alkaline / neutral
C	*Rosa* 'Buff Beauty'	shrub	1-1.5 metres, to 6 feet	1-1.5 metres, to 5 feet	summer / autumn	full sun	moist but well-drained / well-drained	very hardy, USDA 5-10	acid / alkaline / neutral

good sunset. I find that "coral" confuses many of us and conjures up different tones to different people—some linking it to orange, while others plump for pink or even red. Essentially, it's a pink with yellowish tones.

So it is the centre of this peony which inspires the use of the apricot and pale yellow *Rosa* 'Buff Beauty': again, the flowers change according to their position and alter as they age, but they always are in harmony with the very centre of the peony. These warm shades of yellow bring light to the whole grouping.

These two colours—the coral and the yellow—need linking, and the trick here is to select a colour which harmonises with them both as well as with the dark bluish green tones of the rose foliage. The reds and purples of the outer petals of *Astrantia major* 'Rubra' act as an ideal bridge between the stand-out colours, the shades of red drawing the eye to the peony and providing the perfect contrast to the rose. It is important to look at how the colours of a flower change, and this is especially important in the case of this astrantia: tight dark buds start to open in a vivid crimson, eventually becoming more muted and seeming paler as the flower opens fully. In *A Compleat Body of Planting and Gardening* (1770–71), William Hanbury wrote of astrantias, "Being flowers of no great beauty, the very worst part of the garden should be assigned them." How times change. Harnessing this colour movement allows for a planting whose effect changes as the days pass—bright reds, pinks, and oranges settle into peaches and wine as the buds open and develop.

- 15 -

Traditional Pastels

A long narrow London garden was an empty canvas when the property was purchased by an enthusiastic rosarian from California; roses had been harder to grow there, and she wanted to pack in as many as she possibly could at her new home. The challenge, as ever, was to have a sense of continuity throughout the garden as well as a feminine, elegant, classic atmosphere. So it was that pinks and lilacs and roses were the order of the day.

Pink and lilac is a colour scheme often suggested when I am asked to create a classic planting; pale pink roses rambling and scrambling over a cottage door is the quintessential English country garden. These colours work extremely well in a confined area and were thus perfect for this space. Pale colours don't fight for the brain's attention, and they make a space appear to recede: this is especially evident with pale blues and lilacs.

Hardy geraniums are very efficient at creating a haze of colour, a blur which makes everything else work; depending on the season and cultivar, they can be extremely effective fillers. Here, purple-blue *Geranium* Rozanne = 'Gerwat' and the almost pure blue of *G.* ×*johnsonii* 'Johnson's Blue' do their job perfectly, providing the link between the shapely pink flowers of *Rosa* Gertrude Jekyll = 'Ausbord' and the rest of the planting; they are accompanied by the promise of the electric blue globes of *Echinops ritro* 'Veitch's Blue' and the lavender spires of *Veronicastrum virginicum* 'Fascination', which give a more lavender-toned blue at height, the layers of illusory blue pushing the colours back and ensuring the space doesn't feel too crammed.

We really did manage to get many roses into this garden: structural supports across the width at intervals along the space ensure that all three dimensions are used. Roses grow up and over the supports, creating arbours of pink, white, and cream prettiness as we travel along the space. Crimson-tipped cream *Rosa* 'Félicité Perpétué' and blush-white *R.* 'Adélaïde d'Orléans' (both known in Victorian times as evergreen roses, and they do actually hang on to their leaves for a long time) are paler overhead, while the light pink loosely double flowers of *R.* Mortimer Sackler = 'Ausorts' continue the flower-filled theme along the walls.

Early and later colour comes in the form of pinky white *Clematis* 'Foxy' and the sharp blue *C. macropetala* 'Wesselton', whose luminescent light violet-blue is a real attention-seeker when bulbs are in flower. The purple of alliums looks at home in this colour scheme: *Allium hollandicum* 'Purple Sensation' is planted en masse here, and this true purple is picked up again later in the season by the dark purple flowers of *C.* 'Étoile Violette' standing out against any pale pink rose that is still flowering.

A counterpoint is provided here by *Cirsium rivulare* 'Atropupureum', which is similar in colour to a well-loved

Design: Jo Thompson

phalaeonopsis just visible in the kitchen. Any colour link with the interior of a house, even fleeting ones, is an important part of making a garden space feel restful, and where I can, I try to respect the colour choices that have been made inside without overtly matching up tones.

It's a wildlife foodfest here. Bees and butterflies congregate on the cirsium, and E.A. Bowles was spot on when he wrote thus of echinops: "I have often recommended them for entomologists' gardens, where plants are wished for that can be visited after dark with a lantern, to surprise a noctuid moth."

There is a function to all these choices. This is a real garden for a large family, and these classic pinks and pastels form a sort of veil that screens a seating area and dining area, complete with pizza oven, at the far end of the garden. The colours all lend themselves to the pretty, elegant, relaxed space, one that gives much pleasure and is enjoyed by an entire family who truly loves being in the garden, absolutely surrounded by flowers.

A

B

C

	NAME	TYPE	HEIGHT	SPREAD	SEASON	LIGHT	MOISTURE	HARDINESS	SOIL PH
A	*Rosa* Gertrude Jekyll = 'Ausbord'	shrub	1-1.5 metres, to 5 feet	0.5-1 metre, to 3.5 feet	summer / autumn	full sun	moist but well-drained / well-drained	very hardy, USDA 4-11	acid / alkaline / neutral
B	*Echinops ritro* 'Veitch's Blue'	perennial	0.5-1 metre, 3-3.5 feet	0.1-0.5 metre, 1.5-2 feet	summer / autumn	full sun / partial shade	well-drained	very hardy, USDA 3-8	acid / alkaline / neutral
C	*Cirsium rivulare* 'Atropurpureum'	perennial	1-1.5 metres, 4 feet	0.1-0.5 metre, 1.5-2 feet	summer	full sun	moist but well-drained	very hardy, USDA 4-8	acid / alkaline / neutral

– 16 –

Blue and Green

The accepted opinion in small gardens is to keep things simple—to have not too much of anything and to choose only a few varieties. We absolutely wanted to avoid introducing any more shade into this already-dark garden; the space is small, and so any distraction of colours was going to be too much. So how to create the laid-back atmosphere that the clients so wanted?

A jungle of green and blue felt like the right approach for this colour-loving family. The fresh greens of *Dicksonia antarctica* vary with the heights of the individual specimens, changing up and down as their fronds hit different levels of light, while the brown of their trunks links with the trellis installed to conceal the boundary. A multi-tasking summerhouse/play structure/seating/storage shed/shaded dining area was the second line of defence in trying to camouflage the huge height of the neighbouring fence that had been installed. Painted in a dark grey to pick up the colours of the kitchen, the building was going to need the planting palette to play an important role: grey can appear just so dull against a grey city sky. Always worth bearing in mind as you're about hit the buy button on grey hardscaping—is that grey, that looks so inoffensive inside, going to work under gloomy leaden clouds?

Fresh green and blue stop potential dullness. The tree ferns' soft foliage, its colour and form picked up on by perennial ferns and yellowy green *Hakonechloa macra* at ground level, paints the perfect backdrop for dots of colour, with easy geraniums and salvias in blues and purple and *Agastache* 'Blackadder' following on from the spires of the purple *Salvia nemorosa* 'Caradonna'.

Nothing too bright in terms of flowers, though, as I had something else up my sleeve. A bright blue water spout, inspired by the owners' existing furniture, in turn inspired further dots and highlights of colour through the garden. *Sanguisorba* 'Tanna' is at the edges of the borders; a possibly controversial choice you may think, as its flowerheads are red and moving away from the blue and green, but viewed from a couple of feet away or more, they appear burgundy to brown, and the silhouette creates a natural punctuation of form rather than striving to obey a necessity to match tone.

Stipa tenuissima emerges, a long green wispy grass; as it yellows with age it continues the idea of a kind of prehistoric meadow. Looking at the plant list, you can see how neutral the scheme is: essentially it is formed of browns and greens with blue in order to avoid any busy-ness and to stop flowers appearing to jump out of the planting and demand centre stage.

It's very easy to concentrate on the lower planting in an inward-looking garden such as this one, but it is important to remember to introduce colour at different heights. Again, anything too bright demands attention; pale is good. *Thalictrum aquilegiifolium* 'Album' is invaluable here in adding to the slightly otherworldly feeling, its frothy cream flowerheads creating a cloudy veil which further softens the building.

Design: Jo Thompson

	NAME	TYPE	HEIGHT	SPREAD	SEASON	LIGHT	MOISTURE	HARDINESS	SOIL PH
A	*Sanguisorba* 'Tanna'	perennial	0.1-0.5 metre, 1.5 feet	0.1-0.5 metre, 1 foot	summer / autumn	full sun / partial shade	moist but well-drained / well-drained	very hardy, USDA 4-8	acid / alkaline / neutral
B	*Geranium* Rozanne = 'Gerwat'	perennial	0.5-1 metre, 1-1.5 feet	0.5-1 metre, 1-2 feet	summer / autumn	full sun / partial shade	moist but well-drained / well-drained	very hardy, USDA 5-8	acid / alkaline / neutral
C	*Agastache* 'Blackadder'	perennial	0.5-1 metre, 2-3 feet	0.1-0.5 metre, 1.5-2 feet	summer / autumn	full sun	well-drained	very hardy, USDA 6-9	acid / alkaline / neutral
D	*Salvia nemorosa* 'Caradonna'	perennial	0.1-0.5 metre, 1-2 feet	0.1-0.5 metre, 1-2 feet	summer	full sun / partial shade	moist but well-drained	very hardy, USDA 4-8	acid / alkaline / neutral
E	*Dicksonia antarctica*	tree fern	to 6 metres, 12-18 feet	to 4 metres, 8-12 feet	autumn	full sun / partial shade / full shade	moist but well-drained	half hardy, USDA 9-10	acid / alkaline / neutral
F	*Hakonechloa macra*	grass	0.1-0.5 metre, 1-1.5 feet	0.1-0.5 metre, 1-1.5 feet	autumn	full sun / partial shade / full shade	moist but well-drained	very hardy, USDA 5-9	acid / alkaline / neutral

- 17 -

Spring Combination with a Twist

When we think about the colours of spring, fresh yellows and bright blues come to mind—bluebells, daffodils, and massed plantings of crocus and scilla, narcissi and chionodoxa. It's a foolproof colour combination, a definite crowdpleaser. The yellows can range from warm butter to cool lemon, the blues from cool light blue back into a warmer pinker violet-blue.

We are pretty safe in knowing that any combination of these will sit happily alongside each other, although this might be less to do with chromatic theory and more to do with colour psychology, and psychology in general. I am always so utterly relieved to see the first suggestions of colour starting to emerge in January after the dreary greyness of the preceding months that I'll happily embrace any garden colour, whatever and wherever.

Sometimes you might want to play with this palette and nudge it along a little into something a bit more adventurous, and this is what has happened here. *Narcissus* 'Irina's Choice' is pretty in primrose, neatly collaborating with the bluebell blue multi-stemmed *Hyacinthus orientalis* 'Anastasia', a fabulous form, looser than the usual more tightly packed, chunky hyacinth that we are used to seeing being forced up and out of a pot. And the nudge? Well, the glaucous foliage of *Fritillaria persica* is incredibly useful at giving a bit of grey-blue bulk to the palette, but it is its little flowers, whether of *F. p.* 'Ivory Bells' or the deep purple ones of the straight species, which move this scheme from the expected to the interesting.

It's a hint of what is to come, giving us enough colour and something to think about while we wait for the next bulbs to pop up; it is so refreshing to see new combinations, which (I can't help feeling) is part of the point of tulips. Spring comes round every year; our roses will be the colour they were last year, as will our perennials, but with tulips we can create a proper show of matching or mismatched colour, and if it doesn't work, it doesn't matter. The bulbs can be lifted and be moved into a cutting patch or pot, or even onto the compost heap. A little ruthlessness ensures desperately needed variety.

	NAME	TYPE	HEIGHT	SPREAD	SEASON	LIGHT	MOISTURE	HARDINESS	SOIL PH
A	*Hyacinthus orientalis* 'Anastasia'	bulb	0.1-0.5 metre, 0.5-1 foot	0.1-0.5 metre, 0.25 foot	spring	full sun / partial shade	moist but well-drained / well-drained	very hardy, USDA 4-8	acid / alkaline / neutral
B	*Fritillaria persica* 'Ivory Bells'	bulb	0.5-1 metre, 2-3 feet	0.1 metre, 0.5 foot	spring	full sun	well-drained	very hardy, USDA 4-7	acid / alkaline / neutral
C	*Narcissus* 'Irina's Choice'	bulb	0.1-0.5 metre, 1-1.5 feet	0.1 metre, 0.25 foot	spring	full sun / partial shade	moist but well-drained / well-drained	very hardy, USDA 5-9	acid / alkaline / neutral

Opposite | Design: Keukenhof Gardens

- 18 -

A Tumble of Light

Standing at the foot of this planting at the Dry Garden at RHS Hyde Hall, one senses that the plants are defying Nature. Drought-tolerance is the common denominator in this planting, seen here at its peak in summer, yet there's a surprising, interesting feel of fresh abundance. I'm convinced that this feeling is due in no little part to the palette here: the blues and primrose yellows, readily associated with the colours of spring and new hope, have been used to create a drama which plays backwards and forwards through the light as each plant captures it and uses it to show off to its very best.

The Dry Garden was developed in the early 2000s to showcase the huge variety of plants that can be grown in the driest part of the UK. The garden has no artificial irrigation; it receives only natural rainfall. It was designed to represent an undulating, rolling, rocky Mediterranean landscape; large mounds of soil and huge pieces of gabbro stone tie all together. A backbone of textural and evergreen plants, including conifers, small trees and shrubs, and grasses, supports a fantastic range of drought-tolerant perennials, biennials, and annuals planted in a soft and naturalistic style.

Design: RHS Hyde Hall

The queens of the display are *Verbascum bombyciferum* and *V. olympicum* (and their probable hybrid progeny), their buttery primrose tones moving usefully into pure yellows. Extraordinary candelabras of colour shoot upwards, rather cleverly blending in with the long, pale cream plumes of *Ampelodesmos mauritanicus* (Mauritania grass) and working well with the far more restrained and even paler yellow santolina.

The silver and grey foliage of the verbascum catches the light and provides an introduction to the silvery green stems of *Galactites tomentosa* (purple milk thistle); the light is positively shimmering through this foliage and the nigella seedheads in the foreground.

The grouping shown here is a fabulous example of how skeleton forms can play with the light and continue to have an important role in the palette long after the heyday of the flowers themselves: look at how the allium seadheads drift casually down, still attention-seekers weeks after their prime.

Despite the fact that this garden is dry, the foliage shades subvert any notion that dry might mean parched. The dark green *Pinus mugo* 'Ophir' throws its green to the giant *Echium pininana*, while the blue-green leaves of *Helleborus argutifolius* are good partners to the fresher green santolina in the foreground. There has clearly been an excellent, thought-through process in foliage choice here; we wouldn't expect anything less of an RHS garden, of course. A subtle yet apparent journey from silver into blue and through to green creates a tapestry of colours—and I don't use the word *tapestry* lightly. There's an intricate interweaving of tones as threads are picked up and put down across the planting, alternately dampening and then brightening the light in a colour scheme that's dreamy and soft.

	NAME	TYPE	HEIGHT	SPREAD	SEASON	LIGHT	MOISTURE	HARDINESS	SOIL PH
A	*Galactites tomentosa*	annual	0.7-1 metre, 1.5-3 feet	0.3- 0.6 metre, 1.5 feet	summer	full sun	well-drained	hardy, USDA 2-11	acid / alkaline / neutral
B	*Helleborus argutifolius*	perennial	0.5-1 metre, 1.5-2 feet	0.5-1 metre, 1.5-2 feet	spring	full sun / partial shade	moist but well-drained	hardy, USDA 6-8	alkaline / neutral
C	*Verbascum bombyciferum*	biennial	1.5-2.5 metres, 4-5 feet	0.5-1 metre, 1-2 feet	summer	full sun	well-drained	very hardy, USDA 3-9	alkaline
D	*Verbascum olympicum*	biennial	1.5-3.5 metres, to 8-10 feet	0.5-1 metre, 3 feet	summer	full sun	well-drained	very hardy, USDA 5-10	alkaline
E	*Ampelodesmos mauritanicus*	grass	2-3 metres, 9 feet	1 metre, 3-4 feet	spring / summer / autumn	full sun	well-drained	hardy, USDA 8-10	acid / alkaline / neutral
F	*Pinus mugo* 'Ophir'	shrub	0.5-1 metre, 1-3 feet	0.5-1 metre, 1.5 feet	evergreen	full sun	well-drained	very hardy, USDA 2-8	acid / alkaline / neutral
G	*Echium pininana*	perennial	2.5-4 metres, to 12 feet	0.5-1 metre, 3 feet	spring / summer	full sun	well-drained	half hardy, USDA 9-10	acid / alkaline / neutral

- 19 -

Deep Reds and Pinks

Dahlias present never-ending colour possibilities, moving from restrained deep reds and almost blacks, such as *Dahlia* 'Rip City', through to the ridiculously and seemingly unreal combinations of pinks and yellows in *D.* 'Banana Cabana'—all extraordinary shades and extraordinary flower shapes. I admit to leaving dahlias in the ground in the south of the UK; in colder places they do need to be lifted, but with that is the opportunity to shake all the colours about: treat them almost as an annual, and put the previous year's tubers in a vegetable patch to be used for cutting and bringing into the house.

Wonderfully and reassuringly, colour is more and more treated as something to experiment with, something playful, something to spark even more joy than a decluttered wardrobe. You don't really need to commit yourself to one colour combination in this brave new approach, and dahlias are just perfect for this—in fact, all tubers, bulbs, and corms are ideal for ringing in the new growing season with colour changes.

In this garden of a pub in Sussex, the colour scheme is played with each year, and however much I intend to make a colour clash, the dahlias, in all their here-I-am glory, always put on a fabulous show. In this part of the garden the vivid purplish red of *Dahlia* 'Ambition' is the standout colour from which all other colour choices derive; the dark red of *D.* 'Dark Spirit' is a subtle echo, while the red *D.* 'Tahoma Moonshot' in the foreground catches the eye—a beautiful red with no orange within its petals. When scarlet moves into the almost-luminous, it's tough to match it up with other plants, having (as Gertrude Jekyll put it) "a harsh quality that gives discomfort rather than satisfaction to a sensitive colour-eye." I know exactly what she means.

The foil to these brighter colours are the permanent fixtures of the rosemary and the olive trees; blue-grey and green provide a strong background colour and a base for all temporary colour experimentation. *Geranium* 'Orion' and the delicate white to pale pink daisies of airy self-seeding *Erigeron karvinskianus* blur the junction between the hard stone and steel of the gabion cages that hold the contours of this garden together.

I've used one of my all-time favourite grasses here. I'm very strict with ornamental grasses: mass plantings of them always work best when the light is absolutely right. They can look wonderful backlit in photographs, but it's vital to bear in mind that they will be viewed at different times of the day: they need to perform when viewed from wherever and whenever in order to earn their place. Having said all that, *Molinia caerulea* subsp. *arundinacea* 'Transparent' is a grass that does brilliantly in the spots where you know that the light is going to catch it at key moments, its small brown flowers creating that veil that softens everything. I don't plant it in block plantings, using it instead where I think it will partially mask a focal point. Counterintuitive perhaps to block that which I want seen, but this grass is just so very good in its blurring of colour.

Calamagrostis ×acutiflora 'Karl Foerster' is the other grass used here—the garden's ups and downs mean that low evergreens, good for dark green, don't have enough movement about them to work in these contours and curves; with a wilder looser structure needed, the upright yellow-beige sentries of the calamagrostis perfectly punctuate the garden's nooks and crannies.

Design: Jo Thompson

	NAME	TYPE	HEIGHT	SPREAD	SEASON	LIGHT	MOISTURE	HARDINESS	SOIL PH
A	*Dahlia* 'Ambition'	perennial	0.5-1 metre, 3-3.5 feet	0.5 metre, 1.5-2 feet	summer / autumn	full sun	moist but well-drained / well-drained	half hardy, USDA 3-10	acid / alkaline / neutral
B	*Dahlia* 'Dark Spirit'	perennial	0.5-1 metre, 3 feet	0.1-0.5 metre, 1.5-2 feet	summer / autumn	full sun	well-drained	half hardy, USDA 3-10	acid / alkaline / neutral
C	*Erigeron karvinskianus*	perennial	0.1-0.5 metre, 1-2 feet	0.5-1 metre, 3-5 feet	summer	full sun	well-drained	very hardy, USDA 3-8	acid / neutral
D	*Molinia caerulea* subsp. *arundinacea* 'Transparent'	grass	1.5-2.5 metres, 6-8 feet	1-1.5 metres, 2-4 feet	summer / autumn	full sun / partial shade	moist but well-drained / well-drained	very hardy, USDA 5-8	acid / neutral
E	*Calamagrostis ×acuti-flora* 'Karl Foerster'	grass	1-1.5 metres, 3-5 feet	0.5-1 metre, 1.5-2.5 feet	summer / autumn	full sun / partial shade	moist but well-drained / well-drained	very hardy, USDA 5-9	acid / alkaline / neutral

Inspiration from RHS Garden Hyde Hall

Curator Robert Brett describes impressive spring planting in the Robinson Garden at Hyde Hall, Essex:

1. Tinged with gold

In the Robinson Garden, drifts of reliable favourite *Narcissus* 'Tête-à-Tête' bloom beside clumps of geraniums and other emerging herbaceous perennials. As the daffodils die down after flowering, the perennials will quickly expand to fill the space.

2. Clumps of hellebores

The nodding bells of *Helleborus ×hybridus* in a range of hues, from purple to white, provide splendid underplanting. The old evergreen foliage is removed to show off the flowers as they open, ready for a new flush of leaves in mid-spring.

3. Resplendent edgeworthia

The bare, slender branches of *Edgeworthia chrysantha* are decorated with delightfully fragrant and long-lasting white and yellow flowerheads.

- 20 -

Orange, Grey, Red, and Green

Here's a planting where the less-is-more concept is shown to perfection—an absolute triumph of restraint in terms of both choice of plants and choice of tone. The designer Daniel Nolan doesn't generally use a lot of colour in his gardens, but I am really glad he went off-piste here as he demonstrates just how good he is at choosing harmonising tones and shades.

This simple house in the San Francisco Bay area is set in a foliage garden of predominantly dark green, olive green, and silver-grey. Designed elements of an outside space are often a little more formal nearer the house and then become more natural moving away into the garden; here, Daniel has introduced colour into a planter visible from almost every angle of the house, leaving the rest of the garden to shades of green. The intention was to have a concentration of colour near to where people sit, both inside and out, and he selected just three plants which would link the human, habited space to the surrounding greens. Expressive and refined, lush and minimal.

Leucadendron 'Safari Sunset' works so well here, with yellow-green flowerheads, leathery red-flushed leaves, and purple-red bracts fading to golden yellow—all in one plant. It's a brilliant choice, and not just in terms of stature. It provides year-round colour, and it's the seasonal shifts in those colours which make this such a worthy selection in a planting that in theory—with only three different plant choices—could very well risk the need for a bit more interest. But instead there's a journey through green, red, purple, and yellow, and what I find so pleasing is the colour that he has chosen to put next to this. Although they are obviously orange when inspected close-up, viewed from just a few steps away, the long-lasting flowers of *Anigozanthos flavidus* 'Orange Cross' aren't simply orange. The tubular flowers, arrayed in the genus's namesake kangaroo paw shape, means that the orange melts into tones of saffron and tangerine as the background foliage performs a form of colour magic.

André Lhote was quite right: "To use colour well is as difficult as for a fish to pass from water to air or earth." Nolan has certainly used his colours well here, building up the tones and placing bright "Portrait of a Lady" Post-Impressionist colours against angular features in a combination that chimes well with Lhote's description of his own work as "ambient Cubism."

So a layer of red-green and a layer of oranges—and for these two hues the designer has created a catalyst in the form of the large grey-green shrub at the corner of the house, *Bocconia frutescens*. Of the three chosen plants, this is the only one with a colour in the grey-green range, linking it to the pale walls and the sky and olive greens which appear in the wider garden. As I say—perfection.

Design: Daniel Nolan

A

B

C

	NAME	TYPE	HEIGHT	SPREAD	SEASON	LIGHT	MOISTURE	HARDINESS	SOIL PH
A	*Leucadendron* 'Safari Sunset'	shrub	1.5-2.5 metres, 8-10 feet	1.5-2.5 metres, 6-8 feet	evergreen	full sun	well-drained	half hardy, USDA 8-11	acid / neutral
B	*Bocconia frutescens*	shrub	2.5-4.5 metres, 10-16 feet	1.5-3.5 metres, 8-12 feet	spring / summer	full sun	well-drained	tender, USDA 9-12	acid / neutral
C	*Anigozanthos flavidus*	perennial	1-1.5 metres, 4-5 feet	0.5-1 metre, 2-3 feet	spring / summer	full sun	well-drained	tender, USDA 9-12	acid / neutral

– 21 –

Red and Neutrals

Designers talk at great length about respecting the surroundings. However much we may want to express ourselves and experiment with colour and form, sometimes the location has a very strong (not to say final) say in the garden content.

Nowhere is this more evident than in this coastal garden, open to the English Channel and exposed to sand, salt, and wind, where more than anything the owners wanted shelter and privacy in a garden that can be viewed directly from the adjoining beach. Creating a seating area in dunes to link with those surrounding the houses was the first step; the planting has a huge role to play in terms of interest, creating privacy and also sheltering from the winds. And also, it has to survive: no mean feat in this spot.

In an inhospitable location, an examination of what actually grows and thrives nearby is always a wise move. A careful study in this case revealed that tamarisk did well, and that those plants which have the giveaway *maritima* in their name sow themselves with gusto along the beach. These plants have been embraced in the garden: crambe, erigeron, armeria, and poppy are brought together against a palette of yellow sand and blue-green marram grass. A secondary layer of white from the silene provides a backdrop for pale blue leymus. The highlight in this garden is the horned poppy with its bright vivid red: once planted, it's never absent, and it really does love these conditions. I embrace self-seeders in the garden: they seem to know where to go, and if they don't, they get moved along, animating the landscape's palette wherever they land.

The showstopping red flower of the poppy is echoed by the purple of the armeria, and the sea thrift ties the blue leymus to the sky, in itself an enormous part of this garden: shape and form and colour against it have impact all year. An interesting challenge as the sky is never the same, but we know that the reds will look excellent against it, grabbing our attention and looking perfectly matched. It's always worth remembering that our skies change: in the UK they can often be grey, which is why we have to be so careful when inspired by colour combinations we see abroad. Majorelle Blue looks extraordinary in Morocco; it doesn't look quite so mesmerising against a grey London sky.

Design: Jo Thompson

A

B

C

D

	NAME	TYPE	HEIGHT	SPREAD	SEASON	LIGHT	MOISTURE	HARDINESS	SOIL PH
A	*Papaver rhoeas*	annual	0.5-1 metre, 0.75-1.5 feet	0.1-0.5 metre, 0.5-1 foot	spring / summer	full sun	well-drained	very hardy, USDA 3-10	acid / alkaline / neutral
B	*Armeria maritima*	perennial	0.1-0.5 metre, 0.5-1 foot	0.1-0.5 metre, 0.5-1 foot	spring / summer	full sun	well-drained	very hardy, USDA 4-8	acid / alkaline / neutral
C	*Leymus arenarius*	annual	0.5-1 metre, 2-3 feet	0.1-0.5 metre, 2 feet	spring / summer	full sun	well-drained	very hardy, USDA 4-9	acid / alkaline / neutral
D	*Crambe maritima*	perennial	0.5-1 metre, 2.5-3 feet	0.1-0.5 metre, 2-2.5 feet	summer	full sun / partial shade	well-drained	very hardy, USDA 5-9	acid / alkaline / neutral

- 22 -

Green and Wine

Gardens of foliage are elegant and restful to look at, and a foliage planting with white flowers has the same effect: one can look at the garden in a calm way when no one plant is fighting for attention against serene green.

When is a green and white garden not a green and white garden? When it has dark purple foliage too. These deep purple to blacks need to be deployed with care in a planting scheme: they can create wonderful variety, enabling a distinction between an array of greens, but they can also create the sense of a void, so take care where you place them. I would also suggest that if you use one plant with dark foliage, you use more than one, repeating these purple-black leaves in order to consolidate their presence.

This totally new garden, overlooked by neighbouring houses and visible from the street, had to be in conversation with the starkly contemporary interior of a restored sixteenth-century bakery (home to an artist and gallery-owner) as well as with the vernacular architecture on all sides. Foliage—which links to the leaf colour of existing trees as well as to the reclaimed

Design: Jo Thompson

brick wall—helps this garden look as if it's truly meant to be there. Layers of colour both shelter us and give us something to look at, so that we aren't quite sure where the garden ends and the street begins.

The grey stems of amelanchier tone with the greys of the sculptures that appear at intervals through the garden. Against the orange-brown of the clay bricks these sculptures nestle into a simple shade-tolerant planting of digitalis, ferns, and dicentra; the weathered oak gate provides the third shade of grey in this space. Amelanchier and liquidambar bring their autumn shot of red and yet for the rest of the year are a humble green, playing bridesmaid to the stunning purples, browns, and crimsons of *Cercis canadensis* 'Forest Pansy'. The cercis continues the colour rhythm of a mature *Prunus cerasifera* 'Nigra', creating and almost merging into its own shadows on the wall.

Euphorbia characias subsp. *wulfenii* is the bringer of light here; its acid green bracts go to work alongside the fresh green of the liquidambar, lighting up the mid- and lower storeys. Clumps of *Epimedium* ×*youngianum* 'Niveum' travel throughout, the fresh green and red-bronze young foliage and starry white flowers connecting the dots and covering the ground with a satisfying mass of leaves.

	NAME	TYPE	HEIGHT	SPREAD	SEASON	LIGHT	MOISTURE	HARDINESS	SOIL PH
A	*Digitalis purpurea*	perennial	1.5-2.5 metres, 2-5 feet	0.1-0.5 metre, 1-2.5 feet	summer	full sun / partial shade	moist but well-drained / well-drained	very hardy, USDA 4-8	acid / alkaline / neutral
B	*Digitalis purpurea* f. *albiflora*	perennial	0.5-1.5 metres, 3-5 feet	0.1-0.5 metre, 1.5-2 feet	spring / summer	full sun / partial shade	moist but well-drained / well-drained	very hardy, USDA 4-8	acid / alkaline / neutral
C	*Lamprocapnos spectabilis* 'Alba'	perennial	0.5-1 metre, 2-2.5 feet	0.5-1 metre, 1.5-2 feet	spring / summer	partial shade	moist but well-drained / poorly drained	very hardy, USDA 3-9	alkaline / neutral
D	*Geranium phaeum* 'Album'	perennial	0.8 metre, 1.5-2.5 feet	0.6 metre, 1-1.5 feet	spring / summer	full sun / partial shade / full shade	moist but well-drained / well-drained	very hardy, USDA 5-7	acid / alkaline / neutral
E	*Epimedium ×youngianum* 'Niveum'	perennial	0.1-0.5 metre, 0.5-0.75 foot	0.1-0.5 metre, 1-1.5 feet	spring	partial shade	moist but well-drained	very hardy, USDA 4-8	acid / neutral
F	*Cercis canadensis*	shrub or small tree	4-8 metres, 20-30 feet	4-8 metres, 25-35 feet	spring	full sun / partial shade	well-drained	very hardy, USDA 5-9	acid / alkaline / neutral

- 23 -

Isabelline

Isabelline is a beautiful term for one in a range of underrated shades. The neutrals—beige, cream, grey, light brown, and, that most Eighties of colours, taupe—stem from brown and from white, and it seems that everyone has a different perception of what each of these actually is. Whatever the name, they are a jolly useful group of shades and can provide a splendid backdrop as the mainstay in a colour palette.

I rejoice at this colour scheme. The neutral—let us call it Isabelline, but you might plump for brownish white, or even more prosaically, dirty white—is provided by *Stipa tenuissima*. Soft green hairy foliage becomes fluffier and fluffier and lighter and lighter as the season progresses, until it reaches this wonderful light shade, which creates light throughout.

This would be such an exciting scheme to recreate, dotting jewels amongst the neutrals and waiting for the sun to illuminate the whole planting. *Liatris pycnostachya* sends its bright yet palest-of-purple meerkat flower spikes up throughout. The added bonus is that butterflies adore this plant, and seeing them bobbing over the cloud of grass flowers is a very lovely sight indeed. *Verbena hastata* carries the purple along in more slender branching spikes, and *Cleome spinosa* picks up the purple mantle, infusing it with a strong dose of deep pink, working well with the dusky pink fountains of *Pennisetum orientale* 'Karley Rose' at the rear.

This range of colour associations would in itself satisfy quite a few people, but I thoroughly agree with what has happened next. Pink and pale purple against a neutral is pretty; it is charming and looks effective. But there's a surprise here in the form of an orange, neatly contrasting with the purple. No ordinary orange, *Rudbeckia hirta* 'Cappuccino' has hints of russet and mahogany in its petals, bleeding into crimson-orange-yellow, toning so well with the grasses yet providing that one unexpected element in the palette.

Eugène Delacroix was one of the first French artists to observe that no hue existed in isolation but would always be altered by neighbouring complementary or contrasting colours. In *The Expulsion of Heliodorus*, the harmonious earthen and neutral tones of the architecture are smattered with light and colour, a frenzy of vibrant and expressive turquoise, violet, purple, and gold. Cézanne—who believed as a general rule that the greater the contrast, the greater the brilliance—once praised Delacroix's palette as being "the most beautiful in France."

Above | Design: Jaap de Vries
Right | Eugène Delacroix, *The Expulsion of Heliodorus*, 1853–63

Isabelline

The dictionary of L'Académie Française describes Isabelline as a colour halfway between white and yellow, with yellow being predominant. A version of the word first appeared in English 1600, in an inventory of the wardrobe of Queen Elizabeth I: "one rounde gowne of Isabella-colour satten." Others think Isabelline predates the Virgin Queen, being a corruption of *zibellino*, the Italian word for "sable." But in yet another amusing story, the beautiful-sounding Isabelline has a not-so-beautiful origin: it is associated with underwear.

Legend has it that as her husband Albert VII, the Archduke of Austria, was leaving to fight at the Siege of Ostend, Isabella Clara Eugenia of Spain made one of those peculiar "deals" that we sometimes make with ourselves. She declared that she would not change or wash her undergarments until he came back safely—who knows how on earth she came up with that one. The really bad part of this tale is that it took Albert three years to return. The colour of the neglected underwear does not need to be described, but let's just say it was distinctive enough to need its own name—and lo, Isabelline was born.

Rather boringly, the Oxford English Dictionary pours cold water on this theory and states that the term was in use well before the Siege of Ostend, in descriptions of bird plumage and palomino horses.

	NAME	TYPE	HEIGHT	SPREAD	SEASON	LIGHT	MOISTURE	HARDINESS	SOIL PH
A	*Cleome spinosa*	annual	0.9-1.5 metres, 3-5 feet	0.3-0.5 metre, 2 feet	summer	full sun	moist but well-drained	half hardy, USDA 10-11	acid / alkaline / neutral
B	*Liatris pycnostachya*	perennial	1-1.5 metres, 2-5 feet	0.5-1 metre, 1-2 feet	summer	full sun	moist but well-drained / well-drained	very hardy, USDA 3-9	acid / alkaline / neutral
C	*Rudbeckia hirta* 'Cappuccino'	biennial	0.5-1 metre, 2-2.5 feet	0.1-0.5 metre, 1.5-2 feet	summer	full sun / partial shade	moist but well-drained	half hardy, USDA 3-8	acid / alkaline / neutral
D	*Verbena hastata*	perennial	1-2 metres, 2-6 feet	0.5-1 metre, 1-2.5 feet	summer	full sun	moist but well-drained / well-drained	very hardy, USDA 3-8	acid / alkaline / neutral
E	*Pennisetum orientale* 'Karley Rose'	grass	0.5-1 metre, 2-3 feet	0.5-1 metre, 2-3 feet	summer	full sun	well-drained	half hardy, USDA 5-8	acid / alkaline / neutral
F	*Stipa tenuissima*	grass	0.5-1 metre, 1-2 feet	0.1-0.5 metre, 1-2 feet	spring / summer / autumn	full sun	moist but well-drained / well-drained	hardy, USDA 7-10	acid / alkaline / neutral

– 24 –

Violet-Lilac

There is such a thing, I promise you, as Wisteria Hysteria. Each May, as the ground begins to warm up, this Chinese beauty feels a stirring at its roots and, with an almost palpable rush of excitement, causes a tingle all over Britain as its porcelain-blue buds start to emerge.

Wisteria are often seen against house walls, but don't forget that the traffic-stopping beauty of these flowers, most familiar in shades of purple, lilac, and violet, can be even further heightened by a background of sky. At Iford Manor near Bath, we get the best of both vantage points: the wisteria is gorgeous against the warm honey-coloured walls of the casita that it's planted against; it is equally magnificent as you stand inside this garden building and look out through the stems it sends out, creating boughs of welcome against the Wiltshire landscape.

The wisteria here is *Wisteria sinensis*, and with the simplicity of the species comes an absolutely magnificent scent. The lucky owners, William and Marianne Cartwright-Hignett, know that the specimen on the casita was planted in around 1900 by the garden's creator, famed Edwardian architect Harold Peto, but what isn't known is its origin. Perhaps it was one he brought back

Design: Marianne Cartwright-Hignett, Harold Peto

	NAME	TYPE	HEIGHT	SPREAD	SEASON	LIGHT	MOISTURE	HARDINESS	SOIL PH
A	*Wisteria sinensis*	woody vine	> 12 metres, 10-25 feet	> 8 metres, 10-25 feet	spring / summer	full sun / partial shade	moist but well-drained	hardy, USDA 5-8	acid / alkaline / neutral

himself from his travels to Asia; perhaps it was propagated from the one on the front of the house (which is c. 1830 and rumoured to be one of the oldest in the country) or was sourced from elsewhere.

Whichever it is, there truly is a sense of joy created by the colours against sky and stone. Large clusters of deep purple-violet flowers with hints of blue and lilac fading to grey pick up all the colours of the sky behind and at the same time melt beautifully in front of the golden tones of the local Bath stone, cool against warm.

Yet again, colour rules, and theories on primaries, secondaries, and tertiaries sit in second place when seeking to understand why a planting of violet is so successful.

To me it seems that it's more than in part due to the connotations carried by the wisteria flowers: unexpected beauty, the arrival of an old friend, the improbably huge racemes of flowers which look so heavily light. Combine all these notions with the flowers' knack for capturing a textured patchwork of shimmering light—a coup any Impressionist would have been proud of—and perhaps we get somewhere near to understanding why wisteria works so well everywhere: against walls, over pergolas, as a freestanding tree. Colour as light: when we reduce a planting to this notion, it's hard to go wrong.

– 25 –

Green and Silver-Blue with a Hint of Pink

Who wouldn't like to live in a putty-pink bungalow? The shade of this facade references the sun-kissed stucco so often seen in LA's Echo Park neighbourhood. It's a pink which isn't blue and isn't brown: there's a definite splash of yellow in there, which makes it a perfect backdrop for this street-side planting. David Godshall of Terremoto had breeziness in mind when he created the planting palette for this space; at the same time he intended it as a meditative transitional space through which the client could freely move.

Green is important here. It isn't the colour we see straight away: try looking away right now and what colours can you recall? Perhaps the bright orange dots of the wild nasturtiums, or the pale blue of the low-flowering *Salvia* 'Bee's Bliss' slowly ebbing towards the silver of *Santolina chamaecyparissus* maybe? The vivid oranges certainly bob along as an echo of yellow from the house walls, and the dissected silvery fluffiness of the cotton lavender is a brilliantly effective background to the purple-blue flowers and silvery-blue foliage of the mass of the California native sage. A Mannerist palette of exquisite colours washes over and through the planting as delicately as the buffs and corals of Leonard Rosoman's dreamlike *Interior, Elk River, Maryland*.

But there's something else going on this planting.

A mini-orchard of rare heirloom fruit trees, whose structure you might well have noticed, provide the perfect shade of green in front of the pink. It's a green which isn't too fresh; it's just on the muted side of green with a tiny bit of yellow in there. Close your eyes again, and imagine for a moment these leaves as silver instead of green. You'll realise how that would have been too obvious a matching. Any try-hard effect is cleverly avoided with the fruit trees' yellow-green, picked up on the lower plane by the darker green leaves of *Santolina rosmarinifolia* subsp. *rosmarinifolia*. This in turn just nods to a conifer in the rear garden. The designed landscape blurs with the wilderness of Echo Park, hazy with wild nasturtiums. It's hard to tell what the designer did and what he didn't. I, as he, revel in this ambiguity.

Design: David Godshall/Terremoto

	NAME	TYPE	HEIGHT	SPREAD	SEASON	LIGHT	MOISTURE	HARDINESS	SOIL PH
A	*Salvia* 'Bee's Bliss'	perennial	0.1-0.5 metre, 2 feet	1-2.5 metres, 6-8 feet	summer / autumn	full sun / partial shade	well-drained	hardy, USDA 8-10	acid / alkaline / neutral
B	*Santolina rosmarinifolia* subsp. *rosmarinifolia*	perennial	0.5-1 metre, 2-3 feet	0.5-1 metre, 2-3 feet	summer	full sun	moist but well-drained / well-drained	very hardy, USDA 6-11	acid / alkaline / neutral
C	*Santolina chamaecyparissus*	shrub	0.1-0.5 metre, 1-2 feet	0.5-1 metre, 2-3 feet	summer	full sun	well-drained	very hardy, USDA 6-9	acid / alkaline / neutral

- 26 -

Green, Pale Lilac, and Yellow

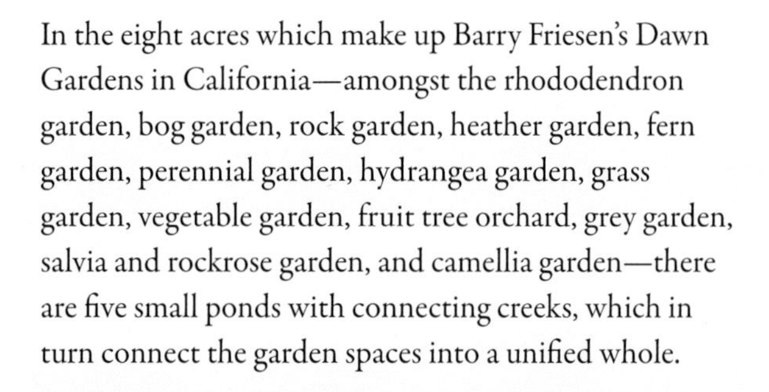

In the eight acres which make up Barry Friesen's Dawn Gardens in California—amongst the rhododendron garden, bog garden, rock garden, heather garden, fern garden, perennial garden, hydrangea garden, grass garden, vegetable garden, fruit tree orchard, grey garden, salvia and rockrose garden, and camellia garden—there are five small ponds with connecting creeks, which in turn connect the garden spaces into a unified whole.

Moving from area to area, colours brighten and then become more subtle. Along the creeks we see this idea of the ebbing and flowing of shades in action; plants whose tones are derived from a calm and restful palette peacefully blend with other, more lively colours. Yellow-green and blue-green grasses contrast with the strong greenish yellow of *Carex elata* 'Aurea' (Bowles' golden sedge), whose foliage forms graceful fountains. Its gold and green striped leaves gleam bright in the spring and then flatten to a duller gold as brown flowers appear. This sedge was discovered naturalising in a Norfolk marsh by a young E.A. Bowles—how beautiful must that marsh have looked with clumps of yellow weaving throughout.

This yellow-gold appears again, just a little bit more sharply, in the bright yellow flowers of *Eriogonum umbellatum* var. *polyanthum* 'Shasta Sulfur', a selection of sulphur buckwheat. Its blue-grey leaves are evergreen and provide an excellent groundcover.

So how to provide a wash of highlighted colour in this area? Barry has selected here a California native, *Collinsia heterophylla* (purple Chinese houses), its tiny flowers looking like miniature pagodas when viewed up close. From afar, the mix of deep purplish pink and pale pink petals creates a haze of shimmering lavender highlights, which move into lighter and darker hues depending on your viewpoint. This idea of moving colour is effective and pretty, completely appropriate by the shallow creek.

Design: David Godshall/Terremoto

A

B

C

	NAME	TYPE	HEIGHT	SPREAD	SEASON	LIGHT	MOISTURE	HARDINESS	SOIL PH
A	*Collinsia heterophylla*	annual	0.1-0.5 metre, 0.3-1.5 feet	0.1-0.5 metre, 0.25 foot	spring / summer	partial shade	moist but well-drained	very hardy, USDA 1-10	acid / alkaline / neutral
B	*Eriogonum umbellatum* var. *polyanthum* 'Shasta Sulfur'	perennial	0.1-0.5 metre, 0.5-1 foot	0.1-0.5 metre, 1-3 feet	spring / summer	full sun	well-drained / moist but well-drained	very hardy, USDA 4-8	acid / alkaline / neutral
C	*Carex elata* 'Aurea'	perennial	0.5-1 metre, 1.5-2.5 feet	0.5-1 metre, 1.5-2.5 feet	summer	full shade / partial shade	poorly drained	very hardy, USDA 5-9	acid / alkaline / neutral

- 27 -

White, Silver-Blue, and Green

We will never tire of white gardens. They are serene, elegant, tasteful, and generally easy on the eye. They convey a sense of thoughtful restraint: however much we enjoy colour, a garden full of white flowers suggests that the owner knows how to hold back and exercise extreme self-control.

In this corner of the Cool Garden at RHS Rosemoor, the planting feels as if it's just escaping from any pure white constraints. The garden itself is a mix of blues, silvers, and whites. However, even within these essentially cool colours, it's still possible to ring the changes and to experiment with different palettes in different areas, while still having a unified whole.

Flowing throughout are a couple of wonderful Shasta daisies. With their prolific nature, they don't have the best reputation, and they announce their presence rather proudly—not the most elegant of plants. Yet within a restrained palette, they gain a bit of class. *Leucanthemum* ×*superbum* 'Real Galaxy' is the star of this bed, its creamy white frilly petals smearing light alongside a streak of *Artemisia lactiflora* and through the neighbouring silver-grey daubs of *Phlomis grandiflora* 'Lloyd's Silver' and *P. fruticosa*.

These bold daubs, which can sometimes overpower and overwhelm, work here because they are the only daubs; everything else is dots and hazes and the lightest of brush-strokes. Gentle shimmers of blue from *Nepeta* ×*faassenii* 'Kit Cat' and points of canary yellow *Hemerocallis* 'Lark Song' nudge this colour scheme over from restrained into a looser, more natural expression of colour. Vertical dashes of brown and bright green, from *Calamagrostis* ×*acutiflora* 'Overdam' and *Panicum virgatum* 'Northwind' create a veil, which just stops the eye before it reaches *Buddleja davidii* Nanho Blue = 'Mongo'.

As ever, the backdrop to a scheme is critical; here the dark green *Taxus baccata* hedge is the perfect rear curtain to the lighter green leaves of *Betula pendula* subsp. *pendula* Fastigiata Joes = 'Jolep 1'. Everything else is in relief.

Design: Jo Thompson

	NAME	TYPE	HEIGHT	SPREAD	SEASON	LIGHT	MOISTURE	HARDINESS	SOIL PH
A	*Phlomis grandiflora* 'Lloyd's Silver'	perennial	0.5-1 metre, 3-4 feet	0.5-1 metre, 3-4 feet	summer / autumn	full sun	well-drained	very hardy, USDA 7-11	acid / alkaline / neutral
B	*Leucanthemum* ×*superbum* 'Real Galaxy'	perennial	0.5-1 metre, 3 feet	0.1-0.5 metre, 1.5 feet	summer / autumn	full sun / partial shade	moist but well-drained	very hardy, USDA 5-9	acid / alkaline / neutral
C	*Hemerocallis* 'Lark Song'	perennial	0.5-1 metre, 3 feet	0.5-1 metre, 3 feet	summer	full sun	moist but well-drained	very hardy, USDA 3-9	acid / alkaline / neutral
D	*Phlomis fruticosa*	perennial	1-1.5 metres, 2-4 feet	0.5-1 metre, 3-5 feet	summer	full sun	moist but well-drained / well-drained	half hardy, USDA 8-10	acid / alkaline / neutral
E	*Nepeta* ×*faassenii* 'Kit Cat'	perennial	0.1-0.5 metre, 1-1.5 feet	0.1-0.5 metre, 1-2 feet	summer / autumn	full sun / partial shade	well-drained	very hardy, USDA 3-8	acid / alkaline / neutral
F	*Artemisia lactiflora*	perennial	1-1.5 metres, 4-5 feet	1-1.5 metres, 2-3 feet	summer / autumn	full sun	moist but well-drained	very hardy, USDA 3-8	acid / alkaline / neutral

A
B
C
D
E
F

- 28 -

Meadow White

When light hits the cones of our eyes, a message pinballs to the hypothalamus—the part of the brain that governs, amongst other things, our autonomic nervous systems, our metabolism, our appetites: essentially, colour presses the button for emotional experience. Apply this to the world of plants, and it's immediately clear why walking through the forest is good for us, why forest bathing is an actual thing, and why this woodland-edge meadow at RHS Rosemoor is somewhere that makes us breathe a sigh of relief. Those greens and whites, simplicity of tone, of light, of colour—all these come together to create a feeling of absolute calm and serenity.

Opposite | Design: RHS Rosemoor
Below | Vincent van Gogh, *Green Wheat Fields, Auvers*, 1890

How to name all the greens that are here? This is where I could really do with the linguistic capability of the Himba people of Namibia who, thanks to their abundance of terms for different nuances of green, are able to "see" and appreciate many shades that others, with a paucity of terms, find much harder to distinguish.

The dark green of the tree canopy is a comforting embrace of serenity, filtering the light and offering glimpses of the fresh greens in the meadows beyond, the branches creating shadows and bands of more muted greens below. Emerald green, lime green, bottle green, grass green, and jade—all shades that exude and engender balance and harmony. Imagine standing right here: you couldn't help but feel rested and calm, that all is good.

No other colour is needed: the different greens in the alternating light and dark patches show themselves as subtly blue and grey, while little spots of yellow in the wildflowers pick up the yellow in the grass itself.

And then we have white. The mass planting of *Camassia leichtlinii* subsp. *leichtlinii* is perfection itself in this location. Spires of ivory stars catch the light, positively sparkling as they shimmer across and away, becoming steadily bluer as they recede. The whole scheme is so very simple yet so utterly seductive, hypnotic in its minimalist bountifulness.

	NAME	TYPE	HEIGHT	SPREAD	SEASON	LIGHT	MOISTURE	HARDINESS	SOIL PH
A	*Camassia leichtlinii* subsp. *leichtlinii*	bulb	1-1.5 metres, 3-4 feet	0.1-0.5 metre, 1-2 feet	spring	full sun / partial shade	moist but well-drained	very hardy, USDA 3-8	acid / alkaline / neutral

I see exactly the same stillness in van Gogh's *Green Wheat Fields, Auvers*. Even in the dynamic swirls and swoops of his brush, the feeling is one of tranquil calm. Consider the context of this painting: the artist had left the Saint-Paul-de-Mausole asylum and settled in a small village north of Paris; at last he felt that he had come home. You start to see how the cool greens, blues, and whites exude a sense of complete peace; gently undulating cool colours have completely replaced the south's fiery yellows and oranges, in a celebration of landscape brimming with gentle energy as opposed to dramatic exploration. If you have ever stood by a wheatfield and seen how even the softest breeze creates a ripple of light across the blue-green, you'll understand that sense of magic which is so hard to convey in words yet so simple to create by using a mass of green. A field of long grass with ox-eye daisies creates that same feeling of the night sky in the day: constellations of sparkly light leaving us in wonder at the magic of the universe itself.

- 29 -

Green and White

Creating something out of nothing is one of the joys of working with a landscape, and nothing is more nothing than a blank canvas. This spa garden was once just a hole in the ground—the owners wanted an area which felt young and fresh and yet which still worked with the surrounding English countryside. The ensuing planting, featuring a restrained palette of whites and greens, was intended to create a feeling of elegant simplicity.

A dark green backdrop created by tall yew hedges provides an effective foil for the fresher green leaves of box-pleached *Carpinus betulus*, while a lower base of colour structure comes from blocks of *Buxus sempervirens*. These layers of green, in shades chosen to link with the crowns of the trees in the wider landscape, support one of the main players in this colour scheme: the gleaming stems of *Betula utilis* subsp. *jacquemontii*, which contrast strikingly with the greens of the manicured topiary. The restriction of form, inherent in topiary, signifies for me that everything else needs to be far more relaxed.

White—elegant and fresh, contemporary and classic—is the one colour apart from green that is used here: *Rosa rugosa* 'Alba', considered a thug but deliberately placed in the knowledge that it would quickly colonise these brand-new borders, provides colour with whiter-than-white blooms followed by orange-red hips. The white of the roses fades away and returns with a supreme flourish in the form of *Hydrangea arborescens* 'Annabelle', whose enormous lime green flowerheads become white and then fade into a muted cream.

The dark green leaves of *Viburnum cinnamomifolium*, besides providing evergreen structure, offer themselves as a backdrop for changing displays of bulbs throughout the growing season. After *Narcissus* 'Thalia' and *Tulipa* 'Hakuun', alliums are allowed to stay on way past their flowering season, right up until their stems fall over in autumn. *Allium stipitatum* 'Mount Everest' is a stunner, its pure white heads fading to a green-yellow skeleton which catches the sun perfectly as well as creating a haze of colour—a ghostly suggestion of what went before.

The entire sunken area is given a subtle foundation with a mass planting of *Hedera helix* 'Green Ripple' against the brown brick of the terrace walls. The ivy's striking light-green-veined leaves are superb for clothing and covering, as they have done with the walls here, their glossy leaves adding light and shade and solidity to all.

Design: Jo Thompson

	NAME	TYPE	HEIGHT	SPREAD	SEASON	LIGHT	MOISTURE	HARDINESS	SOIL PH
A	*Allium stipitatum* 'Mount Everest'	bulb	1-1.5 metres, 3.5 feet	0.1-0.5 metre, 0.5 foot	spring / summer	full sun	moist but well-drained / well-drained	very hardy, USDA 3-9	acid / alkaline / neutral
B	*Hydrangea arbo-rescens* 'Annabelle'	shrub	1.5-2.5 metres, 3-5 feet	1.5-2.5 metres, 4-6 feet	summer	full sun / partial shade / full shade	well-drained	very hardy, USDA 3-9	acid / neutral
C	*Buxus sempervirens*	shrub	2.5-4 metres, 5-15 feet	4-8 metres, 5-15 feet	evergreen	partial shade / full shade	well-drained	very hardy, USDA 5-8	acid / neutral
D	*Taxus baccata*	tree	> 12 metres, 30-60 feet	> 8 metres, 15-25 feet	spring / autumn	full sun / partial shade / full shade	well-drained	very hardy, USDA 6-7	acid / alkaline / neutral

- 30 -

Oranges, Purples, and Greens

The fresh green leaves of the pleached hornbeam provide a satisfying link to the ancient trees lying beyond this swimming pool. When they were planted, I decided that instead of using one unchanging, unshifting shade of green from the ground all the way up, there was a need for a neutral colour, something darker which would recede as well as provide a backdrop for the planned tapestry of colours. So—inspired, oddly enough, by the merging colours of a Battenberg cake—I brought in a contrast that would spread its leafy fingers into the greens: the deep purple of copper beech accomplishes this perfectly, as well as balancing with (and separating the hornbeam from) the pool's expanse of blue-green.

Sambucus nigra f. *porphyrophylla* 'Eva', *Cercis canadensis* 'Forest Pansy', and *Cotinus coggygria* all pick up the purple-black leaves of the copper beech: purple foliage repeated randomly through a planting creates a lovely kind of negative amongst the bright greens of other foliage. Their rich purplish reds, the darkest of garnet,

Design: Jo Thompson

are sumptuously effective when teamed, as here, with the dusky washed-out orpiment orange of *Achillea* 'Walther Funcke' and yellow-leaved acers. An aside here—Patrick Syme, in *Werner's Nomenclature of Colours*, likened this orange to "the Belly of the Warty Newt." Hands up here that I've never had the opportunity to inspect said belly, but I'll take his word for it.

Providing relief in the centre, the silver foliage of *Elaeagnus* 'Quicksilver' complements the orange and also provides a sense of relief, allowing one to pause for a while. Silver- and grey-leaved plants can be used unstintingly—you can never have too many of them—yet in this planting, I felt that one large shrub on each side was enough. They pick up the silveriness of the light reflecting on the water—for this scheme, this is sufficient light, sufficient "positive."

Bronze-grey-leaved fennel, and the grey foliage of the achillea and lavender all gently and subtly echo the elaeagnus, avoiding a statement Mediterreanean planting. I find orange is incredibly effective when it punctuates a border, the more untidily the better.

Achillea millefolium 'Cerise Queen', with its deep cherry red flowers, touches on the fact that there's a little bit of heat in this planting. Just a little bit.

	NAME	TYPE	HEIGHT	SPREAD	SEASON	LIGHT	MOISTURE	HARDINESS	SOIL PH
A	*Sambucus nigra* f. *porphyrophylla* 'Eva'	shrub	2.5-4 metres, 6-8 feet	1.5-2.5 metres, 6-8 feet	summer / autumn	full sun / partial shade	well-drained / moist but well-drained	very hardy, USDA 4-7	acid / alkaline / neutral
B	*Achillea millefolium* 'Cerise Queen'	perennial	0.5-1 metre, 1.5-2.5 feet	0.1-0.5 metre, 1-2 feet	summer / autumn	full sun	well-drained / moist but well-drained	very hardy, USDA 2-9	acid / alkaline / neutral
C	*Achillea* 'Walther Funcke'	perennial	0.1-0.5 metre, 1-2 feet	0.1-0.5 metre, 1-2 feet	summer / autumn	full sun	moist but well-drained / well-drained	very hardy, USDA 3-8	acid / alkaline / neutral
D	*Carpinus betulus*	tree	> 12 metres, 40-60 feet	> 8 metres, 30-40 feet	autumn	full sun / partial shade	moist but well-drained / well-drained	very hardy, USDA 4-8	acid / alkaline / neutral
E	*Elaeagnus* 'Quicksilver'	shrub	2.5-4 metres, to 8 feet	2.5-4 metres, to 4 feet	summer / autumn	full sun	well-drained / moist but well-drained	very hardy, USDA 4-9	acid / alkaline / neutral
F	*Fagus sylvatica* Atropurpurea Group	tree	> 12 metres, 50-60 feet	> 8 metres, 30-45 feet	spring / summer / autumn	full sun / partial shade	moist but well-drained / well-drained	very hardy, USDA 5-7	acid / alkaline / neutral

- 31 -

Vividly Pink in Deepest Purple

The colour scheme in this planting is inspired by the landscape—a glorious backdrop in shades of green and purple, a palette that effectively fades away into the sky. Mounds of *Buxus sempervirens* are a reinterpretation of the majestic parkland trees in the distance, the box's simple green working well with every colour. It's a shame that we have to be so careful now with the planting of *B. sempervirens* due to the rampaging box caterpillar; so far, I have found *Ilex crenata* and *Euonymus* 'Jean Hugues' to be the best substitutes for the fresh green mass that buxus provides.

Right | Design: Jo Thompson
Below | Juan Gris, *Seated Harlequin*, 1923

Why the alliums? It's not just the heavy hint from the featured sculpture. Look at the grey-blue of the sky and the dark purple of the copper beech in the distance: the bright purple-blue of *Allium hollandicum* 'Purple Sensation' brings the two together perfectly. Hardy geraniums such as *Geranium* Rozanne = 'Gerwat' would provide the same colour, but the transparency of the allium's drumstick flowerheads at height lets in some of the colour of the grass and the sky. The huge inflorescences of *A. cristophii* are of a lighter, more silvery violet, which is then picked up by the flat-topped lilac-pink heads of the gorgeous hairy chervil, *Chaerophyllum hirsutum* 'Roseum'. You could use another pink umbellifer here, the dainty ferny-leaved *Pimpinella major* 'Rosea', but I find it very pink, nearer to red, whereas the chaerophyllum hangs on to its blue tones prettily.

Highlights help colours stand out just a little bit from the green background, creating some distance between shades of pink and blue, and this is achieved here by the use of *Geranium phaeum* 'Album', whose small white transparent flowers have a certain greyness about them. They create an element of relief, but the flowers need to be small, and the dots of white are enough. Any larger clumps of white would be too much and fight for attention, which is not to say that we can't have *any* more white: creamy white spires of *Aconitum* 'Ivorine' hold the green of the allium stems.

And then for the counterpoint. What colour would be a contrast—for this planting needs something of a colour pop in order to keep our attention—and yet at the same time fit well with everything surrounding it? Again the deep purple-red tones of the *Fagus sylvatica* Atropurpurea Group in the background give us the clue. Taking these tones and then looking at verticals that one could carry across this colour scheme, the fuchsia-pink *Gladiolus communis* subsp. *byzantinus* comes top of the list for creating dashes of pink throughout.

Why do alliums just work? Everywhere you pop them, there's something about the ethereal colours of these round forms which is simple and calming. Juan Gris' *Seated Harlequin* is a celebration of the round form: Gris felt that the round was the most expansive shape and suited to bright colours. The combination of colour and shape is still and yet moves our eye along at the same time—perfect plant, perfect in every place.

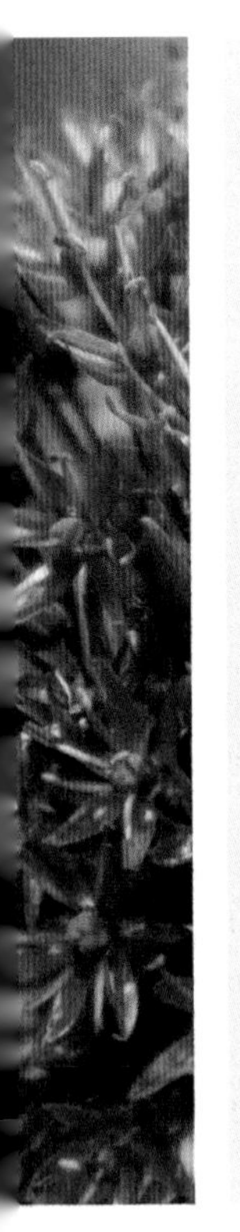

Tyrian Purple

Tyrian purple (aka Phoenician red, Phoenician purple, royal purple, imperial purple, or imperial dye) is a reddish purple natural pigment extracted from the marine mollusc *Bolinus brandaris*. It was first produced by the Phoenician city of Tyre some three thousand years ago and for centuries was used nearly exclusively by kings, noblemen, and high-ranking officials. King Darius the Great of Persia (c. 550–486 BCE) wore snail-dyed garments, and cloaks "aglow with Tyrian dye" are mentioned in Virgil's *Aeneid*.

	NAME	TYPE	HEIGHT	SPREAD	SEASON	LIGHT	MOISTURE	HARDINESS	SOIL PH
A	*Allium hollandicum* 'Purple Sensation'	bulb	0.5-1 metre, 2-2.5 feet	0.1-0.5 metre, 0.5-0.75 foot	summer	full sun	well-drained / moist but well-drained	very hardy, USDA 4-9	acid / alkaline / neutral
B	*Chaerophyllum hirsutum* 'Roseum'	perennial	0.5-1 metre, 2 feet	0.1-0.5 metre, 1 foot	spring / summer	full sun / partial shade	moist but well-drained / poorly drained	very hardy, USDA 6-9	acid / alkaline / neutral
C	*Aconitum* 'Ivorine'	perennial	0.5-1 metre, 2-3 feet	0.1-0.5 metre, 1-1.5 feet	spring / summer	full sun / partial shade	moist but well-drained	very hardy, USDA 3-7	acid / alkaline / neutral
D	*Gladiolus communis* subsp. *byzantinus*	perennial	0.5-1 metre, 1-2 feet	0.1-0.5 metre, 0.75-1.5 feet	spring / summer	full sun	well-drained	hardy, USDA 7-10	acid / alkaline / neutral

– 32 –

Deep Purplish Pink and Red

The inky black and white flowers of *Aquilegia vulgaris* 'William Guiness' never fail to inspire me. I imagine them in a monochrome Eighties interior, looking fabulous against black-lacquered furniture, their architectural forms elegant both in reality and in shadow. Make no mistake though—the versatility of this plant means that it works as well in a rambling, soft palette as it does in a more restrained scheme.

The trick with using the band of shades in and around deep purple to black is to treat them as negatives—they will form "holes" in a border or bed, spaces devoid of colour, so it's worth looking at where you want to highlight in a contrary way. Masses of pale colours benefit from dots of nothingness from afar, and as we move closer we can appreciate the mysteries of this almost-colour. Barely noticeable when first looking at the grouping in this photograph, the intricacies of the form and the depths of delicate dots of black—somewhere near a noble Tyrian purple—can be appreciated at leisure.

So how can we enjoy this colour without creating a black hole in the scheme? Paler colours form an excellent backdrop, and if one is thinking about harmonising, a good shade-tolerant partner for such a dark tone comes in the form of the digitalis. The white form, *Digitalis purpurea* f. *albiflora*, would tie in with the aquilegia's white petals, but a softer contrast would come from the native *D. purpurea*. Many people weed out the mauve-pink-purple plants, but I'd recommend leaving the snobbery behind and embracing this shade—just remember to break up the pink with other colours where you can.

Here I've used the paler *Digitalis purpurea* 'Sutton's Apricot'—this particular strain has the tiniest hint of apricot (essentially, it's a pleasing pale pink), and I brought in actual pink with *Rehmannia elata*. The flowers of this Chinese foxglove are pretty slippers of a warm mauve-pink, a shade which is also satisfyingly present in *Lysimachia atropurpurea* 'Beaujolais'. Once you embrace the fact that this loosestrife is short-lived, you'll find it really useful in the border. Here, its sugar pink/mauve/crimson/magenta/purple spikes of flowers bend strangely yet elegantly above equally helpful silver foliage. The silver isn't too "present": it will advance and highlight or subtly recede, depending on the amount of competing green foliage nearby.

Opposite | Design: Jo Thompson for M&G Garden/RHS Chelsea 2015

	NAME	TYPE	HEIGHT	SPREAD	SEASON	LIGHT	MOISTURE	HARDINESS	SOIL PH
A	*Rehmannia elata*	perennial	1-1.5 metres, 2-4 feet	0.1-0.5 metre, 1.5-3 feet	summer / autumn	full sun / partial shade	well-drained	half hardy, USDA 7-10	acid / alkaline / neutral
B	*Digitalis purpurea* 'Sutton's Apricot'	biennial	1-1.5 metres, 3-4 feet	0.1-0.5 metre, 1-1.5 feet	summer	full sun / partial shade / full shade	moist but well-drained / well-drained	very hardy, USDA 4-8	acid / alkaline / neutral
C	*Lysimachia atropurpurea* 'Beaujolais'	short-lived perennial	0.5-1 metre, 1-1.5 feet	0.1-0.5 metre, 0.75-1 foot	summer	full sun / partial shade	moist but well-drained / poorly drained	very hardy, USDA 4-8	acid / alkaline / neutral
D	*Aquilegia vulgaris* 'William Guiness'	perennial	0.5-1 metre, 2-2.5 feet	0.1-0.5 metre, 1.5-2 feet	summer	full sun / partial shade	well-drained	very hardy, USDA 3-8	acid / alkaline / neutral

Inspiration from RHS Garden Wisley

Curator Matthew Pottage on mixed rose displays in the Bowes-Lyon Rose Garden:

1 Pretty in pink

Roses are more versatile than is often supposed. Here, a wide range of selections are grown in association with other shrubs and herbaceous plants; *Rosa* The Mayflower = 'Austilly' is seen at its peak.

2 Bank of blue

Among the most useful and easily grown of all perennials are cranesbills, plants that often grow well teamed with roses; *Geranium* 'Orion' is a superlative hybrid, producing masses of rich blue flowers for weeks in summer.

3 Mighty Indian bean tree

A noble and long-standing resident of this part of Wisley is a superb and wide-spreading *Catalpa bignonioides*, here forming a fine backdrop. It is grown for its bold foliage, superb summer flowers, and long bean-like seed pods. A purple sea of *Salvia nemorosa* 'Caradonna' flourishes in front.

– 33 –

Silver, Pink, Green, and Blue

However widely used it is (and what is wrong with that—doesn't "widely used" equal much-loved, tried, tested, and trusted?), the restful combination of pink and blue will always make us smile in nostalgic recognition. The softer shades of pink—blush, sugar, rose—may mean something slightly different to each of us, but all these terms have in common the effect of making us feel that all is well with the world, leaving us just a bit more relaxed and quite happy. In my career as a designer only two clients have ever told me they don't like pink—and both were female, so let's not get into the blue for a boy, pink for a girl discussion quite yet.

The combinations of cool colours which sit so near to each other on the colour wheel don't as individual hues seize our gaze. More often than not it's the assembling of easygoing colours which elicits a general *aah* of contentment. That's not to say it always works: I have seen and objected to the overt frilliness of a pale blue, white, pink, and lavender mash-up, made worse by the fact that the planting was described as a "feminine" palette. Feminine doesn't need to be frilly: I want feminine to be relaxed, fun-loving, laid-back, intelligent, considered, and free.

Here, the rich pink of *Rosa* 'Louise Odier', pink yet with hints of blue, provides a splash of pink clouds in areas, rather than a general paintballing of the colour; Graham Stuart Thomas called it "a rose to be treasured for all time." To break up the pink and soften any possible marshmallow effect, a good dose of neutral highlights is needed. To provide this, the tiny mid-green leaves of *Westringia fruticosa* (Victorian rosemary) create an optical illusion—a silvery underside and tiny hairs on the end of the leaves give an impression of hazy silver light. *Geranium* 'Brookside' gently picks up the subtle blue tones in the palest lilac flowers of this tender evergreen shrub, and further light is delivered by the little bright-white sparkles of the annual *Gypsophila elegans* 'Covent Garden'. Can you imagine how this would look if the gypsophila ran throughout this pink and blue? Too much sickly fluffiness for sure. Think of the silver foliage as a squeeze of lemon juice counteracting the sugariness.

Design: Jo Thompson for M&G Garden/RHS Chelsea 2015

	NAME	TYPE	HEIGHT	SPREAD	SEASON	LIGHT	MOISTURE	HARDINESS	SOIL PH
A	*Westringia fruticosa*	shrub	1-1.5 metres, 4-6 feet	1-2 metres, 6 feet	spring / summer / autumn	full sun / partial shade	well-drained / moist but well-drained	half hardy, USDA 9-10	acid / alkaline / neutral
B	*Gypsophila elegans* 'Covent Garden'	annual	0.1-0.5 metre, 1-2 feet	0.1-0.5 metre, 1-2 feet	summer	full sun	well-drained / moist but well-drained	very hardy, USDA 3-9	acid / alkaline / neutral
C	*Geranium* 'Brookside'	perennial	0.1-0.5 metre, 1.5-2 feet	0.1-0.5 metre, 2-3 feet	summer	full sun / partial shade	well-drained / moist but well-drained	very hardy, USDA 5-8	acid / alkaline / neutral
D	*Rosa* 'Louise Odier'	shrub	1-1.5 metres, to 5 feet	1-1.5 metres, 4 feet	summer	full sun / partial shade / full shade	well-drained	very hardy, USDA 5-11	acid / alkaline / neutral

- 34 -

Yellow, White, and Green

Yellow means spring and sunlight and new life. Eye-catching and merry, it lightens up the grey winter and signifies hope and warmer weather alongside daffodils and baby chicks.

Yellow in the garden gets bad press; an aversion to this sunny colour is particularly prevalent amongst those who request a "traditional" scheme of pink and blue. Perhaps it's a hangover from years of sticking too closely to the colour wheel, and to the idea that yellow and pink, neither complementary nor near enough to each other to slot into usefully defined "matches," can't be defined, and therefore will "not go"—whatever that means. Or is it the associations with weeds, jaundice, and feeling "off-colour"? It's hard to know where an aversion comes from—colour psychologists would say that yellow has an impact on the nervous system and that it triggers a response. Clearly.

In *Colour in the Garden*, M.E. Stebbing offered some advice to the yellow-averse: "When dealing with yellows we shall have no trouble in placing the golden and 'buttery' shades. It is the lemon and mustard tints that present a real difficulty, and we may well study Chinese embroideries and learn there how to handle these colours with exquisite certainty."

Let's come back to the idea of freshness and new hope. And sherbet lemons and custard tarts. Here, *Aquilegia chrysantha* 'Yellow Queen' gleams—at once golden, lemon, and canary yellow—up and out of this early summer planting. The white spurs of the elegant *A.* 'Kristall' are a perfect match for it, the white and yellow teaming up cleanly, sharp and neat against the green and blue-green foliage of the ferns and *Polygonatum ×hybridum*. The plants are not massed; rather, they provide pinpoints (not great swathes) of colour. The yellow and white look happy—not a hint of garishness here. This is the only brightness that is needed.

Astrantia 'Snow Star', rippling away at a lower level, carries on illuminating and enhancing without stealing the limelight, its greenish white flowers nodding to both the flowers and foliage of other plants. It is such a simple combination and one worth remembering; it is especially appropriate for a spot whose ability to eye-catch is compromised by the fact that it sits in a little shade. Sprinkle in some yellow and white, go easy on the quantities, and concentrate instead on the qualities of each flower.

	NAME	TYPE	HEIGHT	SPREAD	SEASON	LIGHT	MOISTURE	HARDINESS	SOIL PH
A	*Astrantia* 'Snow Star'	perennial	0.5-1 metre, 2-2.5 feet	0.1-0.5 metre, 1-1.5 feet	spring	full sun / partial shade	moist but well-drained / poorly drained	very hardy, USDA 5-7	acid / alkaline / neutral
B	*Aquilegia* 'Kristall'	perennial	to 1 metre, 1-2 feet	0.5 metre, 1-2 feet	summer / autumn	full sun / partial shade	moist but well-drained / well-drained	very hardy, USDA 3-10	acid / alkaline / neutral
C	*Aquilegia chrysantha* 'Yellow Queen'	perennial	1-1.5 metres, 2-3 feet	0.1-0.5 metre, 2-3 feet	spring / summer	full sun / partial shade	well-drained / moist but well-drained	very hardy, USDA 3-9	acid / alkaline / neutral
D	*Polygonatum ×hybridum*	perennial	1-1.5 metres, 2.5 feet	0.1-0.5 metre, 2.5 feet	spring	full sun / partial shade / full shade	moist but well-drained	very hardy, USDA 4-9	acid / alkaline / neutral

Opposite | Design: Jo Thompson for the Wedgwood Garden/RHS Chelsea 2018

- 35 -

Browns, Peach, Blue, and Yellow-Orange

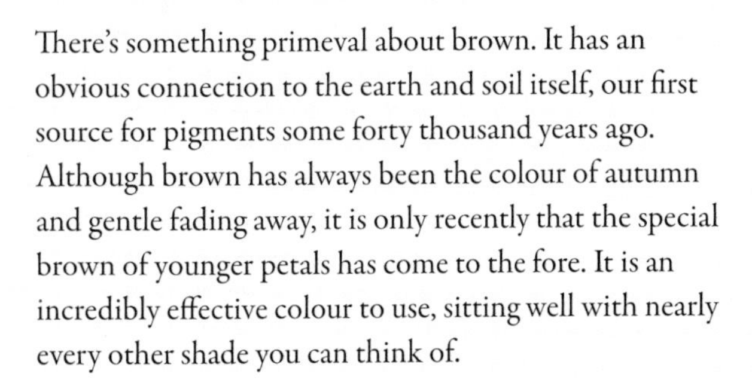

There's something primeval about brown. It has an obvious connection to the earth and soil itself, our first source for pigments some forty thousand years ago. Although brown has always been the colour of autumn and gentle fading away, it is only recently that the special brown of younger petals has come to the fore. It is an incredibly effective colour to use, sitting well with nearly every other shade you can think of.

As ever, bringing in light is vital when using earthy shades; *Iris* 'Carnival Time' does this here in spades. Upon first examination, you wouldn't assign such a mundane colour to this glorious tall bearded iris, with its falls of amber through copper into red; yet this is where it sits, referencing very subtly the earth beneath, so the blue of the sky seems an obvious match made in heaven. *Iris pallida* subsp. *pallida* has the most exquisite crinkled and crumpled petals of the palest lavender into blue, and with a background of more muted brown, from the stems and flowers of *Geum rivale*, we have here another good

Design: Jo Thompson for the Wedgwood Garden/RHS Chelsea 2018

A

B

C

combination of two showstopping colours. The semi-evergreen *Anemanthele lessoniana* is a happy choice to give structure to this planting—its stems contain shades of red and yellow and orange, all blending together to give the impression of simultaneously natural colours as well as something quite startling. This is what is so very good about brown—it is so natural and yet so unexpected in fresh, living plants.

Brown and blue can be overly strong, and the eye needs some relief from what could look like an attempt at colour matching. Pale yellow *Trollius* ×*cultorum* 'Taleggio' is creamy and buttery alongside the brighter yellow, sweetly scented flowers of *Primula sikkimensis*; both are dotted highlights against the fresh green foliage, catching the light of the shallow stream running through this garden. Note that although several different plants here provide a vivid green background, they are essentially all in the same colour range. The *Iris sibirica*, rodgersia, and hosta form a wash of related shades of green, with only the blue tones of *I. pallida* subsp. *pallida* making a clear statement as something different. Standing back from this arrangement of colour, the leaves of the rodgersia actually form the biggest block of a single colour, but they don't seem to be seeking the limelight, happy instead to lounge in the background while the browns and blues stand out, and the lemons and yellows brighten and relieve all.

D

E

F

	NAME	TYPE	HEIGHT	SPREAD	SEASON	LIGHT	MOISTURE	HARDINESS	SOIL PH
A	*Trollius ×cultorum* 'Taleggio'	perennial	0.5-1 metre, 2-3 feet	0.5-1 metre, 1-2.5 feet	spring / summer	full sun / partial shade	moist but well-drained / poorly drained	very hardy, USDA 3-7	acid / alkaline / neutral
B	*Primula sikkimensis*	perennial	0.1-1 metre, 1-3 feet	0.5-1 metre, 1-3 feet	spring / summer	full sun / partial shade	moist but well-drained / poorly drained	very hardy, USDA 4-8	acid / neutral
C	*Geum rivale*	perennial	0.1-0.5 metre, 0.75-1.5 feet	0.1-0.5 metre, 0.5-1 foot	spring / summer	full sun / partial shade	moist but well-drained	very hardy, USDA 3-7	acid / alkaline / neutral
D	*Iris* 'Carnival Time'	perennial	0.5-1 metre, 2.5-3 feet	0.1-0.5 metre, 2 feet	spring / summer	full sun	well-drained	very hardy, USDA 3-9	acid / neutral
E	*Iris pallida* subsp. *pallida*	perennial	1-1.5 metres, 3 feet	0.1-0.5 metre, 1 foot	spring / summer	full sun	well-drained	very hardy, USDA 4-9	acid / neutral
F	*Anemanthele lessoniana*	grass	0.5-1 metre, 2.5 feet	1-1.5 metres, 2.5-3.5 feet	summer / autumn	full sun / partial shade	well-drained / moist but well-drained	hardy, USDA 8-10	acid / alkaline / neutral

- 36 -

Blue and Orange-Brown

In the masterpiece that is the Scrovegni Chapel, Giotto used colour to communicate emotion: a vault of heavenly blue, explosions of other cheerful colours, and rumbling, thunderous shades of black and grey. Blue skies and green landscapes are at once uplifting and awe-inspiring.

I agree it might be bordering on the just-slightly-weird side of hyperbole to state that the associations amongst the colours in this planting raise us to a level of ecstatic wonderment, but honestly, the shades of blue within these flowers are pretty amazing—easy on the eye, restrained, elegant. Ranging from the softest sky blue through to violet and lilac, they conjure up a sense of

Right | Design: Jo Thompson for the Wedgwood Garden/RHS Chelsea 2018
Below | Giotto, Scrovegni Chapel frescoes, Padua, 1303–05

Ultramarine

To the surprise of many, ultramarine is not a reference to the colour of the sea—which kind of makes sense. Think about it: we very rarely see an ultramarine sea on a trip to the local seaside. What is actually meant is that the colour comes from "beyond the seas"—a reference to how far the pigment had to travel so many years ago. It is a colour so showy and precious that we can completely understand how, six thousand years ago, Egyptian traders would travel thousands of miles to bring back lapis lazuli, the semi-precious stone from which the ultramarine pigment is derived. Ultraviolet is another literal translation. It doesn't mean a superhero violet; it refers to the lightwaves that lie beyond violet (the colour with the shortest wavelength), which are barely visible to humans.

calm. Lavender-blue *Iris pallida* subsp. *pallida* picks up the paler blue stars of *Amsonia tabernaemontana*, their timidity tempered here by the quality and depth of neighbouring colours.

A successful intermediary between the two is *Geranium pratense* 'Mrs Kendall Clark'—showing off blues of lavender and of the sky, her discreet splashes bringing together the big fat brushstrokes of iris alongside the pointillist dots of the amsonia. The layer-upon-layer blues are exciting here; it's almost as if priceless ultramarine were present.

Note to self: I really must create that iris bed I've been dreaming of forever. Every year I go to plant a mass of Cedric Morris introductions, but every year I hesitate due to the fleeting nature of the flower and the precious sunny spot required. But their beauty is just too uplifting to ignore—and it's their very transience that has given me an idea for the rest of the year. How about this? I'll use a foundation of hardy geraniums in various blues—they'll give a base from May to September. Arising from them, before the iris have their splendid moment, would be a first act of *Tulipa* 'Brown Sugar' and *Muscari armeniacum*, followed by *Anemone coronaria* (De Caen Group) 'Mister Fokker'. All would be rounded out at summer's end by a few spires of *Gladiolus* 'Indian Summer', left to lean and bend their way up through a mass of self-seeded green fennel.

A

B

C

D

	NAME	TYPE	HEIGHT	SPREAD	SEASON	LIGHT	MOISTURE	HARDINESS	SOIL PH
A	*Amsonia tabernaemontana*	perennial	0.5-1 metre, 2-3 feet	0.1-0.5 metre, 2-3 feet	spring / summer	full sun / partial shade	moist but well-drained	very hardy, USDA 3-9	acid / alkaline / neutral
B	*Geranium pratense* 'Mrs Kendall Clark'	perennial	0.5-1 metre, 2-3 feet	0.5-1 metre, 2-3 feet	summer	full sun / partial shade	moist but well-drained / well-drained	very hardy, USDA 4-8	acid / alkaline / neutral
C	*Iris pallida* subsp. *pallida*	perennial	1-1.5 metres, 3 feet	0.1-0.5 metre, 1 foot	spring / summer	full sun	well-drained	very hardy, USDA 4-9	acid / neutral
D	*Iris* 'Carnival Time'	perennial	0.5-1 metre, 2.5-3 feet	0.1-0.5 metre, 2 feet	spring / summer	full sun	well-drained	very hardy, USDA 3-9	acid / neutral

- 37 -

Foliage and Shades of Blue and Green

Vintage Hollywood meets Morocco via the Mediterranean in this foliage-filled garden in the Hollywood Hills. Jenny Jones of Terremoto has created a masterpiece, carefully placing tones of blue and green and earthy shades to define subtly the zones within the space.

Jenny's suggestion to pull the dining terrace away from the house and into the middle of the garden was a stroke of genius. This new entertaining spot is now surrounded with plants that take the places of the actors who once lived here. I can't put it better than the designers themselves: "We dream of a storied and aged Old Hollywood cast of character actors, flooding past us like taxonomic credits: *Hedera helix*, *Cupressus sempervirens*, *Agave attenuata*, *Alsophila australis*, *Philodendron selloum*. Or, like partygoers, other plants approach us: we gossip with *Ficus pumila*, *Bougainvillea*, and *Cedrus deodara*."

Here the glaucous blue-grey foliage of *Cupressus cashmeriana* (Kashmir cypress) hangs languidly at the entrance

Design: Jenny Jones/Terremoto

to this area, its elegant form working perfectly with the light green fronds of the graceful *Cyathea cooperi* (Australian tree fern). The surprise here are the leaves of *Kalanchoe beharensis* (velvet elephant ear). Extraordinary in their shape and felted texture, the olive-coloured leaves of this succulent bring together perfectly the blue of the cypress and the green of the tree fern, as well as pinpointing the entrance to the tiled terrace. The blue is echoed again in the silvery grey, almost reflective leaves of *Agave attenuata* (foxtail agave), while *Polystichum munitum* (western sword fern) repeats the light green.

It isn't all green and blue here, however. The foliage of *Heuchera maxima* does give some cream and pink spikes early on, which in turn sit neatly with the leaves of *Cercis occidentalis* (western redbud). This stunning tree provides fabulous colour in every season: its branches are silvery grey, while the fresh green young foliage darkens to a blue-green and then becomes reddish brown as autumn approaches. Magenta flowers provide a striking display, but to my mind the leaves are just as stunning. Perfect tree for the perfect spot.

	NAME	TYPE	HEIGHT	SPREAD	SEASON	LIGHT	MOISTURE	HARDINESS	SOIL PH
A	*Cercis occidentalis*	shrub or small tree	4-8 metres, 10-20 feet	4-8 metres, 10-15 feet	spring / summer / autumn / winter	full shade / partial shade	well-drained	hardy, USDA 7-10	acid / alkaline / neutral
B	*Polystichum munitum*	fern	1-2 metres, 1.5-6 feet	1 metre, 2-3 feet	evergreen	full shade / partial shade	moist but well-drained	very hardy, USDA 6-8	acid / alkaline / neutral
C	*Agave attenuata*	succulent perennial	0.5-1 metre, 2-3 feet	1-1.5 metres, 3-4 feet	spring / summer	full sun	well-drained	tender, USDA 10-12	acid
D	*Kalanchoe beharensis*	succulent perennial	0.5-1 metre, 3-5 feet	0.5-1 metre, 3-5 feet	winter	partial shade	well-drained / moist but well-drained	tender, USDA 11-12	acid / alkaline / neutral
E	*Cyathea cooperi*	tree fern	2.5-4 metres, 15-20 feet	2.5-4 metres, 8-12 feet	evergreen	partial shade	moist but well-drained	tender, USDA 9-10	acid / neutral
F	*Cupressus cashmeriana*	tree	> 12 metres, 40-60 feet	4-8 metres, 15-20 feet	evergreen	full sun	well-drained	half hardy, USDA 9-10	acid / alkaline / neutral

- 38 -

Reflections

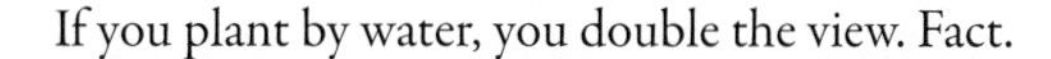

If you plant by water, you double the view. Fact.

What is particularly brilliant about this planting by the lake at RHS Rosemoor is how the selection bears at its forefront the need to respect what happens to our perception of colour where an expanse of light-reflecting water is concerned. Water reflects the colour of the sky, and this Devon sky, on this cold day the bluest of blues, immediately lights up the green around it, turning what might be perceived as emerald, when viewed in isolation, into a rich jade green. The reflections multiply the plants, nearly but not quite replicating them in rippling clarity as light works its magic and tells us, in the same image, that one colour is in fact another colour. Laws of contrast and laws of physics turn things round and make all not quite what it may at first seem. That's just part of the joy of planting by water.

This is one lovely view; your gaze circles around the planting and ends in a flourish at the water, where you then pick up the reflected flaming ochres and siennas of *Sorbus ×kewensis*, the deeper-than-actuality green of *Cornus sericea* 'Flaviramea', the watery white of the birch bark, up to the birches themselves, and back around we go. This broken-up circling of a colour, anchoring it with greys and blues, is as satisfying an eye-journey as that provided by the muted poetry of colours in Niles Spencer's *Waterfront Mill*, warm in its unpeopled stillness.

The splendid late autumn leaf colour of the sorbus is just one of the reasons this tree, a hybrid of two subspecies of *Sorbus aucuparia* (rowan), is a thoroughly deserving specimen in any garden, as good in a smaller plot as it is here framed by larger trees. Fabulously fragrant spring flowers and equally fabulous berries in autumn are further attributes. Cleverly anchored to the ground here, to the right of the cornus, are the orange-echoing coppers and bronzes of the *Parrotia persica* 'Pendula', always a surprise as it is smaller than you'd expect from a parrotia—so another good small garden specimen. The added bonus of this tree is that its nectar and pollen are loved by butterflies and bees.

In the larger landscape around this sumptuous autumnal vignette, whose colours are doubled by the water it surrounds, there is the luxury of an even broader selection of taller specimens. Over the whole scene, birches and beech add their purples, silvers, and greys, while the deep ruby crimsons of *Cornus alba* Baton Rouge = 'Minbat' in the foreground are a beautiful connection to the *Acer palmatum* 'Chitose-yama' which sits over on the other side of the lake.

The fiery yet nurturing colours of autumn are a warming image, and it wouldn't be wrong to assume that the moment captured here is this view's high point, with the greens of foliage taking over as spring and summer return. But there's a summer surprise. Look long enough and you'll spot the hidden hope in the dark silhouette of branches on the left that form a welcoming bough over the lakeside scene. This is *Toona sinensis* (Chinese mahogany), which in summer bears foot-long panicles of creamy white flowers that shimmer over the birch bark and reflect in the water, picking up the circle of light.

Design: RHS Rosemoor

	NAME	TYPE	HEIGHT	SPREAD	SEASON	LIGHT	MOISTURE	HARDINESS	SOIL PH
A	*Sorbus ×kewensis*	tree	2-3 metres, 6-10 feet	2 metres, to 6 feet	spring / autumn	full sun / partial shade	well-drained / moist but well-drained	hardy, USDA 5-8	acid
B	*Cornus sericea* 'Flaviramea'	shrub	1.5-2.5 metres, 5-6 feet	2.5-4 metres, 5-6 feet	autumn / winter	full sun / partial shade	well-drained / moist but well-drained	very hardy, USDA 3-8	acid / alkaline / neutral
C	*Parrotia persica* 'Pendula'	tree	1.5-2.5 metres, 5-8 feet	2.5-5 metres, 8-13 feet	autumn	full sun	well-drained	very hardy, USDA 4-8	acid
D	*Cornus alba* Baton Rouge = 'Minbat'	shrub	1.5-2.5 metres, 5-8 feet	1.5-2.5 metres, 5-8 feet	autumn / winter	full sun / partial shade	well-drained / moist but well-drained	very hardy, USDA 3-7	acid / neutral
E	*Acer palmatum* 'Chitose-yama'	tree	1.5-2.5 metres, 5-8 feet	1.5-2.5 metres, 5-8 feet	autumn	full sun / partial shade	moist but well-drained	very hardy, USDA 5-9	acid / neutral

Inspiration from RHS Garden Hyde Hall

Curator Robert Brett describes Winter Garden planting in Essex, in October:

1 Structural grasses

Repeated across the bank are upright, narrow clumps of *Calamagrostis ×acutiflora* 'Karl Foerster', providing continuity and adding movement in the breeze. Further forward is billowing *Panicum virgatum* 'Rehbraun'.

2 Autumnal perennials

Ever-reliable, drought-tolerant sedum *Hylotelephium* 'Matrona' has flat heads of long-lasting pale pink flowers. Silvery stems and foliage of *Salvia yangii* contrast well with the sedum and the green mounds of bergenia, while silver *Anaphalis triplinervis* 'Sommerschnee' fills in the front line.

3 Foliar inferno

Lit by the glancing autumn sun, the leaves of *Acer ×freemanii* Autumn Blaze = 'Jeffersred' ignite in an eruption of red, orange, and amber.

– 39 –

Colour as Space-Defining

A vast empty area can be a daunting space to fill. Designers' excitable minds can start running to pools and pergolas, frills and furbelows in the quest to furnish a space. Often the most successful approach, one usually made by designers who know and love their plants, is to let the colours of the plants themselves predominate. It is usually enough.

Here in the Walled Garden at Warren House in Coombe Wood, the new planting is a stunning celebration of all the gardeners who have worked there since it was first built. Featured are many iconic garden plants introduced by E.H. Wilson, William Lobb, and other intrepid Victorian plant hunters who travelled the globe for the famous Veitch Nurseries. When they first saw this empty space in 2015, the designers could sense the ghosts of this eminent past, and they sensibly decided that plants were the right and appropriate way to fill it.

The colours they selected—shades of red with a surprisingly successful interweaving of white and the palest yellows and blues—serve to abstract the space, so that being within the garden becomes an experience in itself, rather than just being the notion of looking at flowers.

Design: Andrew Fisher Tomlin, Dan Bowyer

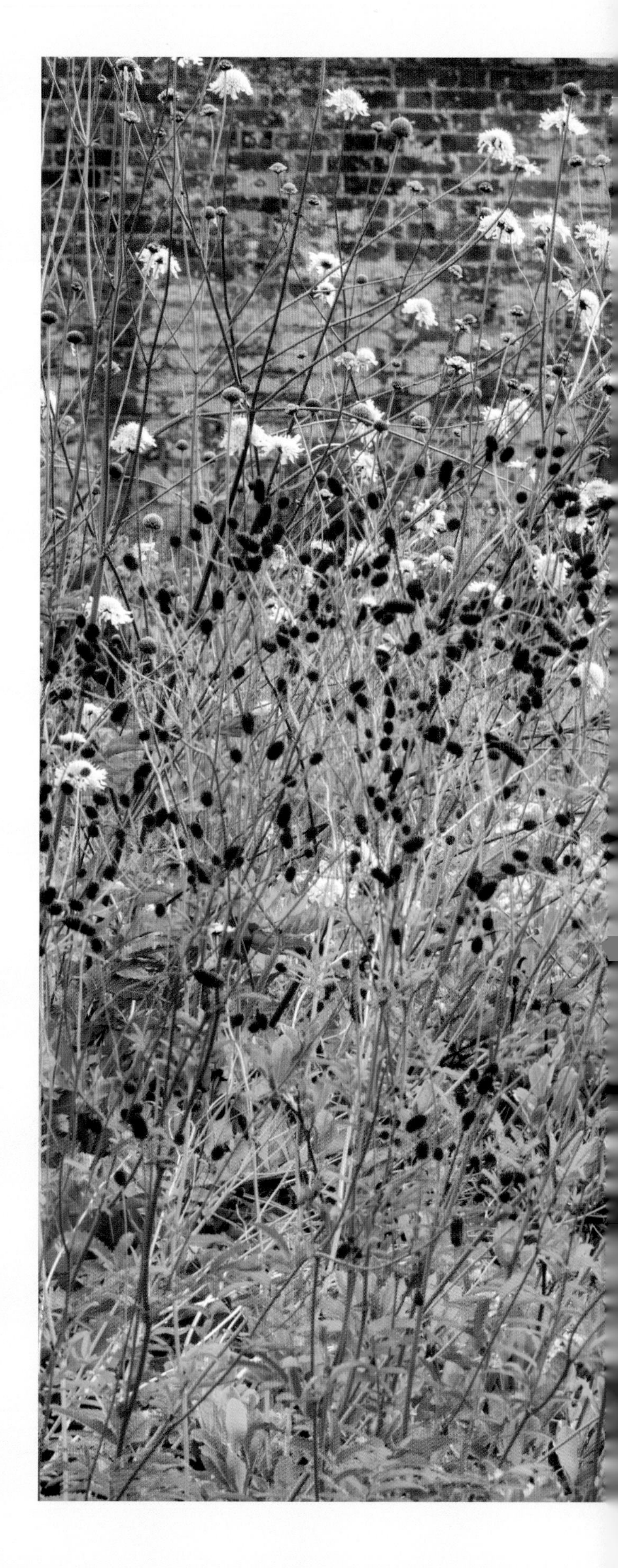

The colour blending is beautiful here. It takes you on a journey where you look along and across, up and down in a gentle meander rather than a speedy back-and-forth. The potential flatness that a mass of red can create is averted by the use of the pales, which delineate the journey of the gaze. *Veronicastrum virginicum* 'Apollo', *Cephalaria gigantea*, and *Astrantia major* subsp. *involucrata* 'Shaggy' are all white light at first glance. But as we wander around, we see that these whites are not all they first seem to be: the cephalaria we know in actuality to be translucent lemon, while the veronicastrum flowers are pale blue. Shimmery light streams away from the mass of astrantia in the foreground.

Looking at the rich red velvet-cut flowers of *Hemerocallis* 'Stafford', I've made a note to make a planting of mixed daylilies in a neglected sunny patch of my own garden. These flowers could have walked straight off the catwalk; they are exquisite and truly in need of a revival in popularity (their foliage, I know, is not for some). Look at how that sumptuous colour, picking up the warm tones of the historic brick walls and echoed by the tiny deep red buttons of *Sanguisorba officinalis*, is beautifully muted here by the shades which surround it. The pale colours just calm it all down.

	NAME	TYPE	HEIGHT	SPREAD	SEASON	LIGHT	MOISTURE	HARDINESS	SOIL PH
A	*Astrantia major* subsp. *involucrata* 'Shaggy'	perennial	0.5-1 metre, 1.5-2.5 feet	0.1-0.5 metre, 1-2 feet	summer	full sun / partial shade	moist but well-drained / poorly drained	very hardy, USDA 4-7	acid / alkaline / neutral
B	*Cephalaria gigantea*	perennial	1.5-2.5 metres, 4-6 feet	0.5-1 metre, 2-4 feet	summer	full sun / partial shade	moist but well-drained	very hardy, USDA 3-7	acid / alkaline / neutral
C	*Hemerocallis* 'Stafford'	perennial	0.5-1 metre, 2-3 feet	0.1-0.5 metre, 1-2 feet	summer	full sun	moist but well-drained	very hardy, USDA 3-9	acid / alkaline / neutral
D	*Veronicastrum virginicum* 'Album'	perennial	1-1.5 metres, 3-4 feet	0.5-1 metre, 2-3 feet	summer	full sun / partial shade	moist but well-drained / well-drained	very hardy, USDA 4-8	acid / alkaline / neutral
E	*Veronicastrum virginicum* 'Apollo'	perennial	1-1.5 metres, 3-4 feet	0.1-0.5 metre, 2-3 feet	summer	full sun / partial shade	moist but well-drained / well-drained	very hardy, USDA 3-8	acid / alkaline / neutral

- 40 -

Unexpected Rainbow

This terrace is the driveway entrance and turning circle to the Cotswolds home of Jade and Julian Dunkerton; the central oval and all surrounding beds are planted entirely with a mass of perennials and bulbs, with a flowering season that extends from spring to late summer. Naturalistic drifts weave the plants' bright colours together: rich purples, deep oranges, reds, pinks, burgundies, and blues from cobalt to deep orchil. The plants are selected for longevity and the ability to hold their form into the autumn and winter months as well as for their colourful blooms, which eventually transform into silvery dark standing seedheads.

Evergreen multi-stemmed specimens of *Osmanthus ×burkwoodii* are raised above the border scheme in chunky reclaimed oak planters, set regularly along the drive on either side; white *Wisteria floribunda* weaves along the original stone balcony walls, providing fragrant clouds to walk by in early summer while overlooking views of the valley below.

I'm not even sure the designers Lulu Urquhart and Adam Hunt were aware that they were subtly embracing the spectrum, but there is definitely a rainbow here.

Design: Urquhart & Hunt

Let's start at the very beginning. At the far end of the rainbow we have small dots of *Salvia ×jamensis* 'Red Velvet'. Then, the red-orange of *Helenium* 'Moerheim Beauty' shows itself to be a fabulous match for the neighbouring *Echinacea purpurea*'s central bosses, appropriately lauded by Christopher Lloyd as prominent features, their vivid orange anthers "in startling contrast" to the rosy purple rays.

The landscape's trees bring yellow and green; *Nepeta ×faassenii* 'Blue Wonder' is exactly that, and *Salvia* 'Indigo Spires' indeed has very lovely spires. Speaking of indigo—it was a bit of a sticky subject, as far as Newton's theorising was concerned: originally both it and orange were missing from his spectrum, but he was keen on making Classical and musical analogies, and seven was a much more appropriate number than five. Perhaps *S.* 'Indigo Spires' could also be violet? Violet, the colour of air, is definitely here: *Lavandula angustifolia* sits behind the indigo-blue flowers of the salvia.

So why doesn't this shout "spectrum" to us? I suggest it's the clever use of blue and all its relatives: *Salvia* 'Blue Spire', which runs along the balcony walls, really has taken on the colour of air in the evening light, while *S. ×sylvestris* 'Mainacht', *Agastache* 'Blackadder', and *Baptisia australis* weave in and out of the rest of the colours. Their flower stems catch the late light in the way you'd expect a grass to, but notice that, although it feels as if they are present, there aren't actually any grasses in this relaxed, laid-back scheme. That loose, slightly wild, at-one-with-nature atmosphere comes completely from the colours and forms of ornamental plants, which works with the majesty of the location so well: at times, the entire sky is tied to the blues in the flowers.

So many elements, in this "linking to the landscape." Capturing light as well as forms, capturing atmosphere as well as tangibles. Both are executed magnificently here.

C

D

E

F

G

	NAME	TYPE	HEIGHT	SPREAD	SEASON	LIGHT	MOISTURE	HARDINESS	SOIL PH
A	*Osmanthus ×burkwoodii*	shrub	2.5-4 metres, 8 feet	2.5-4 metres, 8 feet	spring / autumn	full sun / partial shade	well-drained	very hardy, USDA 7-11	acid / alkaline / neutral
B	*Salvia ×jamensis* 'Red Velvet'	perennial	0.5 metre, 1.5-2 feet	0.5 metre, 1.5-2 feet	spring / summer	full sun / partial shade	well-drained	half hardy, USDA 7-11	acid / neutral
C	*Echinacea purpurea*	perennial	0.5-1.5 metres, 2-5 feet	0.1-0.5 metre, 1.5-2 feet	summer / autumn	full sun / partial shade	well-drained	very hardy, USDA 3-8	acid / alkaline / neutral
D	*Helenium* 'Moerheim Beauty'	perennial	0.5-1 metre, 2-3 feet	0.1-0.5 metre, 1-1.5 feet	summer	full sun	moist but well-drained	very hardy, USDA 3-8	acid / alkaline / neutral
E	*Nepeta ×faassenii* 'Blue Wonder'	perennial	0.3 metre, 0.75-1.5 feet	0.6 metre, 1-1.5 feet	summer	full sun	well-drained	hardy, USDA 3-8	acid / neutral
F	*Salvia* 'Indigo Spires'	perennial	1-1.5 metres, 3 feet	0.5-1 metre, to 3 feet	summer / autumn	full sun	moist but well-drained	half hardy, USDA 7-10	acid / alkaline / neutral
G	*Baptisia australis*	perennial	1-1.5 metres, 3-4 feet	0.5-1 metre, 3-4 feet	summer	full sun	well-drained	very hardy, USDA 3-9	acid / neutral

– 41 –

By the Water

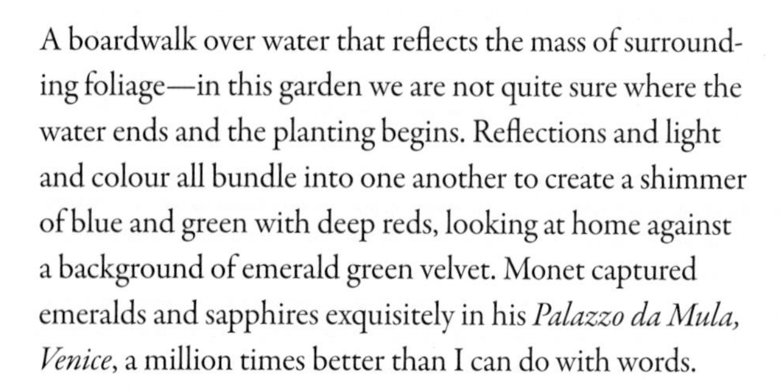

A boardwalk over water that reflects the mass of surrounding foliage—in this garden we are not quite sure where the water ends and the planting begins. Reflections and light and colour all bundle into one another to create a shimmer of blue and green with deep reds, looking at home against a background of emerald green velvet. Monet captured emeralds and sapphires exquisitely in his *Palazzo da Mula, Venice,* a million times better than I can do with words.

It is the light which leads the eye throughout this planting, zigzagging from red to blue to green and yellow. The light makes green appear yellow, and the blue seems green—but rather than being made to feel dizzy by this hovering between one colour and another, we are content to accept the fact that nothing is quite as it seems and that colours will change according to our point of view. Once we process that notion, everything else makes sense.

Ridolfia segetum (false fennel) carries the colour scheme here—a tall, lanky annual, it illuminates everything with its acid green plates of flowers, creating constellations of light. In this image we can see the ridolfia in the foreground—it was important to use a similar brightest-of-bright green in the background to keep the interest and to maintain a very discreet harmony of colour.

The deep red of the *Acer palmatum* is here used sparingly to avoid the sensation of dark gaps which the overuse of purple foliage can sometimes create; it just acknowledges the dark velvety reds and burgundies of *Rosa* 'Nuits de Young' and *R.* 'Tuscany Superb'. Deep blue *Salvia nemorosa* 'Caradonna' and *Iris sibirica* complement each other: I have realised that when colours start to behave in a complementary way like this, my reaction can be one of colour anarchy. I want to stop or tame the contrast; I want to raise a question, to start a conversation. Hence the inclusion here of *Pimpinella major* 'Rosea', its dusky pink plates echoing the form of the ridolfia but in no way its colour. Neatly working with the blues and purples of the iris immediately behind, the pink umbellifer isn't an obvious choice—but like the perfect host, it introduces to each other various guests at the party.

Opposite | Design: Jo Thompson
Below | Claude Monet, *Palazzo da Mula, Venice*, 1908

	NAME	TYPE	HEIGHT	SPREAD	SEASON	LIGHT	MOISTURE	HARDINESS	SOIL PH
A	*Pimpinella major* 'Rosea'	perennial	1-1.5 metres, 2-4 feet	0.1-0.5 metre, 1-2 feet	summer	full sun / partial shade	moist but well-drained / well-drained	very hardy, USDA 5-8	acid / alkaline / neutral
B	*Ridolfia segetum*	annual	0.5-1 metre, 3 feet	0.1-0.5 metre, to 2 feet	summer	full sun / partial shade	moist but well-drained / well-drained	very hardy, to USDA zone 5	acid / alkaline / neutral
C	*Salvia nemorosa* 'Caradonna'	perennial	0.1-0.5 metre, 1-2 feet	0.1-0.5 metre, 1-2 feet	summer	full sun / partial shade	moist but well-drained	very hardy, USDA 4-8	acid / alkaline / neutral
D	*Rosa* 'Nuits de Young'	shrub	1-1.5 metres, 3 feet	0.5-1 metre, 2-3 feet	summer	full sun	moist but well-drained / well-drained	very hardy, USDA 4-9	acid / alkaline / neutral
E	*Rosa* 'Tuscany Superb'	shrub	0.5-1 metre, to 5 feet	0.5-1 metre, to 3 feet	summer	full sun	moist but well-drained / well-drained	very hardy, USDA 4-11	acid / alkaline / neutral
F	*Acer palmatum*	tree	4-8 metres, 10-25 feet	4-8 metres, 10-25 feet	spring / autumn	full sun / partial shade	moist but well-drained	very hardy, USDA 5-8	acid / alkaline / neutral

Inspiration from RHS Garden Wisley

Curator Matthew Pottage on spring pot displays in Surrey:

1 Tulips and other bulbs

Massed pots of flowering tulips and fritillaries inject vibrant colour to a display grouped on the terraces that step down from the Laboratory to the Jellicoe Canal.

2 Blue spires of echium

Overwintered under glass, a potted *Echium candicans* with its towers of blue flowers adds an exotic note to the collection of plants. This plant is tender across most of the UK and needs sun and sharp drainage.

3 Elegant cordyline

With its handsome architectural form and bright striped foliage, *Cordyline australis* 'Torbay Dazzler' makes a great and long-lasting choice for a pot if protected from severe winter cold.

– 42 –

Foliage and Shades of Grey

Verdigris is not a colour term usually applied to plants. To the finishes of pots and planters and railings, yes, it pops up everywhere, but not so much when we are talking about the horticultural side of things.

In a corner of this garden designed by Jenny Jones of Terremoto, a splash of verdigris catches the eye in an elegant, weathered-metal kind of way. Lightish green-blue towards the right of this planting earns it the lead role in this most subtle of gatherings of shades of blues and greens and grey. Light bounces off it and catches the powder-blue fans of *Brahea armata* (big blue hesper palm). Pinballing to the foreground is *Agave attenuata* (foxtail agave) with its seductively curving pale green leaves. A trio of pale greens and blues all taking their cue from verdigris.

The more I look at this palette, the more I see the designer's skill, her intuition in being able to limit her choices to one "colour," and to dot backwards and forwards within this restricted range. Venturing towards the greener end of blue, the tall tree-like *Aloe* 'Hercules' creates an impressive silhouette in front of the palm, and then *ping*: the aloe throws its green to the cactus-like arms of *Euphorbia ingens* (candelabra tree)—good green verticals in front of the verticals of the green cedar fence.

Two plants tie together this sprint through greens. The first, *Echium candicans* (pride of Madeira), displays an intriguing textural-colour combination with hairy leaves of soft silver-grey; it is completely dramatic when in flower, but I love the fact that when simply in leaf, the foliage colour is nearly as muted as the almost indistinguishable yellow-green of *Centranthus ruber* and the dull emerald of *Cedrus deodara*—both perfect greens for bringing all these showstoppers together.

This array of green makes me want to step into this gently jewelled jungle corner and stay there. No wonder that the owners chose to get married in this garden—it's as if you are stepping out from the wardrobe into Narnia, LA style.

Design: Jenny Jones/Terremoto

	NAME	TYPE	HEIGHT	SPREAD	SEASON	LIGHT	MOISTURE	HARDINESS	SOIL PH
A	*Centranthus ruber*	perennial	0.5-1 metre, 1.5-3 feet	0.1-0.5 metre, 1-2 feet	spring / summer / autumn	full sun	well-drained	half hardy, USDA 5-8	alkaline / neutral
B	*Echium candicans*	sub-shrub	1-1.5 metres, 5-6 feet	1-1.5 metres, 6-10 feet	spring / summer	full sun	well-drained	tender, USDA 9-11	alkaline / neutral
C	*Agave attenuata*	succulent perennial	0.5-1 metre, 2-3 feet	1-1.5 metres, 3-4 feet	spring / summer	full sun	well-drained	tender, USDA 10-12	acid
D	*Brahea armata*	tree	> 12 metres, 25-40 feet	2-4 metres, 6-8 feet	summer / autumn	full sun	well-drained	tender, USDA 9-11	acid / alkaline / neutral

	NAME	TYPE	HEIGHT	SPREAD	SEASON	LIGHT	MOISTURE	HARDINESS	SOIL PH
E	*Euphorbia ingens*	succulent tree	> 12 metres, to 40 feet	> 8 metres, to 25 feet	autumn / winter	full sun	well-drained	tender, USDA 10-11	acid / alkaline / neutral
F	*Aloe* 'Hercules'	perennial	8-12 metres, 25-40 feet	4-8 metres, 15-20 feet	evergreen	full sun	well-drained	tender, USDA 9-11	acid / alkaline / neutral
G	*Cedrus deodara*	tree	> 12 metres, 40-50 feet	> 8 metres, 30-40 feet	evergreen	full sun	well-drained	half hardy, USDA 7-8	acid / alkaline / neutral

- 43 -

Brown and Green

In a successful design, the journey and the anticipation along its way are always at least as good as the eventual destination, and back in Old Hollywood, Jenny Jones successfully uses tones and shades of brown and green to create a sense of a botanical adventure.

Inspiration came from the array of amazing existing plants surrounding the property in Whitley Heights: deodar cedars, palm trees, and tree aloes. As Jenny says, "We decided to go maximalist with textures, planting natives, non-natives, spiky things, and soft things—the clients, thankfully, loved the idea and encouraged us to get weird."

It is always completely and utterly brilliant when clients not only get the concept but then push the designer to develop it. The results can be seen in this relatively small garden where the fat-leaved *Monstera deliciosa* thrives alongside the feathery green fans of *Butia capitata* (pindo palm), and the darker green slow-growing *Cycas revoluta* (sago palm), bringing with it a mysterious air of prehistory. Bright green foliage in the understorey comes from *Acanthus mollis*, whose dark brown and white spikes of flowers appear occasionally through the foliage.

Showing respect for the existing deodar cedars with their pendulous branches and needles of silver-blue, the designer hasn't overlooked the most obvious element here: the trees' trunks. The dark brown of the bark is celebrated by the hardwood decked path, which picks up just a hint of red in the cedars' trunks.

Attention to detail of this kind makes for a harmonious atmosphere: the trees are clearly old and the path is clearly new, but they are brought together by the use of toning browns, intersecting at the right angles of Cézanne's *The Pool at Jas de Bouffan*, where the browns of the chestnut trees and the browns of the walls meet each other at the same angles amongst the multiple blues and greens.

Opposite | Design: Jenny Jones/Terremoto
Below | Paul Cézanne, *The Pool at Jas de Bouffan*, c. 1885-86

	NAME	TYPE	HEIGHT	SPREAD	SEASON	LIGHT	MOISTURE	HARDINESS	SOIL PH
A	*Acanthus mollis*	perennial	1-1.5 metres, 3-5 feet	0.5-1 metre, 2-3 feet	summer	full sun / partial shade / full shade	well-drained	very hardy, USDA 7-10	acid / alkaline / neutral
B	*Butia capitata*	palm	4-8 metres, 20-35 feet	2.5-4 metres, 10-15 feet	evergreen	full sun	moist but well-drained	half hardy, USDA 9-11	acid / alkaline / neutral
C	*Monstera deliciosa*	shrub	4-8 metres, 30-70 feet	1.5-2.5 metres, 6-10 feet	spring / summer	partial shade	moist but well-drained	tender, USDA 10-12	acid / alkaline / neutral
D	*Cycas revoluta*	perennial	1-1.5 metres, 3-10 feet	1-1.5 metres, 3-10 feet	evergreen	partial shade	moist but well-drained	tender, USDA 9-10	acid / neutral
E	*Cedrus deodara*	tree	> 12 metres, 40-50 feet	> 8 metres, 30-40 feet	evergreen	full sun	well-drained	half hardy, USDA 7-8	acid / alkaline / neutral

– 44 –

Your Red Is My Green

What to say about colour as it is experienced by colour-blind people? Is what a colour-blind person sees wrong and what a normally sighted person sees right? Of course it's always best to ask the experts, and so I asked designer Andrew Fisher Tomlin—whose colour discrimination means that he sees red as yellow—how this all works for him. It is fascinating to see the colour palettes he creates; as here, they remain beautiful, however we see the colours.

Placing three different ferns together against the rust-paper brown bark of the *Acer griseum*, with a backdrop of *Actaea simplex* Atropurpurea Group, creates a tapestry of colours which move gently towards and away from us. There's a serenity and simplicity in a planting that's actually quite hard to do. Is it something to do with the fact that he sees green in a way that might differ from my idea of green? It's a question that's been asked down the ages. This is his response: "Well, what is interesting is that I get a lot of comments about how I make plantings work: over the years I've come to realise I can do combinations of the same colour, especially green, really well. Simplifying my palette has the effect of emphasising the foliage texture and shape more than the colour itself. It's not an accident and takes some time to do."

That's the key. Texture, together with tone and light, are of enormous significance: the partly dark leaves of *Athyrium niponicum* var. *pictum* (Japanese painted fern) are almost metallic and create the most wonderful sheen that is still—somehow—low-key. Light bounces off the lighter, more matt tones of *Matteuccia struthiopteris* as it pushes its fronds up into a vase shape, while the bristled croziers of *Polystichum polyblepharum* in spring become filigree lace later on: notice that's all without any colour description. The warm yellows, cool greens, cool bronzes, and warm purples fold around the russets from the bark, all coming together to create a complete eiderdown of luxurious loveliness.

I am not going to dare to go anywhere near explaining how colour blindness works, but what I have learned, and what we see so clearly from this photo, is how in the case of the colour-blind and the colour-normal, a subsystem of colour vision still divides colours into warm and cool. Hermann von Helmholtz, a pioneer in the scientific study of human vision, once commented that if an engineer sent him the human eye, he'd send it back as needing further development. But I think this planting demonstrates that one form of colour vision isn't always necessarily better than the other as far as creating a colour scheme is concerned.

Design: Andrew Fisher Tomlin

	NAME	TYPE	HEIGHT	SPREAD	SEASON	LIGHT	MOISTURE	HARDINESS	SOIL PH
A	*Actaea simplex* Atropurpurea Group	perennial	1.5-2.5 metres, 3-4 feet	0.5-1 metre, 2-3 feet	autumn	partial shade	moist but well-drained	very hardy, USDA 4-8	acid / alkaline / neutral
B	*Athyrium niponicum* var. *pictum*	fern	0.1-0.5 metre, 1-1.5 feet	0.1-0.5 metre, 1.5-2 feet	spring / summer / autumn	partial shade / full shade	moist but well-drained	very hardy, USDA 3-8	acid / alkaline / neutral
C	*Polystichum polyblepharum*	fern	0.5-1 metre, 1.5-2 feet	0.5-1 metre, 1.5-2 feet	evergreen	partial shade / full shade	well-drained	very hardy, USDA 5-8	acid / alkaline / neutral
D	*Matteuccia struthiopteris*	fern	1-1.5 metres, 3-6 feet	1.5-2.5 metres, 5-8 feet	spring / summer / autumn	partial shade / full shade	moist but well-drained	very hardy, USDA 3-7	acid / alkaline / neutral
E	*Acer griseum*	tree	8-12 metres, 20-30 feet	4-8 metres, 15-25 feet	spring / summer / autumn	full sun / partial shade	moist but well-drained / well-drained	very hardy, USDA 4-8	acid / alkaline / neutral

- 45 -

Greens and Blues by Water

When we think of landscape colours, we tend to think in various shades of green. However, if that landscape is Paradise Valley, Arizona, we really do need to put aside our presumptions and consider instead that most organic palette of the earth—soil itself.

We tend to want to cover up soil. We don't want to see the gaps of this essential medium without which there would be no planting, but here the designer places it in pole position and celebrates its necessity. Talking about her planting choices, Michele Shelor refers to galleries, palettes, stippling, and there is definitely a painterly, mannered approach to the colours here. Layers of cacti and succulents indeed create a painting, with a low ground plane enhancing the focal points of the sculptural columnar cacti.

You may be thinking that this is simply an attractive sculptural arrangement by a pool, but what we have here isn't just a bunch of arid plants in shades of green. It is so much cleverer than that. Look beyond the garden, and you'll see the starting point for this subtle conversation in colour.

Design: Michele Shelor/Colwell Shelor Landscape Architecture

There, in the distance, is the earthy backdrop of Camelback Mountain, the starting point for this clean, simple placement of cacti and succulents. The mountain isn't the first thing that we notice, but once we do, we can see how everything comes from the Sonoran desert landscape, not least the unashamed expanses of soil between each plant.

The colour focal point for me is the *Opuntia santarita*, a prickly pear beyond compare. Soft blue-grey pads are flushed with purple in winter and then slowly fade back to grey—the changing colours create movement as well as a fabulous hook on which to hang the rest of the planting. The grey-blues appear again in the majestic *Agave beauleriana* and *A. parryi* var. *truncata* (artichoke agave).

With enough blue to form a middle-ground colour link between pool and sky, the rest of the planting relaxes back into a green that we might see more of in the plants in the landscape beyond. Fat low barrels of *Echinocactus grusonii*, the pads of *Opuntia microdasys* (bunny ears cactus), *Cereus repandus*, *Pachycereus weberi* (candelabro)—all hover between green-yellow and silvery green depending on your vantage point. *Dodonaea viscosa* straggles a mid-green all the way along the rear of this planting, knitting all together.

The black pool is itself a large reflective sculpture, punctuating the gardens around it, capturing the reflection of the sky and this unusual sculptural plant palette, creating wonder in the landscape.

I hope you are glad you stopped and looked a little more closely.

	NAME	TYPE	HEIGHT	SPREAD	SEASON	LIGHT	MOISTURE	HARDINESS	SOIL PH
A	*Opuntia santarita*	perennial	1.5-2.5 metres, to 4 feet	2.5 metres, to 6 feet	summer	full sun	well-drained	tender, USDA 8-11	acid / alkaline / neutral
B	*Opuntia microdasys*	perennial	0.5-1 metre, 2-3 feet	1-1.5 metres, 4-6 feet	summer	full sun	well-drained	tender, USDA 9-11	acid / alkaline / neutral
C	*Agave parryi* var. *truncata*	perennial	0.5-1 metre, 2-3 feet	0.5-1 metre, 3-4 feet	summer	full sun	well-drained	half hardy, USDA 6-9	acid / neutral
D	*Agave beauleriana*	perennial	1.5-2.5 metres, 6-8 feet	2.5-4 metres, 8-10 feet	summer	full sun	well-drained	tender, USDA 10-12	acid / alkaline / neutral
E	*Dodonaea viscosa*	shrub	2.5-4 metres, 12-16 feet	1.5-2.5 metres, 8-12 feet	summer / autumn	full sun	moist but well-drained	tender, USDA 10-12	acid / alkaline / neutral
F	*Aloe vera*	succulent	0.5-1 metre, 1-2 feet	0.5-1 metre, 0.5-1 foot	summer	full sun	well-drained	tender, USDA 10-12	acid / alkaline / neutral
G	*Cereus repandus*	treelike succulent	6-15 metres, 20-50 feet	3 metres, to 10 feet	summer	full sun	well-drained	tender, USDA 9-11	acid / alkaline / neutral
H	*Cleistocactus strausii*	perennial	1-3 metres, to 10 feet	to 0.1 metre, 0.25 foot	summer	full sun	well-drained	tender, USDA 9-11	acid / alkaline / neutral
I	*Echinocactus grusonii*	perennial	0.5-1.5 metres, to 4 feet	0.5 metre, 2.5 feet	summer	full sun	well-drained	tender, USDA 9-11	acid / alkaline / neutral
J	*Muhlenbergia rigens*	grass	1-2 metres, 3-6 feet	0.5-1 metre, 2-3 feet	summer / autumn / winter	full sun	well-drained	hardy, USDA 6-9	acid / alkaline / neutral
K	*Pachycereus weberi*	treelike succulent	4.5-6 metres, 15-20 feet	3 metres, to 10 feet	summer	full sun	well-drained	tender, USDA 9-11	acid / alkaline / neutral

– 46 –

Colour Love

When Georgia O'Keeffe first visited New Mexico, she was entranced by the textures of the landscape forms which surrounded her and the intensity of their colours. Experimenting with new colours, she immortalized this landscape in various palettes, including this memorable coral and blue. Extraordinary as it is, in a very different world, another artist independently landed on the same colour scheme, and it is a triumph in both. This is a dreamy palette.

Pastels, faded jewel tones, and warm neutrals have something of the nostalgic about them. Dusky pinky peach and misty hazy violet bring a calm glow to this planting. Arne Maynard's mastery of colour is evident in his attention to every detail—whether living or inanimate, there's perfection in each element. The pots have cool grey within their brown, which links them to the stone setts on the ground, and yet at the same time enough warmth to snuggle up against the peachy walls. There's just of a hint of blue in their brown, too, which ensures the pots behave well as a low-level anchor to the blue wisteria, grown from a cutting in a client's garden.

This framework of welcoming warmth is set up to show off four very beautiful plants, each having just enough about it to make it stand out from the crowd while somehow still managing to look relaxed and unassuming. Skill at every step.

Wisteria, ever the cheer-bringer, exudes happy freshness and a shout that summer's here, a call to all of us to start thinking about turning off the heating and reminding us that we won't be needing to wear a coat every day. It's a glass-half-full plant, its blue-blue-*blue* crammed full of optimism and stopping us in our tracks as they smother house fronts, which makes for walks taking twice as long. Fresh against white, prettily noble against stone, nodding to history against brick, against this honeyed peach it has a sense of glowing softly.

What makes this palette so extra-delectable is that there is in fact another blue in the mix. Look carefully—can you spot it? Amongst *Tulipa* 'Brown Sugar' and *T.* 'La Belle Époque', almost ethereal in burnished tones that defy description as their colours move and change, there's a peppermint ice, a flash and a dash and a start of palest blue: *Muscari armeniacum* 'Peppermint' peeps up through the stands of tulips.

Opposite | Design: Arne Maynard
Below | Georgia O'Keeffe, *Black Mesa Landscape, New Mexico / Out Back of Marie's II*, 1930

	NAME	TYPE	HEIGHT	SPREAD	SEASON	LIGHT	MOISTURE	HARDINESS	SOIL PH
A	*Wisteria sinensis*	woody vine	> 12 metres, 10-25 feet	> 8 metres, 10-25 feet	spring / summer	full sun / partial shade	moist but well-drained	hardy, USDA 5-8	acid / alkaline / neutral
B	*Muscari armeniacum* 'Peppermint'	bulb	0.1-0.5 metre, 0.25 foot	0.1 metre, 0.25 foot	spring	full sun / partial shade	moist but well-drained / well-drained	very hardy, USDA 4-9	acid / alkaline / neutral
C	*Tulipa* 'La Belle Époque'	bulb	0.1-0.5 metre, 1.5-2 feet	0.1 metre, 0.25 foot	spring	full sun	well-drained	very hardy, USDA 3-8	acid / alkaline / neutral
D	*Tulipa* 'Brown Sugar'	bulb	0.1-0.5 metre, 0.75-1 foot	0.1-0.5 metre, 1-1.5 feet	spring	full sun	well-drained	very hardy, USDA 4-8	acid / alkaline / neutral

– 47 –

Green, Silver, and Orange

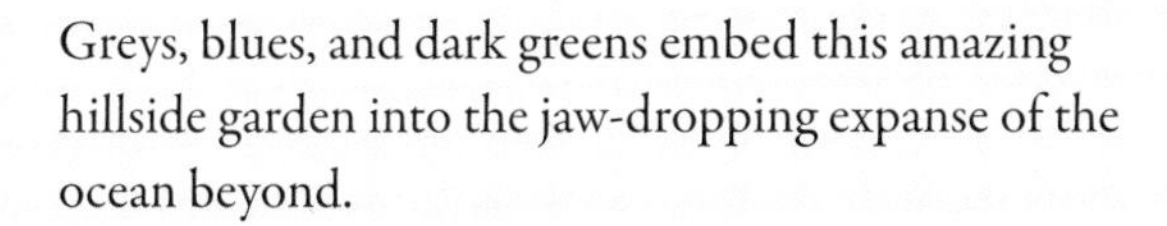

Greys, blues, and dark greens embed this amazing hillside garden into the jaw-dropping expanse of the ocean beyond.

In this setting overlooking the Pacific Coast Highway and the beaches of Malibu, Eric Brandon Gomez weaves an understated, successful colour story of grey and green using climatically appropriate natives of South Africa, Australia, and the Mediterranean. Taking inspiration from the local Malibu chaparral, with its evergreen shrubs growing in coarse-textured soil, he beautifully ties this study of vegetation to the land of its immediate location as well as to its wider, impressive setting.

The silver leaves and pretty blue flowers of *Salvia clevelandii* (Cleveland sage), together with *Artemisia* 'Powis Castle' and *Curio talinoides* subsp. *mandraliscae* in the background, have just enough grey in them to create a neutral link both to the loose aggregate surface and to the ocean in the distance, as well as to the darker green rosemary, which creates the break between the paler colours of hard and soft surfaces. This rosemary in turn is picked up by the blue-green of the agave at the rear.

There's another echo of this dark green foliage in the form of the wonderful *Aloe* 'Cynthia Giddy', whose branched inflorescences of bright orange-red flowers are a highlight in this arrangement of greens, silvers, and blues. This medium-sized aloe clumps to form numerous rosettes to 2 feet tall with dark green, gently white-spotted leaves. Its leaves turn red-brown in autumn, ensuring that this plant continues to give its all to this garden.

Bambusa multiplex 'Alphonso-Karrii' in the foreground provides another break between silver foliage, more of which is provided by the succulent pink-lined *Crassula arborescens* (silver dollar jade) and *Helichrysum petiolare*. The crassula grows in large groups in its native South Africa and loves a rocky outcrop; if deprived of water, its leaves develop a purple flush.

Throughout the rear, *Verbena bonariensis* picks up the blues, greys, and greens, creating a haze of purple-blue at a higher level; it will seed itself around happily. In all, the total effect of this considered colour scheme is one of laid-back welcome and effortless relaxation.

Design: Eric Brandon Gomez

	NAME	TYPE	HEIGHT	SPREAD	SEASON	LIGHT	MOISTURE	HARDINESS	SOIL PH
A	*Aloe* 'Cynthia Giddy'	perennial	0.1-0.5 metre, 1-2 feet	0.5-1 metre, 2-3 feet	summer / autumn	full sun / partial shade	well-drained	tender, USDA 9-11	acid / alkaline / neutral
B	*Salvia clevelandii*	perennial	1-1.5 metres, 3-4.5 feet	1-2.5 metres, to 8 feet	summer	full sun	moist but well-drained	tender, USDA 8-11	acid / alkaline / neutral
C	*Verbena bonariensis*	perennial	1-1.5 metres, 2-4 feet	0.5-1 metre, 1.5-3 feet	summer / autumn	full sun	well-drained / moist but well-drained	hardy, USDA 7-11	acid / alkaline / neutral
D	*Curio talinoides* subsp. *mandraliscae*	perennial	0.5-1 metre, 1-3 feet	0.5-1 metre, 2-3 feet	summer	full sun / partial shade	moist but well-drained	tender, USDA 9-11	acid / alkaline / neutral
E	*Artemisia* 'Powis Castle'	shrub	0.5-1 metre, 2-3 feet	0.1-0.5 metre, 1-2 feet	summer	full sun	well-drained	hardy, USDA 6-9	acid / alkaline / neutral
F	*Crassula arborescens*	succulent	1-1.5 metres, to 4 feet	1-1.5 metres, to 4 feet	summer	full sun	well-drained	tender, USDA 9-11	acid / alkaline / neutral
G	*Helichrysum petiolare*	sub-shrub	0.1-0.5 metre, 0.5-0.75 feet	0.5-1 metre, 0.5-3 feet	spring / summer	full sun	well-drained / moist to well-drained	tender, USDA 9-11	acid / alkaline / neutral

- 48 -

Green, Silver, and Lilac

In his naturalistic Dawn Gardens in California, Barry Friesen has planted one hundred thousand daffodils, one hundred and fifty roses, and fifty Japanese maples—over three thousand different cultivars in total. So, as well you might imagine, there is colour from flowers, fruit, and foliage for every month of the year. At an altitude of twelve hundred feet, this place feels truly serene, and the area of the garden shown in this photograph has a particularly spiritual atmosphere, with almost a cloister of spruce nestled below the Sierra Foothills, which loom behind.

The calming repeated presence of *Picea glauca* var. *albertiana* 'Conica' (dwarf Alberta spruce) conjures up a sense that they are guardians of the garden. Their light green needles move serenely into blue-green as the seasons themselves move onwards. The mass of this standout colour is thrown brilliantly into relief by the gleaming silver stems of *Salvia yangii* (Russian sage), whose deeply divided light grey-green leaves shine brightly behind the spruce.

Simplicity is everything in this palette, and little spots of light purple-violet in the *Liatris spicata*'s flowers pick up the blue in the spruces' needles as well as toning with the lavender-blue and grey of the salvia's tubular flowers. It is so simple: there are only three main focus plants in this grouping, and each works perfectly with the other two.

This harmonious space, so expertly put together, is certainly the ideal spot for its intended purpose as a place conducive to meditation and reflection.

Design: Barry Friesen

	NAME	TYPE	HEIGHT	SPREAD	SEASON	LIGHT	MOISTURE	HARDINESS	SOIL PH
A	*Liatris spicata*	perennial	0.5-1 metre, 2-4 feet	0.1-0.5 metre, 0.75-1.5 feet	summer / autumn	full sun	moist but well-drained	fully hardy, USDA 3-8	acid / alkaline / neutral
B	*Salvia yangii*	perennial	1-1.5 metres, 2-5 feet	0.5-1 metre, 2-4 feet	summer / autumn	full sun	well-drained	fully hardy, USDA 5-9	acid / alkaline / neutral
C	*Picea glauca* var. *albertiana* 'Conica'	tree	1.5-2.5 metres, 10-13 feet	1.5-2.5 metres, 7-10 feet	autumn	full sun	moist but well-drained	fully hardy, USDA 3-6	acid / alkaline / neutral

– 49 –

Blue Heaven

Fresh air is violet. I can't claim to have come up with this; in his excitement when the violet penny dropped, Édouard Manet summarised what we see but what is hard to put into words: colour is transient. What lies between our eye and the object perceived—the air, the atmosphere—has an effect upon the object's colour. (And translating colour words is something else entirely, as statesman-turned-linguist William Gladstone would hasten to add.)

But back to violet. Or blue. Or lavender. What do you see here at Garten der Horizonte? There's a shimmer of silver as the early light catches cream flower fountains above the blue-grey leaves of *Panicum amarum* 'Dewey Blue'. This is one absolute stunner of a grass. The elegantly arching, light-catching foliage and flower combination is superb and in this border works perfectly as the harness between blues.

Molinia caerulea subsp. *caerulea* 'Dauerstrahl' echoes the panicum's blue here. Its proper purple flowers create that all-important air-painting haze, but it's the mid-green foliage which, set in this palette, conjures up a background cloud of grey. Interspersing these grey clouds is the late-summer violet-blue of *Aster amellus* 'Blue King'; violet continues to appear, paler and paler, as the planting moves further and further away. There's a sense of the tones ebbing calmly away as more and more white is added to the palette's purple pigment, lighting all from within.

	NAME	TYPE	HEIGHT	SPREAD	SEASON	LIGHT	MOISTURE	HARDINESS	SOIL PH
A	*Aster amellus* 'Blue King'	perennial	0.5-1 metre, 1 foot	0.5-1 metre, 1.5 feet	summer / autumn	full sun	moist but well-drained / well-drained	very hardy, USDA 5-8	alkaline / neutral
B	*Molinia caerulea* subsp. *caerulea* 'Dauerstrahl'	grass	0.5-1 metre, 3-4 feet	0.5-1 metre, 2-2.5 feet	summer / autumn	full sun / partial shade	moist but well-drained / well-drained	very hardy, USDA 4-8	acid / neutral
C	*Panicum amarum* 'Dewey Blue'	grass	1-1.5 metres, 3-4 feet	0.5-1 metre, 2-3 feet	autumn / winter	full sun	moist but well-drained / well-drained	very hardy, USDA 2-9	acid / alkaline / neutral

Opposite | Design: Maria and Erich Luer

- 50 -

Pastel Veil

I realise I talk a lot about the blurs and veils, the shimmers of transparency, as a way of tying colours to each other. Any plant with a quality of airiness to its arrangement of flowers—often umbellifers such as anthriscus, or thin spires such as those of veronicastrum—can be used to achieve this linking. The key is to look at the flower or leaf colour and decide how it might echo (even if very subtly) the colour tones you are aiming to connect.

Ornamental grasses perform this linking function incredibly well, but they must be sited carefully: they can create big blocks of neutral nothingness in the wrong light. One of the best performers is the exquisite *Sporobolus heterolepis*, so refined in its character, its graceful stems of pink flowers casting a fabulous pastel haze throughout a planting. The mid-green foliage is good too, which earns it a place in many schemes where grasses would otherwise be a drain on the surrounding colour.

Hovering above the pink-lilac cloud are the flowers of *Dianthus carthusianorum*, each a rich restrained dot of magenta. The star in colour terms here, though, has to be *Echinacea pallida* 'Hula Dancer'. More ballerina than hula dancer, its lazy skirts drift nonchalantly through and over the grasses, the palest of pinks to whites perfect against the pale blue sprays of *Limonium platyphyllum*. The latter is another one of those airy plants which catch the light so effectively.

This is such an elegant combination of colours—subtle yet poised, glorious in the evening as it catches the last light, moving the landscape into a lightscape.

Design: Piet Oudolf for Hauser & Wirth, Somerset

	NAME	TYPE	HEIGHT	SPREAD	SEASON	LIGHT	MOISTURE	HARDINESS	SOIL PH
A	*Echinacea pallida* 'Hula Dancer'	perennial	1-1.5 metres, 2-3 feet	0.1-0.5 metre, 1-1.5 feet	summer	full sun	well-drained	very hardy, USDA 3-8	acid / alkaline / neutral
B	*Dianthus carthusianorum*	perennial	0.1-0.5 metre, 2-2.5 feet	0.1-0.5 metre, to 1 foot	summer	full sun	well-drained	very hardy, USDA 5-9	alkaline / neutral
C	*Limonium platyphyllum*	perennial	0.5-1 metre, 2-2.5 feet	0.1-0.5 metre, 2-2.5 feet	summer / autumn	full sun	well-drained	very hardy, USDA 3-9	acid / alkaline / neutral
D	*Sporobolus heterolepis*	grass	0.5-1 metre, 2-3 feet	0.5-1 metre, 2-3 feet	summer	full sun	moist but well-drained / poorly drained	very hardy, USDA 3-9	acid / alkaline / neutral

Inspiration from RHS Garden Hyde Hall

Curator Robert Brett on Floral Fantasia, a dazzling seasonal showpiece which brings together the latest and greatest in summer bedding:

1 Upright anchor plants

Bold clumps of *Miscanthus sinensis* 'Gracillimus' form a permanent background to the Floral Fantasia garden, organised each August by industry champion Peter Seabrook.

2 Compact Peruvian lilies

In 2019 the planting included masses of creamy, yellow-throated *Alstroemeria* Inticancha Series with zingy *A.* Indian Summer = 'Tesronto' in the background.

3 Marguerites for contrast

At the front, gold and pink *Argyranthemum* Grandaisy Series flank rosy *Angelonia angustifolia* Serena Series.

- 51 -

Emerald

Nestled in the deep blue waters of Charleston Harbour in South Carolina, James Island is home to an astoundingly beautiful garden, brought forward from a wooded marshfront containing a mass of overgrown camellias and azaleas. Jim Smeal and Alejandro Gonzalez have made a homage to green in this part of the garden, whose character is stamped by the presence of two majestic specimens of *Quercus virginiana* (southern live oak), their seductively ground-seeking boughs and dark evergreen leaves naturally veiling the marsh grass beyond. And this marsh grass really must be applauded: it is emerald green, reminiscent of the jewel-coloured grass of Ireland, its shades changing with the seasons.

Imagine stumbling upon this area. You walk along a path whose end is marked by clumps of dwarf mat rush; this *Lomandra longifolia* 'Breeze', with its crimped, straplike, dark green leaves, signals both an end and a beginning. The paler yellow-green leaves of *Carex oshimensis* 'Evergold' are the perfect highlight, bringing light to the foreground without distracting the eye from the marsh, a background sea of greens. The darker *Juniperus virginiana* could almost be the full stop in this masterly arrangement of greens, but this juniper has been allowed to sit in its own space and to relax in the light from the marsh. It does not detract from the laconically elegant, lazily drooping and scooping oaks which stand to either side. Even if we didn't know what lies in the distance, we would still have the sense that there is water nearby as the shades of green, so near to sea-green, sit so perfectly before the more watery blue-green of the open expanse beyond. There's a feeling of relaxed, welcoming space, wild yet with just the slightest intervention. A garden on the wild side.

Design: Jim Smeal, Alejandro Gonzalez

	NAME	TYPE	HEIGHT	SPREAD	SEASON	LIGHT	MOISTURE	HARDINESS	SOIL PH
A	*Quercus virginiana*	tree	> 12 metres, 40-80 feet	> 8 metres, 60-100 feet	evergreen	full sun	well-drained / moist but well-drained	half hardy, USDA 8-10	acid / alkaline / neutral
B	*Juniperus virginiana*	tree	> 12 metres, 30-65 feet	4-8 metres, 8-25 feet	evergreen	full sun	well-drained / moist but well-drained	very hardy, USDA 2-9	alkaline / neutral
C	*Carex oshimensis* 'Evergold'	perennial	0.1-0.5 metre, 0.75-1 foot	0.1-0.5 metre, 1-1.5 feet	summer	full shade / partial shade	well-drained / moist but well-drained	very hardy, USDA 5-9	acid / alkaline / neutral

- 52 -

A White Garden

Imitation may be the sincerest form of flattery, but when something is done excellently, the temptation is to think that it will be impossible to replicate. Vita Sackville-West's White Garden at Sissinghurst is the garden that springs to mind, the scrambling milk-white *Rosa* 'Mulliganii' which envelops the arbour setting the tone for the rest of this powerful, seductive garden. But take heart: we may not be able to replicate, but we can certainly take inspiration.

The brief for the garden in these images—created for the RHS Chelsea Flower Show and subsequently rebuilt as a corner of a London square—was "chic and elegant." Elegance can still carry with it variety; the key, as ever, is a good structure. In this planting the structure comes in the form of multi-stemmed *Betula utilis* subsp. *jacquemontii*, selected for its whitest-of-white bark—a nod to the white marble sculpture which was the focal point at the end of the space; a white to sit against the sharp-silver stainless steel bench.

The betula's bark and fresh green leaves inspire the rest of the planting. We speak of not mixing creamy white and white, but I find that as long as there is a contrast of foliage, mixing the two can work well. *Rosa* Macmillan Nurse = 'Beamac' appears here, in both standard and shrub form, alongside *Cornus kousa* and *Viburnum opulus*. The rose's dark green leaves act as a foil, separating it just enough from its white-flowering neighbours; otherwise their shades of white could look a little "off" against its creamy blooms, which have just a hint of a faded pink.

At a lower level, the long racemes of *Hebe salicifolia* start to show themselves a month or so later, taking on the mantle of the white. But earlier in the summer, this evergreen shrub is a satisfying mound of green, allowing the eye to pause for a while before moving on to the other key structure at this level, *Euonymus fortunei* 'Silver Queen'. Some are disinclined to use variegated foliage, but I shall continue to defend it vigorously: in a dark corner this particular variegated evergreen performs brilliantly, almost lighting up the space and behaving however you want it to behave, whether that be keeping it in a mound or letting it scramble through its neighbours or up against a wall, which it loves to do.

In shady areas, *Polystichum setiferum* (Divisilobum Group) 'Herrenhausen' makes a good lacy green pattern against this euonymus, with dots of sharp white from the wonderfully spurred *Aquilegia* 'Kristall', spires of mid-white from *Digitalis purpurea* f. *albiflora*, and starry fireworks of palest cream provided by *Thalictrum aquilegiifolium* 'Album'. These three are all invaluable, linking colours through areas of the garden that have different amounts of light, happy in sun and shade.

An elegant space yet still relaxing, the abundant soft planting softens the central sculptural bench, which weaves its way through, along, down, and around the garden.

White

Leonardo da Vinci called it "the first of all simple colours," one that may be said to "represent light, without which no colour can be seen." On bright winter days, a snowdrop's petals do indeed seem to shine from within. So what is white, exactly? White is the trickiest of colours as well as the absence of colour. White is white because it reflects all colours: white objects absorb no wavelengths. The purest white—the white in a child's paintbox, the chalk-cliff white of Le Corbusier's Villa Savoye—can be hard on the eye. But often what appears to be snow white is in fact pale yellow, ivory, cream, oyster white, greenish white, bluish white, the very palest blue. The emotion white conjures up can be tipped from cold to warm, just by the slightest addition of another colour.

Culturally, white has an intriguing symbolism. It represents death in China and in India is traditionally the colour worn for funerals. In the West, white represents innocence, purity, even virginity, and as such features at weddings and baptisms; but it also carries with it notions of coldness and sterility. The people of the Polynesian island of Bellona attach great importance to white, as one of only three colours they name: *susungu* (white/light), *ungi* (black/dark), and *unga* (red). All other colours are subdivisions of these "mothers of colours."

Long, long ago our ancestors distinguished between matt white (*albus*) and brilliant white (*candidus*). Our empty "blank" is so near to *blanco*, *blanc*, *bianco*—all words for white. Both white sound and white space suggest an absence, a blankness.

White stands out and yet goes with anything. Think of white flowers against green foliage: the flowers show themselves clearly yet work in harmony with the leaves, taking on elements of the green which surrounds them.

Design: Jo Thompson for RHS Chelsea 2014

	NAME	TYPE	HEIGHT	SPREAD	SEASON	LIGHT	MOISTURE	HARDINESS	SOIL PH
A	*Rosa* Macmillan Nurse = 'Beamac'	shrub	0.5-1 metre, 2-3 feet	0.5-1 metre, 3-4 feet	summer / autumn	full sun	moist but well-drained / well-drained	very hardy, USDA 6-9	acid / alkaline / neutral
B	*Viburnum opulus*	shrub	4-8 metres, 8-15 feet	2.5-4 metres, 10-15 feet	summer / autumn	full sun / partial shade / full shade	moist but well-drained / well-drained	very hardy, USDA 3-8	acid / alkaline / neutral
C	*Aquilegia* 'Kristall'	perennial	to 1 metre, 1-2 feet	0.5 metres, 1-2 feet	summer / autumn	full sun / partial shade	moist but well-drained / well-drained	very hardy, USDA 3-10	acid / alkaline / neutral
D	*Cornus kousa*	tree	to 7 metres, 15-30 feet	to 5 metres, 15-30 feet	spring	full sun / partial shade	well-drained	very hardy, USDA 5-8	neutral / acid
E	*Digitalis purpurea* f. *albiflora*	perennial	0.5-1.5 metres, 3-5 feet	0.1-0.5 metre, 1.5-2 feet	spring / summer	full sun / partial shade	moist but well-drained / well-drained	very hardy, USDA 4-8	acid / alkaline / neutral

– 53 –

British Green

I'd like to say a big thank-you to the owner of this garden. Faced with an overgrown bramble-swamped lawn which looked as if it could have been Miss Havisham's actual garden, we knew we had to claw something back from Time's greedy clutches. Shade was needed, as was colour, but there was a concomitant conversation about true respect for the land and in particular for the surrounding landscape, so characteristic of Britain. Green, green, and more green was what we could see, and we decided that we would remain true to this most peaceful of palettes. Another example of gentle intervention rather than gigantic imposition: any notions of flower beds and pergolas were dismissed before I even put pen to paper.

And how glad am I that we had that conversation. Picture in your mind beds of roses: yes, they would look lovely, but the scene is better without. Instead, the colour pops happen in spring; tiny wildflowers stipple the hill-side with dots of pink and white, but after that it's green, with the exception of a few existing acers showing their wonderful autumnal blaze, their fiery oranges and reds catching the sunsets perfectly. Someone cleverly planned that to happen long before I arrived on the scene.

How many greens are in this image? There's fresh green, light green, dark green, sap green, yellow-green, emerald

Design: Jo Thompson

	NAME	TYPE	HEIGHT	SPREAD	SEASON	LIGHT	MOISTURE	HARDINESS	SOIL PH
A	*Anthriscus sylvestris*	perennial	1-1.5 metres, 3 feet	0.1-0.5 metre, 2 feet	spring / summer	full sun / partial shade	moist but well-drained / well-drained	very hardy, USDA 7-10	acid / alkaline / neutral
B	*Prunus avium*	tree	> 12 metres, 15-30 feet	> 8 metres, 15-30 feet	spring / autumn	full sun / partial shade	well-drained / moist but well-drained	very hardy, USDA 3-8	acid / alkaline / neutral
C	*Platanus ×hispanica*	tree	> 12 metres, 70-85 feet	> 8 metres, 50-70 feet	spring / summer / autumn	full sun	well-drained	very hardy, USDA 5-8	acid / alkaline / neutral
D	*Crataegus monogyna*	tree	4-8 metres, 20-30 feet	4-8 metres, 20-30 feet	spring / summer / autumn	full sun / partial shade	well-drained / moist but well-drained	very hardy, USDA 4-7	acid / alkaline / neutral

green, sylvan green, forest green, pine green, moss green, lime green. There are more greens than I have words for here, but what I find interesting is that there is little, if any, green foliage on the blue spectrum. No greys and little silver here.

Perhaps this is why the roof-trained London plane trees seem at home. They shouldn't do, with their structure that has been so clearly and definitely forced by man into a convenient shape. But their leaves, strikingly larger than any other leaves nearby, are of a bright fresh green, light enough to create the sense of light all the way along their canopy. They are the same colour as the grass in the distance, a natural green, no pretension and no trying too hard.

- 54 -

Muted Borders of Wildflower Pastels

In this garden in the south of England, the house needed to appear out of the wilderness of the rest of the garden. It was agreed early on that the key was to relax, to plant varieties and colours that would look equally at home in the surrounding wildflower meadows. This immediately suggested a palette of muted hues in shades and tones that work with one another, with only one or two varieties seeking the limelight at any time.

Using the materials of the house as a starting point, I chose *Angelica sylvestris* 'Vicar's Mead', an unusual selection of wild angelica, for its wonderfully striking deep purple stems and leaves. Its large umbels of purple to pink flowers are in rich harmony with the red brick behind and create a fabulous architectural statement in late summer and autumn. The deep purple stems of *Eutrochium maculatum* Atropurpureum Group, seen at the far end of this border, echo the angelica and take this planting through into late autumn, its skeleton offering interest even when it has turned to darkest brown.

The eutrochium, with its pinkish purple flowers, is a plant that is often overlooked, but in my own garden, I can't do without it in the autumn border. When inspected close-up, the tiny pink spidery stars, loved by butterflies and bees, are difficult to enthuse over, but stand back and they create a flowerhead that becomes ever more hazy as the plant ages. Grouped together, unlike the individual punctuations of the angelica, the Joe-pye weed provides an effective dark shadow of height. Christopher Lloyd, citing the indistinctness of its small flowers, recommended the need for good neighbours; further along this bed, it forms a happy combination with *Molinia caerulea* subsp. *arundinacea* 'Transparent', whose graceful stems end with panicles of dark brown flowers.

So, we have the stars of this border—now to make them feel at home. For this, we need to bring in some highlights of a lighter purple. The effect of the bright points of pale pink of *Verbena hastata* f. *rosea* and its minuscule darker purple flower buds offered the right form to complement the angelica as well as to tie it to the paler wash of pastels from *Leucanthemum vulgare* and *Geranium* Rozanne = 'Gerwat', which together create the foundation of this palette. The verbena's structure is as important as its colours, its candelabras of flowers following the erect stems of the angelica; further along appear the pinkish blue spires of *Salvia nemorosa* 'Amethyst', and even more spires appear in the form of *Veronicastrum virginicum* 'Album'.

Here and there, the dots of dusky pink from the elegantly drooping *Echinacea pallida* are intended to be just visible, appearing through the flower clouds of *Valeriana officinalis*, its pinkish white flowers turning to cream as they fade.

A

B

C

D

	NAME	TYPE	HEIGHT	SPREAD	SEASON	LIGHT	MOISTURE	HARDINESS	SOIL PH
A	*Geranium* Rozanne = 'Gerwat'	perennial	0.5-1 metre, 1-1.5 feet	0.5-1 metre, 1-2 feet	summer / autumn	full sun / partial shade	moist but well-drained / well-drained	very hardy, USDA 5-8	acid / alkaline / neutral
B	*Leucanthemum vulgare*	perennial	0.5-1 metre, 1-3 feet	0.1-0.5 metre, 1-2 feet	summer	full sun / partial shade	moist but well-drained	very hardy, USDA 3-8	acid / alkaline / neutral
C	*Echinacea pallida*	perennial	1-1.5 metres, 2-3 feet	0.1-0.5 metre, 1-1.5 feet	summer	full sun	well-drained	very hardy, USDA 3-10	acid / alkaline / neutral
D	*Salvia nemorosa* 'Amethyst'	perennial	0.5-1 metre, 2.5 feet	0.5-1 metre, 3 feet	summer	full sun / partial shade	moist but well-drained	very hardy, USDA 5-8	acid / alkaline / neutral

Opposite | Design: Jo Thompson

	NAME	TYPE	HEIGHT	SPREAD	SEASON	LIGHT	MOISTURE	HARDINESS	SOIL PH
E	*Veronicastrum virginicum* 'Album'	perennial	1-1.5 metres, 3-4 feet	0.5-1 metre, 2-3 feet	summer	full sun / partial shade	moist but well-drained / well-drained	very hardy, USDA 4-8	acid / alkaline / neutral
F	*Verbena hastata* f. *rosea*	perennial	1-1.5 metres, 3-4 feet	0.5-1 metre, 1.5-2 feet	summer	full sun	moist but well-drained / well-drained	very hardy, USDA 3-8	acid / alkaline / neutral
G	*Eutrochium maculatum* Atropurpureum Group	perennial	1.5-2.5 metres, to 7 feet	1-1.5 metres, to 5 feet	summer / autumn	full sun / partial shade	well-drained / moist but well-drained / poorly drained	very hardy, USDA 4-8	acid / alkaline / neutral
H	*Angelica sylvestris* 'Vicar's Mead'	biennial	1-1.5 metres, 3-4 feet	0.5-1 metre, to 3 feet	summer / autumn	partial shade	moist but well-drained	very hardy, USDA 4-9	acid / alkaline / neutral
I	*Molinia caerulea* subsp. *arundinacea* 'Transparent'	grass	1.5-2.5 metres, 6-8 feet	1-1.5 metres, 2-4 feet	summer / autumn	full sun / partial shade	moist but well-drained / well-drained	very hardy, USDA 5-8	acid / neutral

– 55 –

Rose Tapestry

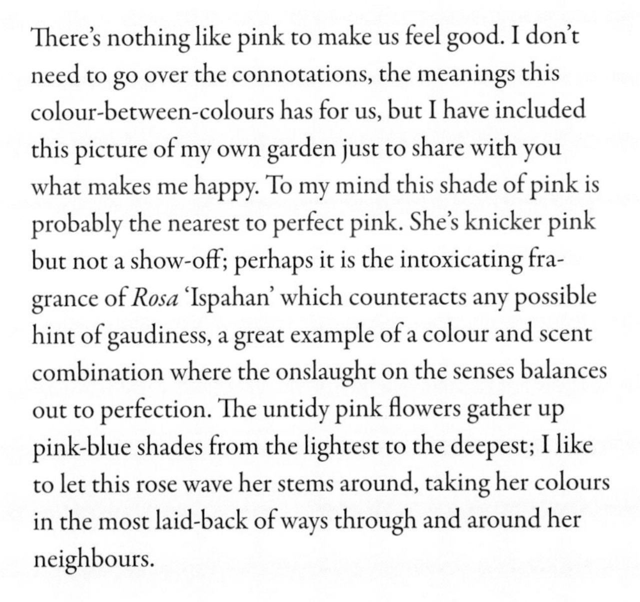

There's nothing like pink to make us feel good. I don't need to go over the connotations, the meanings this colour-between-colours has for us, but I have included this picture of my own garden just to share with you what makes me happy. To my mind this shade of pink is probably the nearest to perfect pink. She's knicker pink but not a show-off; perhaps it is the intoxicating fragrance of *Rosa* 'Ispahan' which counteracts any possible hint of gaudiness, a great example of a colour and scent combination where the onslaught on the senses balances out to perfection. The untidy pink flowers gather up pink-blue shades from the lightest to the deepest; I like to let this rose wave her stems around, taking her colours in the most laid-back of ways through and around her neighbours.

Wanting to enjoy colours and their effects when placed together, I've allowed *Rosa* Port Sunlight = 'Auslofty' to stand to one side, bringing its little peachy orange balls of sunshine into the mix. While I speak of not overthinking, there is, I admit, a thought process behind the introduction of the next colour, the deep red burgundy wine of *R.* Munstead Wood = 'Ausbernard', which sits between *R.* 'Ispahan' and *R.* Port Sunlight = 'Auslofty'. The reason for my letting *R.* 'Ispahan' weave through is simply that I don't want stripes, and I definitely don't want formality in this part of the garden: it encloses an unassuming little, much-used seating area, which fortuitously catches both the morning and the evening sun. I also want to blend and blur the colours, seeing what works with what.

A small self-sown geranium was allowed to stay, as its bluer pinks are echoed in the rose's pink petals, and *Rosa* Falstaff = 'Ausverse' who comes up next is a redder red, to give just a little bit of a flow of colour and encourage the eye to move through the planting. The reds are also a pause, a positive kind of a negative, darker dots amongst the light; more light is achieved by *Stipa gigantea* (giant oat grass), whose flowers create the perfect transparency as well as catching the sunlight and surrounding this planting with a halo of bright gold and muted beige.

I don't ever want to forget about the importance of light—hence the white bracts of *Cornus kousa* in the background and then the vital variegation of the grey and creamy white leaves of *Pittosporum tenuifolium* 'Silver Queen'. Variegated plants are so useful, yet they seem to fall into the same plant-snobbery category as dahlias used to occupy. Just look at dahlias now.

In schemes that experiment with colour, played with, almost thrown around, the key is the blurring colours in between. Think light and airy, think grasses and relaxed foliage. I don't want a statement, a "brave" border. I want to create a place which gives interest in its smallest parts.

Design: Jo Thompson

	NAME	TYPE	HEIGHT	SPREAD	SEASON	LIGHT	MOISTURE	HARDINESS	SOIL PH
A	*Rosa* Port Sunlight = 'Auslofty'	shrub	1-1.5 metres, 4-5 feet	0.5-1 metre, 3-4 feet	summer / autumn	full sun	moist but well-drained / well-drained	very hardy, USDA 5-9	acid / alkaline / neutral
B	*Rosa* 'Ispahan'	shrub	1-1.5 metres, 5 feet	1-1.5 metres, 4 feet	summer	full sun	moist but well-drained / well-drained	very hardy, USDA 4-11	acid / alkaline / neutral
C	*Rosa* Munstead Wood = 'Ausbernard'	shrub	1.5-2.5 metres, 4-6 feet	1.5-2.5 metres, 4-6 feet	summer / autumn	full sun / partial shade	moist but well-drained / well-drained	very hardy, USDA 5-9	acid / alkaline / neutral
D	*Pittosporum tenuifolium* 'Silver Queen'	perennial	4-8 metres, 15-25 feet	1.5-2.5 metres, 10-15 feet	spring / summer	full sun / partial shade	moist but well-drained / well-drained	half hardy, USDA 9-10	acid / alkaline / neutral
E	*Stipa gigantea*	grass	1.5-2.5 metres, to 8 feet	0.5-1 metre, to 4 feet	summer / autumn	full sun	moist but well-drained / well-drained	half hardy, USDA 7-10	acid / alkaline / neutral

- 56 -

Tutti Frutti

When working with a blank canvas, the layout, of course, plays a huge part, but to me, it's the colours that are vital in communicating a story, an atmosphere, an idea of whose garden it is and what the garden is for. Colour gave Matisse "an energy that [seemed] to stem from witchcraft" and, while not wanting to go over to the Dark Side when putting a palette together, I'm always completely absorbed by the energy of the emerging and receding tones and shades of each colour.

Nowhere was this use of colour so important to me as in this garden. I wanted to convey the idea that providing shelter, food, and water for wildlife is more important than trying to create a wildlife garden in one particular style. The garden featured here is a true explosion of colour, thought through clearly but with a let-it-all-hang-out vibe. A tutti-frutti mix of pinks, lemons, burgundy, coral, and magenta all combine to give a feeling of joyous exuberance, of a garden loved for plants' sake.

The pink shades are its starting point: crushed strawberry *Digitalis* ×*mertonensis* proudly backs up the coral *Rosa* 'Fragrant Delight', which anchors the whole scheme. A standout colour, coral lends weight and focus to this combination of colours. Notice that it isn't replicated anywhere else in this portion of the garden. Instead of

Design: Jo Thompson for BBC Springwatch/RHS Hampton Court 2019

doing the whole repeat-in-swathes thing, I'll get a feel for the tones in the main plant and weave out from there, so the fiery red-orange tones of *Achillea* 'Walther Funcke' link to the lemon dahlia, which in turn gives a nod to the golden foliage of an oregano.

At this point, it's time to calm everything down, so the terracottas of the achillea reappear along the border—not so much that they become the dominant feature but just enough to allow the deep crimson-burgundies of *Knautia macedonica* and *Allium amethystinum* 'Red Mohican', together with the adjoining browns of the centres of the echinacea, to link together, giving the eye something to hang on to. The burgundy has an element of pink to it—and this gives the opportunity to use the chunky but fabulous *Oenothera lindheimeri* Belleza Series, with its fuchsia tones looking good against the neighbouring clover lawn backdrop. Green is important in allowing this colour combination to work: blue-green tones are avoided, but blue-pink is in abundance in the *Nepeta grandiflora* 'Dawn to Dusk' which sits next to the digitalis, forming a classic pastel combination. This nepeta is useful as a link, a connector which can be used throughout, as its smoky-pink colour isn't strident and gives the eye a chance to rest.

Pink and yellow here adds a vintage feel to the scheme, the Post-it butter yellow of *Scabiosa atropurpurea* 'Fata Morgana', just glimpsed in the background, harmonising the pinks and lilac of sweet peas.

This is a book about the gardener's palette, not about art, but we take inspiration as it comes. As this garden took shape, I couldn't help but think of Chagall's eclectic, radiant palettes. Wild exuberance, luminous calm. Joy and serenity. If I can create that in a garden, I'm happy—and the way I do it is with colour.

	NAME	TYPE	HEIGHT	SPREAD	SEASON	LIGHT	MOISTURE	HARDINESS	SOIL PH
A	*Phlox drummondii* 'Crème Brûlée'	annual	0.1-0.5 metre, 0.5-1 foot	0.1-0.5 metre, 0.5-1 foot	summer	full sun	moist but well-drained / well-drained	half hardy, USDA 2-11	acid / alkaline / neutral
B	*Oenothera lindheimeri* Belleza Series	perennial	0.5-1 metre, 2.5-3 feet	0.1-0.5 metre, 2.5-3 feet	summer / autumn	full sun / partial shade	moist but well-drained / well-drained	half hardy, USDA 6-9	acid / alkaline / neutral
C	*Achillea* 'Walther Funcke'	perennial	0.1-0.5 metre, 1-2 feet	0.1-0.5 metre, 1-2 feet	summer / autumn	full sun	moist but well-drained / well-drained	very hardy, USDA 3-8	acid / alkaline / neutral
D	*Eryngium* 'Pen Blue'	perennial	0.5-1 metre, 2-2.5 feet	0.1-0.5 metre, 1.5-2 feet	summer	full sun	well-drained	very hardy, USDA 4-9	acid / alkaline / neutral
E	*Knautia macedonica*	perennial	0.5-1 metre, 1.5-2 feet	0.1-0.5 metre, 1.5-2 feet	summer	full sun	well-drained	very hardy, USDA 5-9	alkaline / neutral

- 57 -

Sunrise

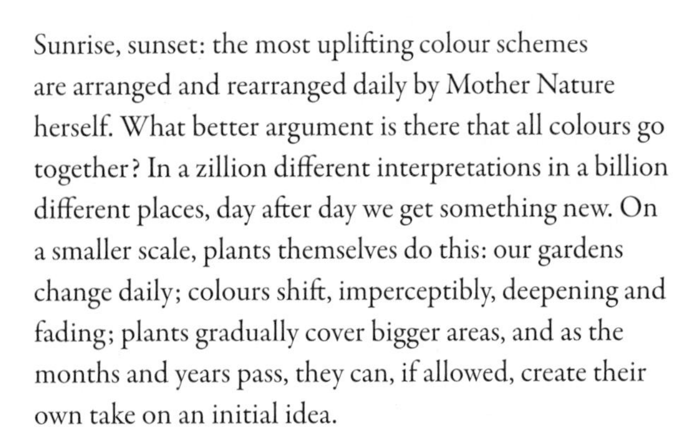

Sunrise, sunset: the most uplifting colour schemes are arranged and rearranged daily by Mother Nature herself. What better argument is there that all colours go together? In a zillion different interpretations in a billion different places, day after day we get something new. On a smaller scale, plants themselves do this: our gardens change daily; colours shift, imperceptibly, deepening and fading; plants gradually cover bigger areas, and as the months and years pass, they can, if allowed, create their own take on an initial idea.

Technical alert: at sunrise and sunset, when it takes longer for light to travel through the air, blue light and green light seem to disappear as they are scattered out of view. Essentially, we lose greens and gain a lot of red and orange; this creates astounding colour schemes, which humans have being trying to capture on paper and in pictures, words, and music, forever. William Ashcroft, who spent considerable time in the 1880s sketching pastels of sunsets, lamented that he could "only secure in a kind of chromatic shorthand the heart of the effect."

We can attempt to do the same in the garden, putting together in different quantities oranges and reds, a little pink, and—inspired by a cooler-coloured sunrise—a scattering of violets and indigos. I think a blend of hardy

Design: Jo Thompson for Perennial

geraniums would be a wonderful groundcover base in this palette: besides *Geranium* 'Brookside', perhaps pale *G.* 'Blue Cloud' skipping through blue-blue *G.* ×*johnsonii* 'Johnson's Blue' and into the violet of *G.* Rozanne = 'Gerwat'.

Geum 'Totally Tangerine' and *G.* 'Prinses Juliana' harness the shades of orange in a sunrise, the muted tangerines becoming more saturated and eye-catching, demonstrating that orange and its associated tones needn't be ringfenced within the hot or warm section of the colour wheel. Orange works equally well with cool colours, creating a mellow atmosphere rather than full-on heat.

Wanting this garden to be a whole picture, not wanting any one colour to stand out, and above all knowing there was no way I could exclude the greens, I decided instead to include light. Light is here in the shape of creamy white heads *Anthriscus sylvestris* 'Ravenswing' and peachy pink *Digitalis purpurea* 'Sutton's Apricot'. This colour scheme would look fabulous interrupted by tulips: imagine *Tulipa* 'Candy Prince' and *T.* 'Christmas Orange' followed by *T.* 'Valentine' and then *T.* 'Dordogne', all with a groundcover of the forget-me-not blue of myosotis—a sunrise of almost edible colours which would certainly get you up in the morning.

	NAME	TYPE	HEIGHT	SPREAD	SEASON	LIGHT	MOISTURE	HARDINESS	SOIL PH
A	*Anthriscus sylvestris* 'Ravenswing'	perennial	1-1.5 metres, 3 feet	0.1-0.5 metre, 2 feet	spring / summer	full sun / partial shade	moist but well-drained / well-drained	very hardy, USDA 7-10	acid / alkaline / neutral
B	*Geranium* 'Brookside'	perennial	0.1-0.5 metre, 1.5-2 feet	0.1-0.5 metre, 2-3 feet	summer	full sun / partial shade	well-drained / moist but well-drained	very hardy, USDA 5-8	acid / alkaline / neutral
C	*Geum* 'Totally Tangerine'	perennial	0.5-1 metre, 1-2.5 feet	0.1-0.5 metre, 0.75-1.5 feet	spring / summer / autumn	full sun	moist but well-drained / well-drained	very hardy, USDA 5-7	acid / alkaline / neutral
D	*Geum* 'Prinses Juliana'	perennial	0.1-0.5 metre, 1.5-2 feet	0.1-0.5 metre, 1.5-2 feet	summer	full sun	moist but well-drained / well-drained	very hardy, USDA 5-7	acid / alkaline / neutral
E	*Digitalis purpurea* 'Sutton's Apricot'	biennial	1-1.5 metres, 3-4 feet	0.1-0.5 metre, 1-1.5 feet	summer	full sun / partial shade / full shade	moist but well-drained / well-drained	very hardy, USDA 4-8	acid / alkaline / neutral

– 58 –

Sunset

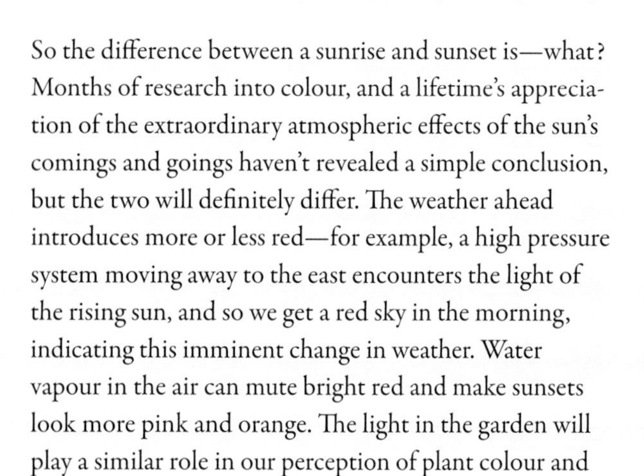

So the difference between a sunrise and sunset is—what? Months of research into colour, and a lifetime's appreciation of the extraordinary atmospheric effects of the sun's comings and goings haven't revealed a simple conclusion, but the two will definitely differ. The weather ahead introduces more or less red—for example, a high pressure system moving away to the east encounters the light of the rising sun, and so we get a red sky in the morning, indicating this imminent change in weather. Water vapour in the air can mute bright red and make sunsets look more pink and orange. The light in the garden will play a similar role in our perception of plant colour and plant effects.

Incorporating shades between blue and red settles a planting, introducing a sense of serenity and glamour. Why this is I'm not entirely sure, as red itself can appear to be an alert, but somehow red morphing nicely into blue results in pleasing wine shades of burgundy and claret. Combined with orange, these deep reds create a rich contrast, stronger or weaker depending on the amount of the colour used.

Here, *Cirsium rivulare* 'Atropupureum' scatters deep red in this sunset palette. The blue has all but gone, with only *Allium hollandicum* 'Purple Sensation' here and there

Design: Jo Thompson for Perennial

A

B

C

	NAME	TYPE	HEIGHT	SPREAD	SEASON	LIGHT	MOISTURE	HARDINESS	SOIL PH
A	*Geum* 'Totally Tangerine'	perennial	0.5-1 metre, 1-2.5 feet	0.1-0.5 metre, 0.75-1.5 feet	spring / summer / autumn	full sun	moist but well-drained / well-drained	very hardy, USDA 5-7	acid / alkaline / neutral
B	*Cirsium rivulare* 'Atropurpureum'	perennial	1-1.5 metres, 4 feet	0.1-0.5 metre, 1.5-2 feet	summer	full sun	moist but well-drained	very hardy, USDA 4-8	acid / alkaline / neutral
C	*Allium hollandicum* 'Purple Sensation'	bulb	0.5-1 metre, 2-2.5 feet	0.1-0.5 metre, 0.5-0.75 foot	summer	full sun	well-drained / moist but well-drained	very hardy, USDA 4-9	acid / alkaline / neutral

as a nod to what has happened earlier in the day. This allium will later hand its blue baton to *Salvia nemorosa* 'Caradonna' in the foreground, but for the moment this salvia is fabulous for its silhouette of its dark stems and spikes of buds.

Geum 'Totally Tangerine' offers the only orange; the brighter *G.* 'Prinses Juliana' is too strident for this settling-down of colours. Ornamental cow parsley comes into its own here: the native species would also work, but the purple-black stems of its selection, *Anthriscus sylvestris* 'Ravenswing', offer shadows and skeletons, ghosts of the day, suggesting just a bit of structure and teaming up with the salvia's stems. The deep purple in these stems is admirable, echoing tints in the cirsium's flowers. What stem belongs with which flower? Who can tell?

– 59 –

Sherbets

Sherbet colours of pinks, lemons, and corals mark this garden out as something different. So many times we are told that one colour doesn't go with another—that black and navy blue should never be worn together, for example—and there seems to be the same sort of thinking with pinks and reds, yellows and pinks. I've never been able to sign up to this approach: I reckon that as long as you pinpoint the right shade, anything can go with anything.

In this scheme, I wanted to achieve something other than classic yet still pretty, without resorting to obvious blues or lilacs. The result evokes a scene glimpsed from an Italian rooftop, where in the buildings below you can see every shade from terracotta through coral and pink and lemon. Knowing that these colours can work together without the clash that is often written about, I took the beautiful apricot-yellow (capucine buff almost) *Rosa* 'Buff Beauty' and the clearest pink *R.* Bonica = 'Meidomonac', placed them together, and built up from there—definitely more colorito than disegno (more casually painted than strictly drawn, in other words). I built up the layers in my head, shifting from palest lemon through to dusky plum.

The orange tones of *Paeonia* 'Coral Sunset' are the stand-out large flower, and it was important that all the tones in its petals were picked up by the surrounding scheme. The pale yellow-cream of *Eschscholzia californica* 'Ivory Castle' reappears in the smaller petals of *Phlox drummondii* 'Crème Brûlée'. The pretty damask of *Verbascum* 'Helen Johnson' has in it a pink that is midway between the roses and *Iris* 'Pink Charm'. The flat-topped heads of the wild carrot *Daucus carota* 'Dara' move from palest pink to deep wine, a happy contrast in form while all the time in harmony with the shades of pink throughout. *Geranium* ×*oxonianum* 'Lace Time' with its petals of mother-of-pearl, gently twinkles pink at the foot of this exuberant planting, which was inspired—looking back on it—by unicorns, fairies, and sweetshop shelves full of multi-coloured jars of Sherbet Lemons and chewy Fruit Salads.

	NAME	TYPE	HEIGHT	SPREAD	SEASON	LIGHT	MOISTURE	HARDINESS	SOIL PH
A	*Geranium ×oxonianum* 'Lace Time'	perennial	0.1-0.5 metre, 1-1.5 feet	0.5-1 metre, 1.5-2.5 feet	spring / summer / autumn	full sun / partial shade	moist but well-drained / well-drained	very hardy, USDA 4-8	acid / alkaline / neutral
B	*Phlox drummondii* 'Crème Brûlée'	annual	0.1-0.5 metre, 0.5-1 foot	0.1-0.5 metre, 0.5-1 foot	summer	full sun	moist but well-drained / well-drained	half hardy, USDA 2-11	acid / alkaline / neutral
C	*Iris* 'Pink Charm'	perennial	1 metre, 3 feet	0.5-1 metre, 2 feet	summer	full sun	well-drained	very hardy, USDA 4-9	acid / neutral
D	*Verbascum* 'Helen Johnson'	perennial	0.5-1 metre, 3-4 feet	0.1-0.5 metre, 1.5-2 feet	summer	full sun	well-drained	very hardy, USDA 5-8	alkaline / neutral
E	*Rosa* 'Buff Beauty'	shrub	1-1.5 metres, to 6 feet	1-1.5 metres, to 5 feet	summer / autumn	full sun	moist but well-drained / well-drained	very hardy, USDA 5-10	acid / alkaline / neutral
F	*Daucus carota* 'Dara'	biennial	0.5-1 metre, 3 feet	0.1-0.5 metre, 3 feet	summer	full sun	moist but well-drained / well-drained	very hardy, USDA 2-11	acid / alkaline / neutral

Opposite | Design: Jo Thompson

- 60 -

Amber Green

Gardens are about personality—to each his own. Keeping this in mind informs my choice of colour scheme, especially when I work on a show garden that is destined to go on to have a real life. From that very first blank-paper moment, before I can add the very first "something," I must conjure up the eventual clients: the people who will use this garden and the colours they might prefer to have.

This garden is now enjoying its real life as a horticultural therapy garden at the charity Thrive's headquarters. I was tasked to create a garden that could be used by Thrive's clients and staff alike, a place which would be accessible to all. I began with a flight of fancy, summoning up one specific person for whom I would be designing the garden. This person soon arrived in my mind: an older gentleman, finding it a little harder to get around but who didn't want to compromise his own style choices—perhaps an ageing designer, who knows?! As soon as he'd arrived, I was able to pinpoint the atmosphere, and following on from that, the exact colour scheme.

To me, masculine doesn't necessarily mean shades of grey or big blocks of planting. I felt strongly that I needed to explore earthy tones of coppers, browns, and orange, experimenting with how they could be used as highlights of bright colour on a backdrop of green.

Two majestic specimens of *Prunus serrula* (Tibetan cherry) are the anchors of this assembly of colour, the gleaming mahogany bark resplendent against a light background and creating a focal point year-round. Their blossom is fairly muted—tiny white flowers appearing for just a moment—but when you look at the bark, you remember that you don't plant this prunus for its blooms.

The modern shrub *Rosa* Hot Chocolate = 'Wekpaltlez', orange to terracotta in some lights, fading to coral/apricot in others, is paired with the warm brown *R.* Edith Holden = 'Chewlegacy', which in turn is picked up by the amber-copper *Iris* 'Copper Classic'. Ambers, oranges, and browns work so well with lime green; the bronze featheriness of *Foeniculum vulgare* 'Purpureum' is an excellent foil for the extraordinary lime green of *Mathiasella bupleuroides* 'Green Dream', its otherworldly heads complementing the oranges perfectly.

Lime green, orange, and blue are what we take from this scheme. *Iris* 'Titan's Glory' and *Aquilegia vulgaris* var. *stellata* 'Blue Barlow' are electric blue pinpoints of brightness and colour, connecting to the blue-purple of *Geranium phaeum* 'Lily Lovell' and to the ever-so-slightly blue-grey walls.

The variegated leaves of *Calamagrostis* ×*acutiflora* 'Overdam', white and green with a flush of pink, are another link to the pale rendered walls, as are the clouds of white flowers of the ornamental cow parsley *Anthriscus sylvestris* 'Ravenswing'.

Opposite | Design: Jo Thompson for RHS Chelsea 2010

A

B

C

D

	NAME	TYPE	HEIGHT	SPREAD	SEASON	LIGHT	MOISTURE	HARDINESS	SOIL PH
A	*Geranium phaeum* 'Lily Lovell'	perennial	0.5-1 metre, 1.5-2.5 feet	0.1-0.5 metre, 1-1.5 feet	spring / summer	full sun / partial shade / full shade	moist but well-drained / well-drained	very hardy, USDA 5-7	acid / alkaline / neutral
B	*Aquilegia vulgaris* var. *stellata* 'Blue Barlow'	perennial	0.5-1 metre, 1.5-3 feet	0.1-0.5 metre, 1-2 feet	spring / summer	full sun / partial shade	moist but well-drained / well-drained	very hardy, USDA 3-8	acid / alkaline / neutral
C	*Rosa* Edith Holden = 'Chewlegacy'	shrub	1-3 metres, to 9 feet	1 metre, 3 feet	spring / summer / autumn	full sun	moist but well-drained	half hardy, USDA 5-9	acid / alkaline / neutral
D	*Rosa* Hot Chocolate = 'Wekpaltlez'	shrub	0.5-1 metre, 3-4 feet	0.5-1 metre, 2-3 feet	summer / autumn	full sun	moist but well-drained / well-drained	very hardy, USDA 5-9	acid / alkaline / neutral

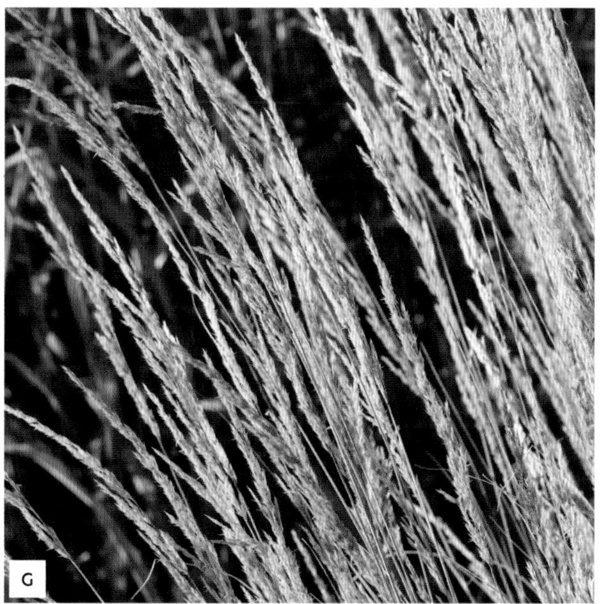

	NAME	TYPE	HEIGHT	SPREAD	SEASON	LIGHT	MOISTURE	HARDINESS	SOIL PH
E	*Iris* 'Titan's Glory'	perennial	0.5-1 metre, 3 feet	0.1-0.5 metre, 2 feet	summer	full sun	well-drained	very hardy, USDA 4-9	acid / neutral
F	*Anthriscus sylvestris* 'Ravenswing'	perennial	1-1.5 metres, 3 feet	0.1-0.5 metre, 2 feet	spring / summer	full sun / partial shade	moist but well-drained / well-drained	very hardy, USDA 7-10	acid / alkaline / neutral
G	*Calamagrostis ×acutiflora* 'Overdam'	grass	0.5-1 metre, 2.5-3 feet	0.1-0.5 metre, 1.5-2 feet	spring / summer / autumn	full sun / partial shade	moist but well-drained / well-drained	very hardy, USDA 4-8	acid / alkaline / neutral
H	*Prunus serrula*	tree	8-12 metres, 20-30 feet	> 8 metres, 20-30 feet	spring / autumn	full sun	moist but well-drained / well-drained	very hardy, USDA 5-6	acid / alkaline / neutral

- 61 -

Wild Pastels

In this garden, planted with wildlife in mind, the intention was to create a cohesive look: it may be loose, relaxed, and generally laid-back, but its wildness is controlled by gentle intervention.

Wildflower meadows are wonderful sights: they touch our souls and remind us that Nature is jolly good at putting things together. This wildflower scheme is at its heart harmonious: whites, lemons, creams, and pastels, with the odd counterpoint here and there.

Right | Design: Jo Thompson for BBC Springwatch/ RHS Hampton Court 2019
Below | Paul Cézanne, *Houses in Provence: The Riaux Valley Near L'Estaque*, c. 1883

The white flowers of *Leucanthemum vulgare* and our native *Achillea millefolium* make our neutral backdrop; the achillea arrives with an added bonus in that it sometimes comes through as pink. The possibility of this occasional pink, teamed with the ox-eye daisy's yellow centres, creates the rationale behind the ensuing colour scheme. Taking care to select plants that look as if they could probably be in a meadow, plants with forms not out of place in a wild environment, I looked for flowers which would celebrate this ode to pale pastels. *Nepeta grandiflora* 'Dawn to Dusk' in palest purple—so pale that it looks pink in some lights—echoes the few *Achillea millefolium* 'Wonderful Wampee' that have appeared in the same tone. Going for a yellow to accompany the centres of the daisies was just a step too far in matching for me, and besides, yellow is already amply provided for in the form of *Galium verum*. So, making the most of the fabulous apricot-peach shades that are increasingly available, I chose the willowy annual *Scabiosa atropurpurea* 'Fata Morgana' for the pinkish orange tones of its pinhead flowers. These oranges sometimes appear as lemon or butter yellow, leaving us with a slightly unpredictable mix of sherbet pastels. Less intense than primary yellow, butter yellow is a really useful neutral: when placed next to most other colours, it recedes. It's a creamy, soft yellow which doesn't offend or excite, instead imbuing a sense of sunny hope.

Look closely and you find another annual stitching this background together: the peaches and creams of *Phlox drummondii* 'Crème Brûlée'. On closer inspection, you'll see that every flower is veined slightly differently: some have delicate threads of violet, others have starry blotches of dark purple. This irregularity of colour may not be for some, but in this loose scheme, the variation is key in creating the sense of wildness.

A counterpoint is needed to prevent this sweep of pale from becoming bland: both dusky pink *Digitalis ×mertonensis* and magenta *Knautia macedonica* have purple tones that catch our eye. Pink ochres against green. Floating on and along this purple theme, the branching tapers of *Verbena hastata* add a strong purple dot here and there.

The wildflowers throw up another colour cue: *Dianthus carthusianorum*, making the knautia look so at home, is picked up by *Allium amethystinum* 'Red Mohican', whose deep red heads slide nicely into the pink-purple of *Buddleja* 'Pink Delight'.

The brown dying uprights of common teasel are almost dark purple here; following on from these, one can embrace these deep purple themes by using other dark statuesque uprights such as *Angelica sylvestris* 'Vicar's Mead', or *A. gigas* in a shadier spot. The bees continue to be happy; the garden continues to feel wild.

	NAME	TYPE	HEIGHT	SPREAD	SEASON	LIGHT	MOISTURE	HARDINESS	SOIL PH
A	*Dianthus carthusianorum*	perennial	0.1-0.5 metre, 2-2.5 feet	0.1-0.5 metre, to 1 foot	summer	full sun	well-drained	very hardy, USDA 5-9	alkaline / neutral
B	*Knautia macedonica*	perennial	0.5-1 metre, 1.5-2 feet	0.1-0.5 metre, 1.5-2 feet	summer	full sun	well-drained	very hardy, USDA 5-9	alkaline / neutral
C	*Achillea millefolium* 'Wonderful Wampee'	perennial	0.1-0.5 metre, 1.5-2 feet	0.1-0.5 metre, 1.5-2 feet	summer	full sun	moist but well-drained / well-drained	very hardy, USDA 4-8	acid / alkaline / neutral
D	*Phlox drummondii* 'Crème Brûlée'	annual	0.1-0.5 metre, 0.5-1 foot	0.1-0.5 metre, 0.5-1 foot	summer	full sun	moist but well-drained / well-drained	half-hardy, USDA 2-11	acid / alkaline / neutral
E	*Leucanthemum vulgare*	perennial	0.5-1 metre, 1-3 feet	0.1-0.5 metre, 1-2 feet	summer	full sun / partial shade	moist but well-drained	very hardy, USDA 3-8	acid / alkaline / neutral
F	*Dipsacus fullonum*	biennial	1.5-2.5 metres, 4-6 feet	0.5-1 metre, 1-2.5 feet	summer / autumn	full sun / partial shade	moist but well-drained / well-drained / poorly drained	very hardy, USDA 3-8	acid / alkaline / neutral

- 62 -

Contrast and Blend

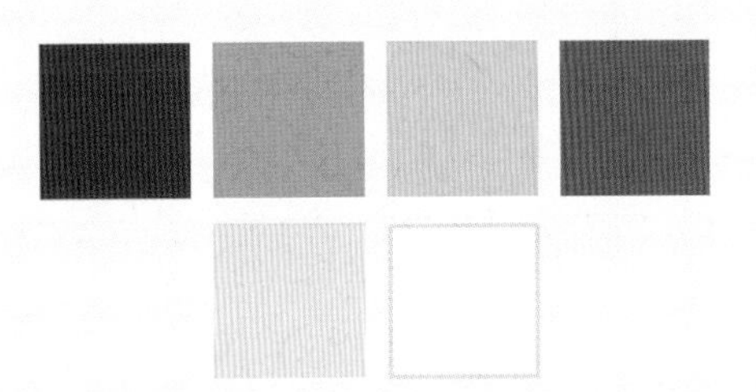

Some plants immediately bring incandescence to a scheme; *Helenium* 'Moerheim Beauty', muted brownish red on close inspection, when viewed from a distance brings a dash of heat and light to this planting by Piet Oudolf at the Hauser & Wirth gallery in Somerset. Oudolf has no concerns about orange and pink together—the neighbouring *Salvia* ×*sylvestris* 'Dear Anja' and *S. verticillata* 'Purple Rain' bring both contrast and almost-contrast, effortlessly chic against the droopy petals of *Echinacea pallida* drifting through golden cream *Stipa tenuissima*. This is the majesty of this grouping of colours: most hues here are understated, mid- to pastel-pale, but the helenium's reddish orange-brown sweeps along, deservedly capturing our attention and earning our appreciation.

The pinky amethyst and blue-purples of the salvias and *Lythrum salicaria* 'Blush' don't stand out too much—they are the enablers here, letting the helenium take the praise. Toning down is achieved by the gradually fading pinks of the spires of *Veronicastrum virginicum* 'Erica' and the even paler *Lysimachia ephemerum*, creating that ever-useful veil, which blurs the join. Smatterings of

Design: Piet Oudolf for Hauser & Wirth, Somerset

	NAME	TYPE	HEIGHT	SPREAD	SEASON	LIGHT	MOISTURE	HARDINESS	SOIL PH
A	*Helenium* 'Moerheim Beauty'	perennial	0.5-1 metre, 2-3 feet	0.1-0.5 metre, 1-1.5 feet	summer	full sun	moist but well-drained	very hardy, USDA 3-8	acid / alkaline / neutral
B	*Echinacea pallida*	perennial	1-1.5 metres, 2-3 feet	0.1-0.5 metre, 1-1.5 feet	summer	full sun	well-drained	very hardy, USDA 3-10	acid / alkaline / neutral

light are provided in the distance by the stipa and to the sides by blocks of *Panicum virgatum* 'Cloud Nine'; these grasses would have created too much light had they been positioned more centrally.

Oudolf uses huge numbers of the same plant in great waves across seemingly endless landscapes, but it's just as effective to use these groupings on a smaller scale. To achieve this sense of layers, think of a brush moving in horizontal sweeps across a canvas—a sweep of three salvias in the foreground, move further back and make a shorter sweep of two plants back across, and then, further back still, a dash of just one. Bring in a couple of heleniums and some stipa to fill the gaps between these three sweeps, and you have your base. Drop in the vertical highlights of echinacea wherever you'd like a smudgy blur of textures and colour.

This is most definitely a scheme for the summer. A similar effect could be achieved earlier on by dotting orange and red geums, but the effect here is so enticing that I'd recommend patience. Year-round colour isn't all it's cracked up to be, and sometimes emergent green in early summer is all that's needed to suggest that what's to come is something rather special. You want to reach out and touch this meadow, so incredibly inviting, its strong sweeps of colour so obviously man-made yet at the same time gentle and soft. I'd wander through this anytime.

	NAME	TYPE	HEIGHT	SPREAD	SEASON	LIGHT	MOISTURE	HARDINESS	SOIL PH
C	*Lythrum salicaria* 'Blush'	perennial	0.5-1 metre, 2-4 feet	0.1-0.5 metre, 2-4 feet	summer	full sun	moist but well-drained / poorly drained	very hardy, USDA 4-9	acid / alkaline / neutral
D	*Salvia verticillata* 'Purple Rain'	perennial	0.5-1 metre, 1-2 feet	0.1-0.5 metre, 1.5-2.5 feet	summer	full sun	well-drained	very hardy, USDA 5-8	acid / alkaline / neutral
E	*Veronicastrum virginicum* 'Erica'	perennial	1-1.5 metres, 3-4 feet	0.1-0.5 metre, 1.5 feet	summer	full sun / partial shade	moist but well-drained / well-drained	very hardy, USDA 4-8	acid / alkaline / neutral
F	*Panicum virgatum* 'Cloud Nine'	grass	1-1.5 metres, 5-7 feet	0.5-1 metre, 2-3 feet	summer / autumn	full sun	well-drained	very hardy, USDA 5-9	acid / alkaline / neutral

– 63 –

Pinks, Purples, and Pale Lemon

Sometimes an unexpected partnering totally works: peanut butter and a sharp green apple, or a juicy pear and a smash of gorgonzola.

Set round a seventeenth-century farmhouse, Town Place Garden in East Sussex has herbaceous borders, a herb garden, topiary inspired by the sculptures of Henry Moore, an eight-hundred-year-old oak, and over six hundred roses. The roses are wonderful—but what particularly grabs my attention, the star of the show, is hanging back in the wings, in the summer-loving Long Borders. Let's demand this star step forward.

This lead player is *Anthemis tinctoria* 'E.C. Buxton'; teamed with *Lythrum salicaria*, a surprise best friend, it dominates this palette and makes it a success. You have to really hunt for the anthemis's pale lemon daisy-like flowers; once you've found them, you understand how they are the element that makes this palette of pinks and purples work. Their light yellow is a quietly brave highlight to the loosestrife's magenta flower spires.

Here you may have thrown your hands over your eyes and weakly whispered "weed"; if so please take another peek, and let the lythrum seduce you: look at that purple which is not purple. The pinks and reds in the flowers blur perfectly into the not-so-low *Nepeta racemosa* 'Walker's Low' and the almost spent flower stems of *Salvia nemorosa* 'Ostfriesland' and *S.* ×*superba*, their hints of brown and orange giving the eye a bit of a rest and a chance to really enjoy the magenta.

The anthemis has another role. The whole border is backed by a tapestry hedge of ×*Cuprocyparis leylandii* 'Haggerston Grey' and golden *Thuja plicata* 'Zebrina'. The yellow in the green of these conifers is the perfect foil to the anthemis—we see how the whole grouping is tied together.

Nepeta grandiflora 'Dawn to Dusk' shows here how it can be so effective as a link between stone and plants, its little greyish pink-to-white flowers doing a grand job and toning perfectly with its neighbours; it's understated, subtle, cool, even a bit smoky, which I am convinced links it to the clouds of thalictrum behind. That may be a step too far in terms of linking, but it stands out to me, as does the neutral colour bridge provided by the sedum: did you spot that?

The Rose Garden lies just beyond, and the colours in this border are an overture to the senses of affection and elegance about to be triggered by the roses. It's important to remember this when considering colour in the garden, and how colour changes as we walk around. I for one am sometimes a bit surprised by "colour themes" in a garden if there hasn't been a bit of a lead-up, if a few hints haven't been dropped—basically, if they haven't been introduced to me by stealth. Here, the visual energy and purity of the magenta, which straddles purple and pink, is the perfect introduction to the roses which we can't yet see but which, thanks to this tapestry of faded romance, we kind of expect.

Design: Town Place Garden

	NAME	TYPE	HEIGHT	SPREAD	SEASON	LIGHT	MOISTURE	HARDINESS	SOIL PH
A	*Anthemis tinctoria* 'E.C. Buxton'	perennial	0.5-1 metre, 2 feet	0.5-1 metre, 1.5 feet	summer	full sun	well-drained	very hardy, USDA 3-8	acid / alkaline / neutral
B	*Nepeta grandiflora* 'Dawn to Dusk'	perennial	0.5-1 metre, 2.5 feet	0.5-1 metre, 2.5 feet	summer	full sun / partial shade / full shade	moist but well-drained / well-drained	very hardy, USDA 4-9	alkaline / neutral
C	*Lythrum salicaria*	perennial	0.5-1.2 metres, 2-4 feet	0.5-1.2 metres, 2-4 feet	summer / autumn	full sun	poorly drained	very hardy, USDA 4-9	acid / alkaline / neutral
D	*Salvia nemorosa* 'Ostfriesland'	perennial	0.3-0.5 metre, 1-1.5 feet	0.2-0.3 metre, 0.75-1 foot	summer / autumn	full sun	moist but well-drained	very hardy, USDA 4-8	acid / alkaline / neutral
E	*Salvia ×superba*	perennial	0.5-1 metre, 1-2.5 feet	0.1-0.5 metre, 1-1.5 feet	summer / autumn	full sun	moist but well-drained	very hardy, USDA 4-8	acid / alkaline / neutral
F	*Thuja plicata* 'Zebrina'	tree	> 12 metres, 30-50 feet	4-8 metres, 8-12 feet	evergreen	full sun	moist but well-drained	very hardy, USDA 5-7	acid / alkaline / neutral
G	*×Cuprocyparis leylandii* 'Haggerston Grey'	tree	12-15 metres, 60-70 feet	4.5-7.5 metres, 10-15 feet	evergreen	full sun / partial shade	well-drained	half hardy, USDA 6-10	acid / alkaline / neutral

- 64 -

Impressionist Violet 1

"I have finally discovered the true colour of the atmosphere," declared Manet. "It is violet." One person's violet is another's lavender, or yet another's lilac, but its luminosity is something that is agreed on by all, and the way that the colours play with the light in this prairie meadow in Niwot, Colorado, is beyond the description of beautiful.

This palette was brought together by Lauren Springer, and its thirty-three hundred constituents were then lovingly planted by its owners. The planting was designed to mimic the surrounding landscape, but what is truly extraordinary is how it blends not only into the land but into the atmosphere of the place. In complete harmony, different values of violet from purple-violet through amethyst into lilac-pinks place an Impressionist's palette on the land.

Symphyotrichum novi-belgii 'Purple Dome' has bold, full flowers that aren't that easy to site gracefully in a planting. But the dreamy partnering of this Michaelmas daisy with *Muhlenbergia reverchonii* 'Autumn Embers', which casts a pinkish haze, softens the impact of the purple and then neatly joins its own rose-brown shades with the pink flowers of *Hylotelephium spectabile* (Brilliant Group) 'Neon', its fleshy green leaves also deserving their place here. A good mid-green and pink-to-lilac together seem to both absorb and reflect light: it's a Monet painting of a planting, suggesting skyscapes and reflections of years gone by and yet feeling so current.

Who knows when we first started to appreciate violet as a new colour with which to depict the world? Did the colours of the Impressionists train us to appreciate nature differently, to use colours that we wouldn't otherwise have put together to create a notion of beauty? Was it the "white quivering sunlight" of France that first introduced us to Nature's "restless violet shadows"? Oscar Wilde thought so. In his essay "The Decay of Lying," he writes: "Where [Nature] used to give us Corots and Daubignys, she gives us now exquisite Monets and entrancing Pissarros. Indeed there are moments, rare, it is true, but still to be observed from time to time, when Nature becomes absolutely modern."

Claude Monet, *Branch of the Seine near Giverny (Mist)*, 1897

	NAME	TYPE	HEIGHT	SPREAD	SEASON	LIGHT	MOISTURE	HARDINESS	SOIL PH
A	*Symphyotrichum novi-belgii* 'Purple Dome'	perennial	0.5-1 metre, 1.5-2 feet	0.5-1 metre, 2-3 feet	autumn	full sun	moist but well-drained	very hardy, USDA 5-8	alkaline / neutral
B	*Hylotelephium spectabile* (Brilliant Group) 'Neon'	succulent perennial	0.5-1 metre, 1-2 feet	0.5-1 metre, 1-2 feet	summer / autumn	full sun	well-drained	very hardy, USDA 3-9	alkaline / neutral
C	*Muhlenbergia reverchonii* 'Autumn Embers'	grass	0.5-1 metre, 2-3 feet	0.1-0.5 metre, 1.5-2 feet	autumn / winter	full sun	well-drained	very hardy, USDA 5-9	acid / alkaline / neutral

Opposite | Design: Lauren Springer

- 65 -

Impressionist Violet 2

Creating a similar atmosphere in the same area using a different palette of plants, with one unifying grass, is masterly. Still in the Scripter garden, Lauren Springer continues her celebration of violet, with tiny little sparklers of *Schizachyrium scoparium* (little bluestem) fizzing alongside the pinker muhly grass. The bluestem's upright to arching sea blue-green leaves are a prompt for the introduction of a lavender, and so the petals of *Symphyotrichum laeve* (smooth aster) weave through, looking the content natives that they are.

The murkily acidic yellow-green of *Solidago ohioensis* is a surprise here, but it works. This goldenrod's compact form means that the yellow is a true neighbour to the pinkish red-brown of *Hylotelephium* 'Matrona' and the lavender-lilac aster, rather than hovering above as a taller solidago would.

The palette of violet, blue, off-yellow, and muted pink-red is the scheme's imprimatura, the first layer, which comes through to a lesser or greater extent depending on the colours used elsewhere. All combines to create a feeling of lightheartedness, of light itself.

The colours and light—how the colours make light as well as being light themselves—are reminiscent of those in Seurat's *Model, Back View*. Here Seurat achieves his trademark effect of blended colour by precisely placing each individual colour—in a painting that positively buzzes with light. It's easy to picture him enthusiastically declaring, "Let's go and get drunk on light again—it has the power to console."

The light skitters through this atmospheric planting too, through precise layers of tones and shades, placed to sit in the light and catch the spirit of the place.

Opposite | Design: Lauren Springer
Below | Georges Seurat, *Model, Back View*, 1887

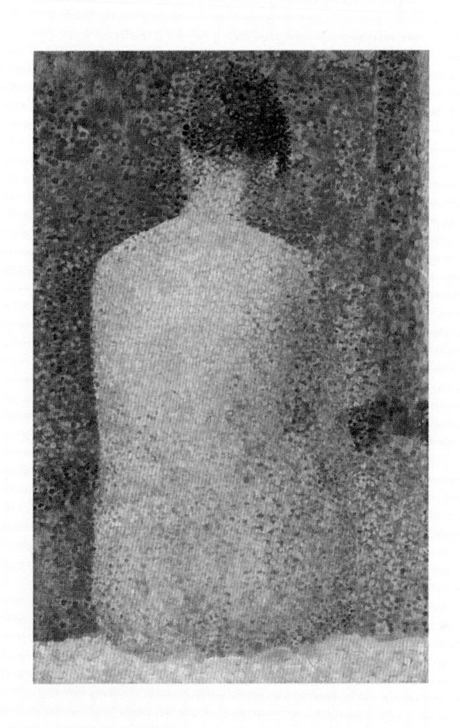

	NAME	TYPE	HEIGHT	SPREAD	SEASON	LIGHT	MOISTURE	HARDINESS	SOIL PH
A	*Symphyotrichum laeve*	perennial	1-1.5 metres, 2-4 feet	0.1-0.5 metre, 1-2 feet	summer	full sun / partial shade	moist but well-drained	very hardy, USDA 3-8	acid / alkaline / neutral
B	*Solidago ohioensis*	perennial	1-1.5 metres, 3-4 feet	0.5 metre, 1.5 feet	summer	full sun	moist but well-drained	very hardy, USDA 4-6	acid / alkaline / neutral
C	*Hylotelephium* 'Matrona'	succulent perennial	0.5-1 metre, 2-2.5 feet	0.1-0.5 metre, 1.5-2 feet	summer / autumn	full sun	well-drained	very hardy, USDA 3-9	alkaline / neutral
D	*Schizachyrium scoparium*	grass	0.5-1 metre, 2-4 feet	0.5-1 metre, 1.5-2 feet	summer	full sun	well-drained	very hardy, USDA 3-9	acid / alkaline / neutral

Aristotle *On Colours*

Those colours are simple which belong to the elements, fire, air, water, and earth. For air and water are naturally white in themselves, while fire and the sun are golden. The earth is also naturally white but seems coloured because it is dyed. This becomes clear when we consider ashes; for they become white when the moisture which caused their dyeing is burned out of them; but not completely so, for they are also dyed by smoke, which is black. In the same way sand becomes golden, because the fiery red and black tints the water. The colour black belongs to the elements of things while they are undergoing a transformation of their nature. But the other colours are evidently due to mixture, when they are blended with each other. For darkness follows when light fails.

Inspiration from RHS Garden Wisley

Curator Matthew Pottage on three smaller conifers in the Rock Garden:

1 Forest tree in miniature

With a splendid backdrop of freshly emerged maple foliage, not to mention flowers of cherries and rhododendrons, *Chamaecyparis obtusa* 'Nana Gracilis' is pruned to enhance its tree-like shape and gnarled trunk. This much-treasured veteran makes a wonderful sight here in Wisley's historic Rock Garden.

2 Pillar of green

Dense and upright, yew-like conifer *Cephalotaxus harringtonia* 'Fastigiata' forms a fine focal point amid the rounded shapes of its surroundings.

3 Spreading canopy

This mature *Picea abies* 'Nidiformis' is carefully pruned like a bonsai to create the shape of a tree of great age. It responds each spring with this spreading dome of glorious green.

– 66 –

Silhouettes

If I were to ask you to name the colour of the towering trees in the very background of the Cool Garden at RHS Rosemoor, you would probably say they are green. They are indeed green, but at this time of day, as the sun sets, the silhouettes become black, and the garden takes on a different character. Our brains see the memory before they see the colour, so an overall sense of green brings with it shadows but never gloom.

Silver-leaved plants grab the light and shine out from what would otherwise be a dark spot in the painter's hour; a camaieu of green and blue is brightened by the palest apricot alstroemeria and the caramel-tawny plumes of *Panicum virgatum* 'Northwind' and *Miscanthus sinensis* 'Morning Light'. Now, I know these colours to be apricot and fallow; I know the silvers of the santolina to be silver and grey: look at them, though, and they appear nearly white, partly because of the light but also because of the colours that surround them.

Leonardo da Vinci figured out the effect of complementary shadows at dawn and sunset, and in the 1760s, the painter Claude-Joseph Vernet, observing

Design: Jo Thompson for RHS Rosemoor

the vast range of greens in nature, noted that if you really wanted to see the colour of things, you must always make comparisons between them. By the early nineteenth century, twilight had come to be known as the painter's hour, as the silhouettes in the lowering sun meant that instead of attempting to capture Vernet's innumerable greens, painters could instead explore the massing of light and dark using colours other than green. They had understood that it was not green that their eyes were seeing. It was what their experience was telling them they were seeing.

Now look again.

	NAME	TYPE	HEIGHT	SPREAD	SEASON	LIGHT	MOISTURE	HARDINESS	SOIL PH
A	*Potentilla fruticosa* 'Primrose Beauty'	shrub	0.5-1 metre, 2-4 feet	0.5-1.5 metres, 3-5 feet	spring / summer	full sun / partial shade	moist but well-drained / well-drained	very hardy, USDA 3-7	acid / alkaline / neutral
B	*Geranium* 'Orion'	perennial	0.1-0.5 metre, 1.5-2 feet	0.5-1 metre, 2-3 feet	summer	full sun / partial shade	moist but well-drained / well-drained	very hardy, USDA 5-8	acid / alkaline / neutral
C	*Phlox paniculata* 'Mount Fuji'	perennial	0.5-1 metre, 3-4 feet	0.1-0.5 metre, 1.5-2 feet	summer	full sun / partial shade	moist but well-drained	very hardy, USDA 3-8	acid / alkaline / neutral
D	*Buddleja davidii* Nanho Blue = 'Mongo'	shrub	1.5-2.5 metres, 3-5 feet	1.5-2.5 metres, 3-5 feet	summer / autumn	full sun	well-drained	very hardy, USDA 5-9	acid / alkaline / neutral
E	*Nepeta racemosa* 'Walker's Low'	perennial	0.1-0.5 metre, 2-2.5 feet	0.1-0.5 metre, 2.5-3 feet	spring / summer	full sun / partial shade / full shade	well-drained	very hardy, USDA 4-8	acid / alkaline / neutral
F	*Panicum virgatum* 'Northwind'	grass	1-1.5 metres, 4-6 feet	0.5-1 metre, 2-2.5 feet	summer / autumn	full sun	well-drained	very hardy, USDA 5-9	acid / alkaline / neutral
G	*Miscanthus sinensis* 'Morning Light'	grass	1.5-2 metres, 4-6 feet	0.5-1 metre, 2.5-4 feet	autumn	full sun	moist but well-drained / well-drained	very hardy, USDA 5-9	acid / alkaline / neutral

- 67 -

Boiled Sweets

I'll attempt to avoid too much rapture, but *Tulipa* 'Dordogne' carries within its petals one of those colour combinations that make you want to dive into the tones, drink them all up, float back out, sit on the edge for a while, and then repeat.

That's probably enough for you, but I just love these boiled sweet oranges, pinks, roses, and reds, all merging in and out of each other, and the possibilities they offer in the flower border in April and May. There's a charm about them which enables them to be the perfect partner of light at both dawn and dusk. A bit of sky at the Taj Mahal sunset moment shown here holds all these shades; sumptuous taffeta moves into a gentle yellow that defies our preconceptions of yellow.

Back in the Cottage Garden at RHS Hyde Hall, *Tulipa* 'Kingsblood' is a perfect partner. In fact, any of the sunset colour range will work with *T.* 'Dordogne'; the key is that the colours chosen have a warmth about them, even a bit of an aura, dare I say? Perhaps, as Annie Besant and C.W. Leadbeater wrote in *Thought-Forms*, rosy pink *does* signify "affectionate sympathy" and clear yellow "intellectual pleasure." Or at least it did for them, and that is the point. (The planting team at Hyde Hall are probably wondering where on earth I'm going with this—) The fact is that any attempt to capture a thought and emotion elicited by a colour combination is subjective, in the same way that the colour we see is subjective.

Back to the harmonies, though. Pink, yellow, orange, and red, all sitting together, warmly harmonising (and very stealthily clashing) while not in any way forming the character of a "hot" planting. A sumptuous and successful range of colours—and yet, if forced to categorise them on the colour wheel, I would definitely be a little bit befuddled.

Opposite | Design: RHS Hyde Hall
Below | The Taj Mahal at sunset.

A

B

	NAME	TYPE	HEIGHT	SPREAD	SEASON	LIGHT	MOISTURE	HARDINESS	SOIL PH
A	*Tulipa* 'Dordogne'	bulb	0.5-1 metre, 2-2.5 feet	0.1 metre, 0.5 foot	spring	full sun	well-drained	very hardy, USDA 3-8	acid / alkaline / neutral
B	*Tulipa* 'Kingsblood'	bulb	0.5-1 metre, 2-2.5 feet	to 0.1 metre, 0.25 foot	spring	full sun	well-drained	very hardy, USDA 3-8	acid / alkaline / neutral

- 68 -

Peachy

People have different names for the same colour: no one can be completely sure whether this is because we each see colours differently, or whether it's because we have associated a name with a colour and that name has simply stuck. So whatever colour you call the facade in this photograph—whether it's peach, coral, orange, pink, terracotta—your chosen term is valid because it means something to you.

Colour certainly means a lot to the owners of this beachside garden in the Bahamas. Passionate about colour, they took advice from a colour consultant for the home's interior palette and then tasked the great Raymond Jungles to create the surrounding landscape. He selected resilient plant material to give texture, depth, colour, and sculptural qualities to the garden. Everything comes together to create a joyous celebration of colour; one enormous uplift of atmosphere greets you wherever you look.

I look at this and am reminded of Paul Klee's *Hammamet with Its Mosque*, whose glorious washes of colour evoke the same atmosphere of calm which flows out of Jungles' planting. The very best plantsmanship is on display here, with restraint shown by selecting only one plant, *Euphorbia milii*, to give that colour-wow. The showy bracts of this long-flowering crown of thorns, in shades of vermilion and aurora red, are perfect dots of colour against its leathery leaves. Oh to live in a tropical or sub-tropical spot, where you can have a plant like this flowering in your garden all year long . . .

We must not overlook, though, the other plants here, the bridesmaids to the bride that is euphorbia. Without their colour and form, the impact of the euphorbia wouldn't be half as successful. Structure comes from *Pseudophoenix sargentii* (buccaneer palm), its light green leaves in conversation with the bright green of the euphorbia, while the interesting trunks of *Cocos nucifera* (coconut palm) and *Bursera simaruba* (gumbo limbo) form brilliant silhouettes against the building.

Silvery green *Salvia rosmarinus* Prostrata Group (creeping rosemary) peeks out and over the edge of the planter, keeping the euphorbia just on the right side of statement-making, while *Muhlenbergia capillaris* captures the pinks, oranges, peaches, and corals in its extraordinary clouds of flowers as they catch the light from various angles.

This garden has been planted by someone who knows exactly what to do with light and colour. I can't stop looking at it—imagine living there.

Design: Raymond Jungles

	NAME	TYPE	HEIGHT	SPREAD	SEASON	LIGHT	MOISTURE	HARDINESS	SOIL PH
A	*Salvia rosmarinus* Prostrata Group	shrub	0.1-0.5 metre, 1 foot	1-1.5 metres, 3.5 feet	spring / summer / autumn	full sun	moist but well-drained / well-drained	half hardy, USDA 8-10	acid / alkaline / neutral
B	*Euphorbia milii*	shrub	1-2 metres, 3-6 feet	0.5-1 metre, 1.5-3 feet	summer	full sun	well-drained	tender, USDA 9-11	acid / alkaline / neutral
C	*Muhlenbergia capillaris*	grass	0.5-1 metre, 2-3 feet	0.5-1 metre, 2-3 feet	spring / summer / autumn	full sun	moist but well-drained / well-drained	very hardy, USDA 5-9	acid / alkaline / neutral
D	*Cocos nucifera*	tree	> 12 metres, 50-100 feet	> 8 metres, 20-40 feet	evergreen	full sun / partial shade	moist but well-drained	tender, USDA 10-12	acid / alkaline / neutral
E	*Pseudophoenix sargentii*	tree	4-8 metres, 10-20 feet	2.5-4 metres, 8-10 feet	evergreen	full sun	well-drained	tender, USDA 10-11	acid / alkaline / neutral
F	*Bursera simaruba*	tree	> 12 metres, 60 feet	> 8 metres, 60 feet	evergreen	full sun / partial shade	moist but well-drained	tender, USDA 10-12	acid / alkaline / neutral

- 69 -

Fiery

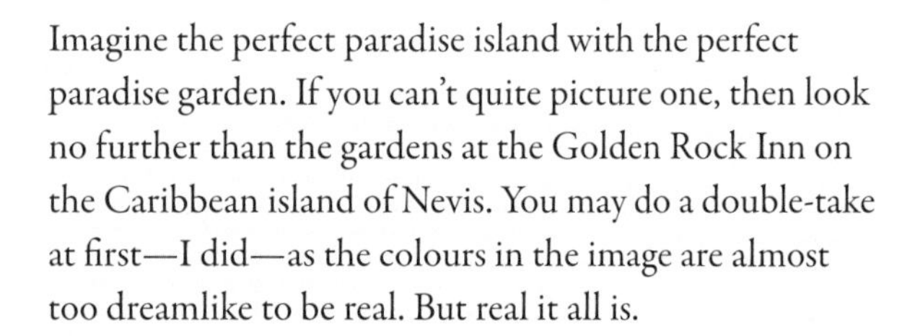

Imagine the perfect paradise island with the perfect paradise garden. If you can't quite picture one, then look no further than the gardens at the Golden Rock Inn on the Caribbean island of Nevis. You may do a double-take at first—I did—as the colours in the image are almost too dreamlike to be real. But real it all is.

Many factors contribute to the mystery-laden atmosphere at the foot of this volcano. From the forms and the layout, to the backdrop of Mount Nevis itself, which beats most other backdrops hands-down for drama. But it's the gentle and confident use of colour that creates the magic. Raymond Jungles devised his character-infused colour palette to harmonise with the plant selections of its original co-creators, New York artists Helen and Brice Marden.

You can't help but see how extraordinarily exquisite is the selection of the colours on Nevis. Yellows and browns are the foliage on the slopes in the background, a nod to the flanks of the volcano further in the distance. A masterclass in taking the location and running with it, the muted base colours become more vibrant in the foreground, but not before the palest yellow-beige *Spartina bakeri* (sand cordgrass) has trickled and flowed through, arriving at a casual grey-blue-green stop of *Aloe ferox* (bitter aloe).

Design: Raymond Jungles

Beaucarnea recurvata (ponytail palm), *Dioon spinulosum* (giant dioon), and a cereus cactus move the grey into green, while the brown silhouette of *Pachypodium lamerei* (Madagascar palm) brings our mind back to the earlier volcanic shades behind.

But what amazes are the bursts of fire that pop throughout, the fiery reds and oranges of *Aechmea blanchetiana* 'Orange' ablaze in the distance and, nearer to us, *A.* 'Dean', the green bases of the bromeliad's leaves allowing its upper reds and browns to perform a different kind of punctuation, blending into the *Aloe brevifolia* (short-leaved aloe) in the foreground, without demanding the attention craved by its peers in the distance.

By manipulating the site's hydrology, Jungles and his team have created different microclimates for specific plant types. This garden is a thousand feet above sea level and very conveniently gets a generous amount of rain for at least half the year from condensation at the peak of the ancient volcano, which is seemingly set in a cloud of golden foliage.

	NAME	TYPE	HEIGHT	SPREAD	SEASON	LIGHT	MOISTURE	HARDINESS	SOIL PH
A	*Aechmea* 'Dean'	bromeliad	1 metre, 3 feet	1-2.5 metres, to 4.5 feet	summer / autumn	full sun / partial shade	moist	tender, USDA 9-11	acid / alkaline / neutral
B	*Aechmea blanchetiana* 'Orange'	bromeliad	1-1.5 metres, 2-4 feet	1 metre, to 3 feet	spring	full sun	moist	tender, USDA 10-11	acid / alkaline / neutral
C	*Aloe ferox*	succulent	2.5-4 metres, to 15 feet	1.5-2.5 metres, to 5 feet	evergreen	full sun	well-drained	tender, USDA 9-11	acid / alkaline / neutral
D	*Dioon spinulosum*	cycad	1.5-3.6 metres, 4-12 feet	1.5-3.6 metres, 4-12 feet	evergreen	full sun / partial shade	moist but well-drained	tender, USDA 9-11	acid / alkaline / neutral
E	*Beaucarnea recurvata*	perennial	1.5-2.5 metres, 6-8 feet	1-1.5 metres, 3-5 feet	evergreen	full sun	well-drained	tender, USDA 10-11	acid / alkaline / neutral

- 70 -

Dazzling Subtleties

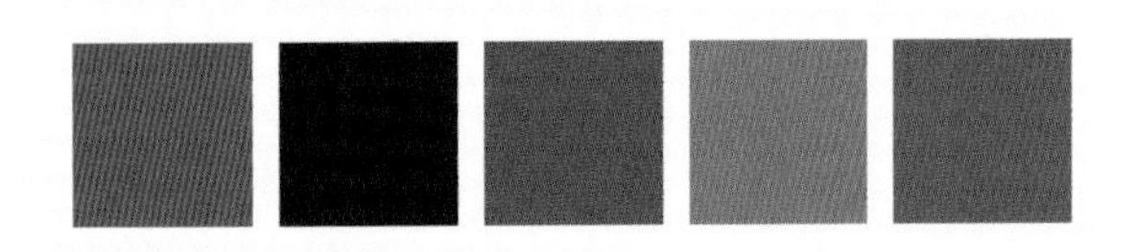

Fluidity of water and sky, a sense of motion, is that "something intangible" Monet struggled to capture in *Regattas at Argenteuil*. He went on: "It's appalling, this light that drifts off and takes the colour with it." Change is constant across the canvas as the light moves and turns one colour to another—blue to grey to white-grey and back to blue, with highlights of an earthy brown that gleams almost bronze in the light he has created.

Here we are in the same garden designed by Raymond Jungles. This time we are viewing it from close up, looking inwards rather than out at the landscape beyond. And I don't need to tell you that as we go through the garden, the magic continues: we are now truly within the secret

Right | Design: Raymond Jungles
Below | Claude Monet, *Regattas at Argenteuil*, c. 1872

A

B

	NAME	TYPE	HEIGHT	SPREAD	SEASON	LIGHT	MOISTURE	HARDINESS	SOIL PH
A	*Aechmea* 'Dean'	bromeliad	1 metre, 3 feet	1-2.5 metres, to 4.5 feet	summer / autumn	full sun / partial shade	moist	tender, USDA 9-11	acid / alkaline / neutral
B	*Euphorbia* Blackbird = 'Nothowlee'	sub-shrub	0.1-0.5 metre, 1-2 feet	0.1-0.5 metre, 1-2 feet	spring	full sun	well-drained	hardy, USDA 6-9	acid / alkaline / neutral

garden, the volcano beyond isn't visible, and we are safe in a landscape of dazzling Impressionist complementaries of blues and oranges, red with green, yellow with violet.

The hillside yellows themselves have disappeared by the time we get to this spot, and the yellow is much subtler: the slope-planted cycad *Dioon mejiae* and *Attalea cohune* (American oil palm) have the merest hint of yellow in their foliage, perfect neighbours to the *Alcantarea odorata* with a bluish violet reflection coming from its green leaves, which are covered with a silvery grey bloom.

The pale cream spartina, in places moving to white, brings a strong dash of light to this planting—peinture claire, in garden form, created with one genus.

The leaves of the extraordinary *Dioon spinulosum* also have bluish tones—as well as being a perfect foreground reflection of the blue-violet *Alcantarea odorata*, their blue contrasts with the bromeliad *Aechmea blanchetiana* 'Orange', while the reddish purples of *A.* 'Dean' and *Euphorbia* Blackbird = 'Nothowlee' contrast with the greens of *Beaucarnea recurvata* and a cereus cactus.

All these colour associations are dazzling in their subtleties: we see the harmony, but it is an effortless harmony. The colours enhance each other by contrasting simultaneously: we know where to look, we can take it all in, and we want to go there.

	NAME	TYPE	HEIGHT	SPREAD	SEASON	LIGHT	MOISTURE	HARDINESS	SOIL PH
C	*Alcantarea odorata*	bromeliad	1-1.5 metres, 3-4 feet	1-1.5 metres, 3-5 feet	evergreen	full sun / partial shade	moist	tender, USDA 9-11	neutral
D	*Dioon mejiae*	cycad	1 metre, 3 feet	1-2 metres, 3-6 feet	evergreen	full sun / partial shade	moist but well-drained	half hardy, USDA 9-11	acid / alkaline / neutral
E	*Attalea cohune*	tree	> 12 metres, to 80 feet	12 metres, to 40 feet	evergreen	full sun	moist but well-drained	tender, USDA 9-12	neutral

- 71 -

Broad Brushstrokes for Larger Spaces

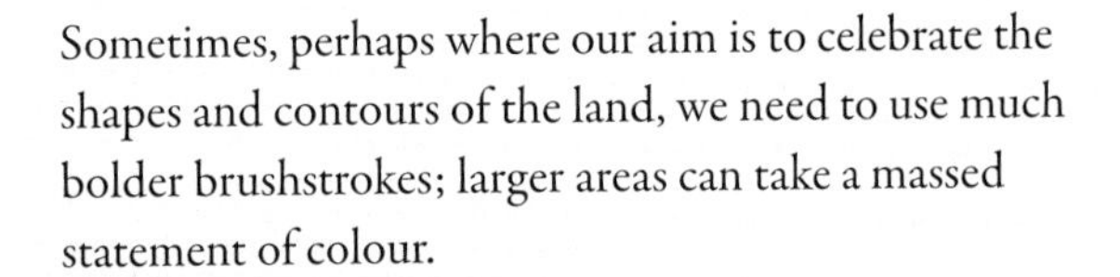

Sometimes, perhaps where our aim is to celebrate the shapes and contours of the land, we need to use much bolder brushstrokes; larger areas can take a massed statement of colour.

Back at RHS Hyde Hall, Clover Hill is a good example of an arrangement of colour suitable for a big space which needs filling but with maintenance time in mind. Its plantings, huge groups of cultivars in a restricted palette, blend with the clover-rich pastures of the neighbouring countryside. The airiness of the plant selections is key to the success of this prairie-influenced grouping, which might otherwise have read as an arrangement of impenetrable blocks of colour.

The sense of both implied and actual movement owes much to the grasses here: for once, the flowers of *Calamagrostis ×acutiflora* 'Karl Foerster' and *Stipa gigantea* aren't in a position to catch the light; instead, they take their tones from the cue given by *Malus ×moerlandsii* 'Red Profusion', whose coppery green foliage is turning to its brooding autumnal bronze. Colours as muted as these brownish and purplish reds and warmer blue-beige and grey are really useful for filling a large space: they don't demand that we look at them. They invite us instead to look through them. Seedheads of *Allium cristophii* bring this neutral silvery grey around to the front with a satisfying sweep.

A great sense of a sweeping hand continues across the landscape: purple-blue *Salvia ×sylvestris* 'Mainacht' and golden yellow hemerocallis reference the pinkish purple of the salvia in the distance. Lightness comes in the brilliant unexpected colour here: a great clump of *Rosa* 'Ballerina' sprawls pink down the hill and dashes a highlight across the whole planting, with a nod to the sunlit grass in the distance.

What dictates the choice of any structural plant is foliage: here it's the purple leaves of the malus, directing the blue tones beneath. The limited palette creates beauty and a sense of serenity: blue, pink, bronze, and yellow, each with little variation in tone as each colour derives from only one cultivar. Recreating this in a smaller garden would need a concentration of texture and form; I'd want to use grasses and plants whose tall naked stems would give a glimpse through to the colour behind rather than filling the view with their own tones.

Being contrary and knowing that it would be difficult to make red work here, I'm therefore wondering if I could make red work. This is how I make trouble for myself. For a start, I know I'd need grasses with a hint of red or pink: *Calamagrostis brachytricha* and a panicum perhaps. Then what? Perhaps a sprawl of sanguisorba and a mass of *Echinacea pallida* 'Hula Dancer'? Would the tones jar? Hmm. I wonder.

Design: RHS Hyde Hall

	NAME	TYPE	HEIGHT	SPREAD	SEASON	LIGHT	MOISTURE	HARDINESS	SOIL PH
A	*Hemerocallis* 'Azor'	perennial	0.5 metre, 1.5 feet	0.5 metre, 1.5 feet	summer / autumn	full sun / partial shade	moist but well-drained	hardy, USDA 3-10	acid / alkaline / neutral
B	*Rosa* 'Ballerina'	shrub	1-1.5 metres, 4-6 feet	1-1.5 metres, 3-5 feet	summer / autumn	full sun / partial shade	moist but well-drained / well-drained	very hardy, USDA 5-9	acid / alkaline / neutral
C	*Allium cristophii*	bulb	0.6 metre, 1-2 feet	0.2-0.5 metre, 0.5-1.5 feet	summer	full sun	well-drained	very hardy, USDA 4-8	acid / alkaline / neutral
D	*Salvia* ×*sylvestris* 'Mainacht'	perennial	0.5-1 metre, 1.5-2 feet	0.1-0.5 metre, 1-1.5 feet	summer	full sun	moist but well-drained	very hardy, USDA 4-8	acid / alkaline / neutral
E	*Malus* ×*moerlandsii* 'Red Profusion'	tree	8-12 metres, 15-30 feet	> 8 metres, 20-35 feet	spring / autumn	full sun / partial shade	moist but well-drained / well-drained	very hardy, USDA 4-8	acid / alkaline / neutral
F	*Stipa gigantea*	grass	1.5-2.5 metres, to 8 feet	0.5-1 metre, to 4 feet	summer / autumn	full sun	moist but well-drained / well-drained	half hardy, USDA 7-10	acid / alkaline / neutral
G	*Calamagrostis* ×*acutiflora* 'Karl Foerster'	grass	1-1.5 metres, 3-5 feet	0.5-1 metre, 1.5-2.5 feet	summer / autumn	full sun / partial shade	moist but well-drained / well-drained	very hardy, USDA 5-9	acid / alkaline / neutral

- 72 -

The Primaries at Great Dixter

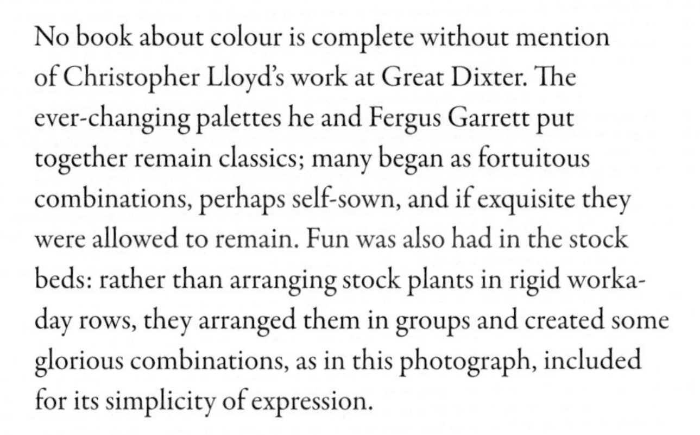

No book about colour is complete without mention of Christopher Lloyd's work at Great Dixter. The ever-changing palettes he and Fergus Garrett put together remain classics; many began as fortuitous combinations, perhaps self-sown, and if exquisite they were allowed to remain. Fun was also had in the stock beds: rather than arranging stock plants in rigid workaday rows, they arranged them in groups and created some glorious combinations, as in this photograph, included for its simplicity of expression.

Here, the strong purplish red of *Penstemon* 'Drinkstone Red' makes a satisfying partner for the rich purple of *Salvia* ×*superba*. The salvia's spires stand almost at right angles to *Achillea* 'Lucky Break', whose yellow flowers, in a softer shade than the strident *A. filipendulina* 'Gold Plate', have just the tiniest hint of green. *Verbascum chaixii*, scattered (perhaps self-sown) throughout, continues the yellow theme; it is a restrained choice, continuing the same colour in a different form rather than going for a contrast in blue, for example. Less is more, and when there's so much pure, unadulterated colour, as here, three different cultivars are enough.

Nori and Sandra Pope knew that the sun always shines from a yellow planting, and that's just the effect that the achilleas and verbascum have here. The shades of yellow in this bed have enough brightness about them to bring light to the rear of the off-red and the off-blue hues in front, as well as gently zigzagging dots of light away into the distance.

This isn't all about the flower colours. The verbascum's grey foliage is an echo of the larger grey leaves of *Cynara cardunculus* in the foreground, the silvery grey highlight increasing the effect of a sophisticated representation of primary colours. A fabulous palette.

	NAME	TYPE	HEIGHT	SPREAD	SEASON	LIGHT	MOISTURE	HARDINESS	SOIL PH
A	*Penstemon* 'Drinkstone Red'	perennial	0.5-1 metre, 3 feet	0.5-1 metre, 3 feet	summer / autumn	full sun / partial shade	well-drained	hardy, USDA 7-9	acid / alkaline / neutral
B	*Verbascum chaixii*	perennial	0.5-1 metre, 2-3 feet	0.1-0.5 metre, 1.5-2 feet	summer	full sun	well-drained	very hardy, USDA 5-8	alkaline
C	*Achillea* 'Lucky Break'	perennial	0.5-1 metre, 2.5 feet	0.5-1 metre, 1.5 feet	summer / autumn	full sun	moist but well-drained / well-drained	very hardy, USDA 3-9	acid / alkaline / neutral
D	*Achillea filipendulina* 'Gold Plate'	perennial	1-1.5 metres, 4-5 feet	0.5-1 metre, 2.5-3 feet	summer / autumn	full sun	moist but well-drained / well-drained	very hardy, USDA 3-8	acid / alkaline / neutral
E	*Salvia ×superba*	perennial	0.5-1 metre, 1-2.5 feet	0.1-0.5 metre, 1-1.5 feet	summer / autumn	full sun	moist but well-drained	very hardy, USDA 4-8	acid / alkaline / neutral

Opposite | Design: Christopher Lloyd

– 73 –

Hot Garden

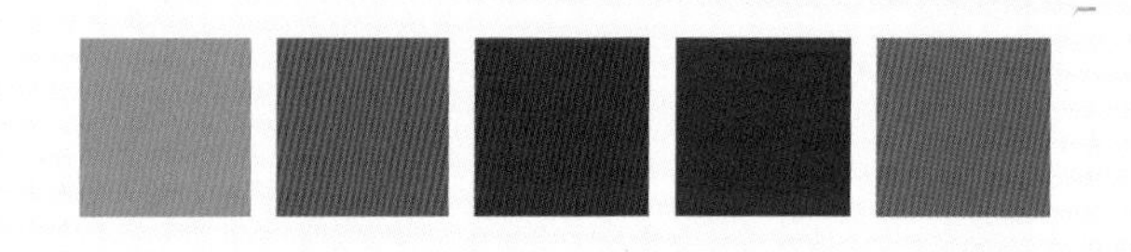

Mention a hot planting or a hot border, and the mind immediately jumps to red and orange and yellow, all grouped together, looking very bold and challenging the pastel perfection so dear to our hearts.

To be truly successful, a hot planting has to have so many more levels than these three colours—just as in Hofmann's *The Golden Wall*: it isn't just about the vivid colours on his palette but about how he puts what next what, and how much of each. Light on top of dark makes the light jump forward and the dark recede. The colours all sing as they lure our gaze backwards and forwards and from side to side. And in a garden, the same decisions are made. Who will be the showstopper? Who will be the supporting band? Which red? How many reds? And so on.

Then the tone, of course, is vital: if more than one yellow plant is going to be chosen, we know it's helpful to separate them, but with what? Another strong colour? And on it goes.

This planting in the Hot Garden at RHS Rosemoor is hot perfection. Restrained isn't necessarily the first word that springs to mind, but there's certainly a restrained use of red. *Lobelia cardinalis* 'Bee's Flame', in the unabashedly flamboyant racing red of Rosso Corsa, stands proudly at the heart of this planting, seizing our attention however we might view red, whether it means to us the colour of love, the colour of hate, the colour of danger, the colour of blood. Towards the far end of this planting, *Monarda* 'Gardenview Scarlet' is a ripple of similar scarlet, distance muting its dazzling effect.

There's a sensitive touch here. By introducing another lobelia, *Lobelia* ×*speciosa* 'Hadspen Purple', in a strong purplish red, everything is tempered just a little bit, enough for the yellow heads of *Kniphofia* 'Bees' Lemon' to avoid the effect of a child's painting and instead look glamorous against the orange-streaked flowers of *Helenium* 'Sahin's Early Flowerer'. The apricot-brown-orange *Crocosmia* ×*crocosmiiflora* 'Star of the East' is fabulous, its pale orange star-shaped flowers popping and fizzing like fireworks against the purples and lemons and reds.

The subtle brilliance of *Lobelia* ×*speciosa* 'Hadspen Purple' deserves another round of applause. I love how here its purple is picked up on and shouted out by the huge clump of *Monarda* 'Prärienacht'. Seen with the crocosmia, pinkish tones in the monarda make their way out of the photograph towards us, but as we then manage to take in the brutal yellow of *Achillea* 'Coronation Gold' and the similarly strident yellow of *Solidago* 'Goldenmosa', the monarda, which isn't blue at all, gives a suggestion of blue.

I'm not going to go into cones and rods and chromatic theory. But I marvel at how what could appear to be a clunky statement of bold heat is instead a gorgeous tapestry of colour. Thanks to a careful placing of colours, with clear attention given to the fact that different sizes of each block makes the grouping appear in turn to recede or advance, what could be deemed exotic in fact sits very well within its UK landscape.

Above | Design: RHS Rosemoor
Right | Hans Hofmann, *The Golden Wall*, 1961. With permission of the Renate, Hans & Maria Hofmann Trust / Artists Rights Society (ARS), New York.

	NAME	TYPE	HEIGHT	SPREAD	SEASON	LIGHT	MOISTURE	HARDINESS	SOIL PH
A	*Crocosmia ×crocosmiiflora* 'Star of the East'	perennial	1-2 metres, 3-6 feet	1-2 metres, 3-6 feet	summer / autumn	full sun / partial shade	moist but well-drained	very hardy, USDA 6-9	acid / alkaline / neutral
B	*Helenium* 'Sahin's Early Flowerer'	perennial	0.5-1.5 metres, 3-5 feet	0.5-1 metre, 3 feet	summer / autumn	full sun	moist but well-drained	very hardy, USDA 4-9	acid / alkaline / neutral
C	*Monarda* 'Gardenview Scarlet'	perennial	0.5-1 metre, 2-3 feet	0.1-0.5 metre, 1-2 feet	summer / autumn	full sun / partial shade	moist but well-drained	very hardy, USDA 4-9	acid / alkaline / neutral
D	*Lobelia cardinalis* 'Bee's Flame'	perennial	0.5-1 metre, 2-3 feet	0.1-0.5 metre, 1-2 feet	summer / autumn	full sun / partial shade	moist but well-drained	very hardy, USDA 3-9	acid / alkaline / neutral
E	*Lobelia ×speciosa* 'Hadspen Purple'	perennial	0.5-1 metre, 2-3 feet	0.1-0.5 metre, 1.5-2 feet	summer / autumn	full sun / partial shade	moist but well-drained	very hardy, USDA 5-8	acid / alkaline / neutral

Inspiration from RHS Garden Rosemoor

Curator Jonathan Webster on planting from the Hot Garden:

1 Globes of alliums

Injecting early interest, *Allium hollandicum* 'Purple Sensation' runs through the planting. This bulb contrasts dramatically with the fiery tones of other carefully selected perennials.

2 Drift of orange geums

Reliable perennials for starting displays in late spring and early summer, many geums, such as orange-flowered *Geum* 'Dolly North', are easy to grow and may continue to bloom for several months.

3 Yellow-green euphorbia

Forming a soft mound of growth, herbaceous *Euphorbia palustris* hits its stride early in the growing season, producing long-lasting heads of acid yellow flowers.

– 74 –

Magentaphobia

To Rudolf Steiner, magenta was more a mood than a colour; for Goethe, the colour radiated both the gracious dignity of old age and the sweet amiability of youth. In 1899 Gertrude Jekyll warned people against crimson, which "covers such a wide extent of ground, and is used so carelessly in plant-catalogues, that one cannot know whether it stands for a rich blood colour or for malignant magenta." Malignant! And she wasn't alone: E.A. Bowles called magenta "that awful form of floral original sin." Plantsman Michael Loftus coined the term *magentaphobia* in one of his wonderful catalogues for Woottens of Wenhaston, noting astutely that "horticultural bigotry is still the worst weed in the garden."

I, for one, am amazed. Magenta is one of those colours that no one is ever really sure about identifying nowadays. Your magenta is my hot pink; my magenta is your light purple. I would stake a lot on two of these zinnias in the Cutting Garden at West Dean being very definitely magenta; we may have to agree to disagree.

The fact is that in the nineteenth century, it really wasn't "the thing" to like this new colour. Aniline dyes, a new man-made product, had produced all sorts of brightly coloured, less expensive textiles for clothing and a home's interior, one of which was magenta, discovered in 1859 by August Wilhelm Hoffman. Adding to this "down-marketing" of the colour, a by-product of magenta's manufacture was London purple, an arsenic compound used as an insecticide in the United States at the time but mainly shunned in Britain: it had accidentally poisoned staff and destroyed bees around fruit trees. Put together this association with the huge growth in glasshouses and gaudy bedding schemes, and you can kind of see how magentaphobia came to be.

But look again at this razzmatazz of colours at West Dean, looking for all the world as if they should be jars in an old-fashioned sweetshop. There's puce and saffron, madder and fuchsia, cochineal and hematite. There's the palest pink with splashes of purple. There's definitely magenta, I insist.

Admittedly, these zinnias are grown for cutting rather than an extended permanent display, but all these hues, tones, and shades create a buzz of energy and a harmony, possibly because we are pretty sure that whoever planted these varieties wasn't in pursuit of a specific effect. There was clearly an optimism that there would be colour, and colour there certainly is. It's worth trying, this throw-it-all-in-and-see-what-happens approach, in a place where you know that vicars and aged aunts won't swoon at your outrageous colour statement.

Design: West Dean Gardens

	NAME	TYPE	HEIGHT	SPREAD	SEASON	LIGHT	MOISTURE	HARDINESS	SOIL PH
A	*Zinnia* cvs.	annual	0.1-1.5 metres, 0.5-4 feet	0.1-0.5 metre, 0.5-1.5 feet	summer / autumn	full sun	moist but well-drained	hardy, USDA 2-11	acid / alkaline / neutral

- 75 -

Red on Red

"Large blocks of undiluted red are a mistake; indigestible as swallowing a lump of uncooked dough." Nobody could put it quite like Christopher Lloyd.

The initial onslaught of wavelength-surfing red catches our attention for sure, but too much of it and we don't know where to look. Vast swathes of scarlet are never a good idea, but mix them thoughtfully, play with the light and suddenly you have beauty that is never too much of a good thing. Look how Matisse did it in *The Red Studio*: he interrupted an uncompromising red with pale pink and white objects and pale yellow lines, subtly lighting and defining the space.

There's a very real reason for me referencing this painting, for the red planting in this Munich garden shouts out the same clever use of one hue. Three bands of red stand out. *Zinnia elegans* 'Benary's Giant Deep Red' does exactly what its name suggests. It creates a tall wash of crimson dots, deeper and deeper in tone as they recede, the flowers nearer to us a brighter red.

Design: Maximilian Park

A

B

	NAME	TYPE	HEIGHT	SPREAD	SEASON	LIGHT	MOISTURE	HARDINESS	SOIL PH
A	*Zinnia elegans* 'Benary's Giant Deep Red'	annual	0.5-1 metre, 1-4 feet	0.1-0.5 metre, 0.75-1 foot	summer	full sun	moist but well-drained / well-drained	very hardy, USDA 2-11	acid / alkaline / neutral
B	*Salvia splendens*	perennial	0.1-0.5 metre, 1-2 feet	0.1-0.5 metre, 0.75-1.5 feet	summer / autumn	full sun	moist but well-drained / well-drained	hardy, USDA 10-11	acid / alkaline / neutral

The zinnias' own foliage gives us a break here, as does the plant height: a clever placing of *Salvia farinacea* Farina Series drops the levels right down to almost ground level, the grey foliage and emergent white and blue flowers creating a welcome break of silver before the red ramps up again, this time with the verticals of *Imperata cylindrica* 'Rubra'. This Japanese red-tipped grass is wonderful placed, as it is here, where it can catch the evening light. Blood reds become pink with flashes of orange, mellow behind a final punch of red in the form of *S. splendens*. It is the foliage of this scarlet sage which allows this plant to get away with its unstinting redness. Not to my taste necessarily in a bedding scheme, but when allowed to loosen up a little as here, alongside just a few pops of dark foliage creating some further welcome respite—"holes" of vision, as *Amaranthus tricolor* 'Red Army' does here—the sage can, I think, be given some space to show what it can really do.

The message is this: break it up. Turn off the red channel sometimes. Red on red is good, but think about allowing that exhalation, pleasure with pauses in between.

C

D

E

F

	NAME	TYPE	HEIGHT	SPREAD	SEASON	LIGHT	MOISTURE	HARDINESS	SOIL PH
C	*Salvia farinacea* Farina Series	perennial	0.5 metre, 1-3 feet	0.3 metre, 1-2 feet	summer / autumn	full sun	moist but well-drained	half hardy, USDA 8-10	acid / alkaline / neutral
D	*Amaranthus tricolor* 'Red Army'	annual	1.2 metres, 2-4 feet	0.5 metre, 1-2 feet	summer / autumn	full sun	well-drained	half hardy, USDA 2-11	alkaline / neutral
E	*Imperata cylindrica* 'Rubra'	grass	0.1-0.5 metre, 2-4 feet	0.1-0.5 metre, 2-4 feet	spring / summer / autumn	full sun / partial shade	moist but well-drained / well-drained	hardy, USDA 5-9	acid / alkaline / neutral
F	*Nassella trichotoma*	grass	0.1-0.5 metre, 2 feet	0.1-0.5 metre, 2 feet	summer	full sun	moist but well-drained / well-drained	very hardy, USDA 7-10	acid / alkaline / neutral

- 76 -

Falling Off the Colour Wheel

Somebody remarked to me recently that they loved a colour scheme that they themselves would never have thought of putting together: "We were taught not to mix warm and cool colours." How soul-destroying is that? To be denied the opportunity to mix corals and mint, warm buttery yellow and icy blue, even warms and cools of the same colour. These do work together—or rather, they can work together, no matter what the colour wheel says.

As I hope I've shown in the rest of this book, I am not by any means advocating throwing everything in together, holding your nose, and metaphorically jumping into a palette of every colour you can think of. There's room for consideration and that gentle approach, but please don't abide by the rules just because they are there.

As soon as we loosen up a little, we can create some fabulous groupings that shouldn't harmonise. In this flower border along a yellowish brick wall, the intention was to create a colour effect which seems to move forwards, to create a focal point by using only the plants themselves.

Verbascum 'Cherry Helen' has flowers of a colour totally indispensable to me. They are pink, but it's a pink that is at the same time raspberry, plum, and grape—shades almost as edible as they sound. To make the most of stand-out pinks like this, the more unexpected you can be with colour, the better. The peachy orange tones of the erysimum are that shock element here. On paper they shouldn't work, but released into the garden, the tones collaborate with the all-important light and create a match that went further than I could have dreamed.

Knowing that the earthy buff of the brick would echo subtle hints of yellow, I'd used the wallflower as part of the all-important background wash. *Erysimum* 'Apricot Twist' has just the right amount of yellow and pink in her flowers to be a perfect match for the wall, and it's a wonderful plant for continuous colour; what I hadn't anticipated, though, was that the combination of the verbascum's pink flowers and silver-grey foliage would reflect light so much that it emphasised the wallflower's pink tones. Happy accidents are an essential part of the gardening process; changing light and changing seasons create colour effects that we could never foresee.

The pink being so beautiful, everything else needed to go up or down a few shades. When creating a scheme of this sort, I have in my mind that there is one stand-out plant (that bride again). You could argue that the blues and purples contrast the orange, and well, yes, they do. I chose them simply because I thought they would work—the deep blue-purple *Iris* 'Dusky Challenger' dark and moody in front of the light blue flowers of the

Opposite | Design: Jo Thompson

	NAME	TYPE	HEIGHT	SPREAD	SEASON	LIGHT	MOISTURE	HARDINESS	SOIL PH
A	*Geranium pratense* (Victor Reiter Group) 'Kaya'	perennial	0.5 metre, 1-1.5 feet	0.1-0.5 metre, 2 feet	summer	full sun / partial shade / full shade	well-drained	very hardy, USDA 4-8	acid / alkaline / neutral
B	*Verbascum* 'Cherry Helen'	perennial	1-1.5 metres, 3-4.5 feet	0.1-0.5 metre, 1-1.5 feet	summer	full sun	well-drained	very hardy, USDA 5-9	alkaline / neutral

ceanothus, while fresh green *Stipa tenuissima* foliage adds freshness to all.

I needed an acid yellow against the strawberries and plums, so I included *Alchemilla mollis* to form the rest of the background at ground level, as its yellow fades out to a barely noticeable lime green.

I've experimented recently with another version of this scheme, replacing the verbascum with *Papaver* (Oriental Group) 'Patty's Plum' and using *Salvia verticillata* 'Purple Rain' instead of the iris, with *Geranium pratense* (Victor Reiter Group) 'Kaya' set slightly further away. This still creates that intriguing reaction: people are surprised that they like something that, in theory, they shouldn't do. This is the moment when they fall off the colour wheel: liberation.

	NAME	TYPE	HEIGHT	SPREAD	SEASON	LIGHT	MOISTURE	HARDINESS	SOIL PH
C	*Iris* 'Dusky Challenger'	perennial	0.5-1 metre, 3 feet	0.1-0.5 metre, 1-2 feet	summer	full sun	well-drained	very hardy, USDA 5-9	acid / alkaline / neutral
D	*Salvia verticillata* 'Purple Rain'	perennial	0.5-1 metre, 1-2 feet	0.1-0.5 metre, 1.5-2.5 feet	summer	full sun	well-drained	very hardy, USDA 5-8	acid / alkaline / neutral
E	*Erysimum* 'Apricot Twist'	perennial	0.1-0.5 metre, 1-2 feet	0.1-0.5 metre, 2 feet	spring / summer / winter	full sun	well-drained	half hardy, USDA 6-9	alkaline / neutral
F	*Alchemilla mollis*	perennial	0.1-0.5 metre, 1-1.5 feet	0.1-0.5 metre, 1.5-2.5 feet	summer / autumn	full sun / partial shade / full shade	moist but well-drained	very hardy, USDA 3-8	acid / alkaline / neutral

- 77 -

Naturally Pretty

People are starting to appreciate that "wild" doesn't necessarily mean "messy," buoyed along by a new movement, one that embraces the fact that we want to enjoy our gardens for what they are, for what they represent to us. For many, that's about getting up close and personal with nature, loving what we see for what it is. Beauty very much in the eye of the beholder. We're starting to want to spend our time enjoying the garden rather than getting stressed when things are out of place. Does it really matter if things are a little unkempt?

I am seeing wildflower planting everywhere now, thank goodness. Wildflowers in meadows, wildflowers around topiary à la Great Dixter, new wildflower plantings in verges where once upon a time they used to introduce themselves. And there's no denying the uplift they arouse in us. Whether it's a natural wildflower planting, or the primary punches of poppies and cornflowers and marigolds growing in a cornfield, they make us happy. These pure colours are proudly delicate, completely uncontrived when scattered through the greens of thousands of stems.

Design: Lippe Polder Park

	NAME	TYPE	HEIGHT	SPREAD	SEASON	LIGHT	MOISTURE	HARDINESS	SOIL PH
A	*Centaurea cyanus*	annual	0.5-1 metre, 1-3 feet	0.1-0.5 metre, 1-2 feet	spring / summer	full sun	well-drained	hardy, USDA 2-11	acid / alkaline / neutral
B	*Lavatera trimestris*	annual	0.5-1 metre, 2-4 feet	0.1-0.5 metre, 2-3 feet	summer	full sun	well-drained	hardy, USDA 2-11	acid / alkaline / neutral

As here in Germany, adding more colours only adds to the joy. Think "pure" in terms of colour to achieve this effect of complete abandon in a sweetshop: pink, white, yellow, green, blue, orange. The blue of *Centaurea cyanus* and *Borago officinalis*, glorious ultramarine. Whenever I remember that borage is brilliant in a gin and tonic and go to snip off a flower, I can't help but think that its odd texture is far better viewed than touched. Its hairy stems are lightcatchers, creating a silver fuzziness that blends in with the whites of camomile and yarrow.

Glebionis segetum (corn marigold) and *Calendula officinalis* (pot marigold) are further sunny uplifts, while the yellow of *Anethum graveolens* (dill) is slightly more acidic. I can just imagine the creator of this collection of seeds: "What next? Hmm . . . let's try *pink*!" and in goes *Lavatera trimestris*, upturned ballgowns of the best proper pink silkily elegant against this joyful scattering of colour.

I'm left wondering how one would make this scheme work as a perennial planting, and I firmly believe what is key here is quantity. The red, which would be too much of an eye-hook scattered throughout, is used sparingly here: I might think about using yellow *Geum* 'Prinses Juliana', yellow *Anthemis tinctoria* 'E.C. Buxton', *Nigella damascena* 'Miss Jekyll' for blue, *Geranium* ×*oxonianum* 'Rose Clair', with *Angelica archangelica* for some good yellow-green structure. And then, only a very few dots of scarlet, perhaps *Crocosmia* 'Lucifer', would be needed. Only a very, very few.

People with a brain more scientific than mine have shown that however much background colour there is, red will always shine through and dominate, so we need use only just a tiny bit of it. I promise you it's true: imagine this wildness with massed poppies: we would see red.

	NAME	TYPE	HEIGHT	SPREAD	SEASON	LIGHT	MOISTURE	HARDINESS	SOIL PH
C	*Borago officinalis*	annual	0.5-1 metre, 1-3 feet	0.1-0.5 metre, 0.75-1.5 feet	summer	full sun / partial shade	well-drained	hardy, USDA 2-11	acid / alkaline / neutral
D	*Calendula officinalis*	annual	0.1-0.5 metre, 1-2 feet	0.1-0.5 metre, 1-2 feet	summer / autumn	full sun / partial shade	well-drained	hardy, USDA 2-11	acid / alkaline / neutral
E	*Anethum graveolens*	annual	0.5-1.5 metre, 3-5 feet	0.5-1 metre, 2-3 feet	spring / summer	full sun	well-drained	hardy, USDA 2-11	acid / alkaline / neutral
F	*Glebionis segetum*	annual	0.5-1 metre, 1.5 feet	0.5-1 metre, 1.5 feet	summer	full sun	moist but well-drained / well-drained	hardy, USDA 2-11	acid / neutral

- 78 -

South African Meadow

Sometimes you come across a colour combination that is truly uplifting: its zing and happiness make your day. That's what happens to me when I see how the South African Meadow is developing at RHS Wisley. Seed-raised plants were chosen for their similar vigour and for their enjoyment of the full-sun location. This spot is rather damp throughout the year and pleases lots of South African perennials, despite their sometimes xeric appearance.

The intention was to mimic a naturalistic direct-sown meadow, but a meadow with a twist. No scarlet poppies or bright blue cornflowers here; instead the red tips of *Kniphofia caulescens* and bright blue agapanthus peep through a satisfying haze of *Watsonia pillansii*, which glimmers and shimmers in shades of the palest pearlescent pink through to shrimp and on to peach.

Berkheya purpurea has a whiteness that I can never quite put my finger on: is berkheya actually pale grey or is it the delicate streaks of lilac-purple in the petals that make it appear silvery? It might even be the colour of the surprisingly spiky leaves, which seem so at odds with the delicate flowers.

Spots of magenta, shocking pink, purplish red, and reddish purple catch our eye here and there, and bell-shaped flowers of dierama land a gentle punch of contrast. It is always worth remembering how effective it is to introduce contrast in a colour combination: it doesn't need to be an obvious one. The angel's fishing rod works well here because the pink of the watsonia's tiny gladioli-like flowers has a bit of purple to it: the two are not next to each other but are a mutual appreciation society, either side of the shades of grey.

Lovely pinpricks of sunlight yellow illustrate perfectly how reference to a colour wheel would be completely useless in creating the colour combinations seen in the pastel loveliness of this palette. The acid yellow of the lower parts of the kniphofia add to this planting's general feeling of exuberance. You cannot look at it without feeling happy. Summer sunshine—it makes us feel good.

Opposite | Design: RHS Wisley

	NAME	TYPE	HEIGHT	SPREAD	SEASON	LIGHT	MOISTURE	HARDINESS	SOIL PH
A	*Berkheya purpurea*	perennial	0.5-1.5 metres, 3-4 feet	0.25-1 metre, 1-3 feet	summer	full sun	well-drained	half hardy, USDA 7-10	acid / alkaline / neutral
B	*Dierama* 'Blackberry Bells'	perennial	1-1.5 metres, 3.5-4.5 feet	0.1-0.5 metre, 3-4 feet	summer	full sun	well-drained	hardy, USDA 7-10	acid / alkaline / neutral
C	*Watsonia pillansii*	perennial	0.5-1 metre, 3 feet	0.5-1 metre, to 3 feet	summer / autumn	full sun	moist but well-drained / well-drained	half hardy, USDA 8-10	acid / alkaline / neutral
D	*Kniphofia caulescens*	perennial	1-1.5 metres, 2-4 feet	0.5-1 metre, 1-2 feet	summer	full sun	moist but well-drained	very hardy, USDA 6-8	acid / neutral

- 79 -

Cherry Pink

We all wait for it. The Japan Meteorological Corporation even issues forecasts for it. Cherry blossom—with its connotations of fragility and the transience of beauty, of seizing the day and celebrating what we know will pass—is a natural wonder of our world. The annual appearance of the confetti of sugared-almond colours against grey skies is predictable yet mesmerising. Of course, sometimes those skies are in fact blue—an added bonus—and then we get the double whammy of pastel and pastel: baby pink and baby blue, soft colours letting us know that a whole explosion of garden colours is yet to come.

The semi-double flowers of *Prunus* 'Accolade', seen here in the gardens at RHS Wisley, are the purest pink. This tree's excellent autumn colour adds to its appeal, as does its smooth reddish brown bark. It's difficult not to stray into descriptive overkill when imagining the sense of enveloping welcome that ensues at its flowering, the feeling created by the arrival of longed-for colour, gentle enough to function perfectly with any colour, strong enough to make us stop and admire.

This shade of pink is of a low intensity, which the colour psychologists say creates a physically soothing sensation of gentle energy, and that certainly seems the reason for the creation of a seating area at this spot, where everything else is in neutral shades so as not to detract (as if that were possible) from its effect. There's no other pink here, interestingly: would we start to find it too much if the ground beneath were carpeted in toning shades of rose-pink and blush? These petals embody the Impressionist and Neo-Impressionist mission to depict light by the use of colour; for the artists, colour perception became pictorial colour. Paul Signac delivers this in various beautiful scenes along the Seine; here at Wisley I see the same scintillating colour mosaics achieved through the use of a palette limited to specific colours in allocated quantities.

Both colours and forms beneath the pink cherry blossoms suggest neutrality. *Gunnera manicata* has enough structure to "hold" the eye, its sculpted leaves and its huge buds protected by brownish red scales, here at their most beautiful catching the sun low in the sky. The white arum-like flowers of *Lysichiton* ×*hortensis* 'Billy' emerge lime green and offer just enough of a light reflection at low level. The seedheads of *Typha latifolia* perform the same function at a mid-level—never underestimate the light-producing power of seedheads. The whole effect is one of colour being allowed its space and its moment. In a smaller garden you would probably forgo the skunk cabbage and the bulrushes, but that pink? There's always a space for that pink in any garden of mine.

Above | Design: RHS Wisley
Right | Paul Signac, *L'Hirondelle Steamer on the Seine*, 1901

	NAME	TYPE	HEIGHT	SPREAD	SEASON	LIGHT	MOISTURE	HARDINESS	SOIL PH
A	*Prunus* 'Accolade'	tree	4-8 metres, to 25 feet	4-8 metres, to 25 feet	spring / autumn	full sun	moist but well-drained / well-drained	very hardy, USDA 4-9	acid / alkaline / neutral
B	*Lysichiton ×hortensis* 'Billy'	perennial	0.5-1 metre, 2-3 feet	0.1-0.5 metre, 2-3 feet	spring	full sun / partial shade	poorly drained	hardy, USDA 5-7	acid / alkaline / neutral
C	*Typha latifolia*	perennial	2-2.5 metres, 4-6 feet	2-2.5 metres, 4-6 feet	summer / autumn	full sun	poorly drained	hardy, USDA 3-10	acid / alkaline / neutral
D	*Gunnera manicata*	perennial	1.5-2.5 metres, 6-10 feet	2.5-4 metres, 8-14 feet	summer / autumn	full sun / partial shade	poorly drained	hardy, USDA 7-10	acid / alkaline / neutral

- 80 -

Antique Pink

Why does the cottage-garden planting style make us so happy? It could be the relaxed, let-it-all-hang-out atmosphere of a wayward tangle and scramble of annuals and perennials, all muddled together without a hint of artfulness, suggesting that this arrangement has just "happened." It could be the sense that nature is having its way, that the flowers will survive and thrive come what may. I have my own theory on this.

Colour has a demonstrated effect on our mood, and colour palettes have the ability to make us feel by degrees content, excited, agitated, calm. Out of all the colours, I'd stick my neck out and say that pink carries with it a

Right | Design: RHS Wisley
Below | *Le Repas de Sancho dans l'Ile de Barataria*, from *L'Histoire de don Quichotte Series*. Woven in Gobelins, France, 1772.

particularly huge range of meaning, as just a cool or warm tone up or down can soothe or stimulate, offend or please. And in this planting in the Cottage Garden at RHS Wisley, pink is all. It reminds us of a place we once knew, either in reality or in a storybook, with happy-making shades tumbling through a garden full of charm.

Cosmos bipinnatus 'Antiquity' is the charmer here; newly emergent petals of crimson, fuchsia, and magenta, fading to antique rose and dusty pink, billow softly as all good cottage-garden plantings should. Any deeper a red (for pink is, of course, a pale red) and the scheme of three hues would move from gentle to strident, which would look well on a flag but wouldn't necessarily be that easy on the eye. The violet-blue of the geranium is gorgeous here—pink tones within this violet conjure up feelings of serenity and reflection, and this *Geranium* Rozanne = 'Gerwat' carries the blues perfectly as it travels through and up and around the taller stems of the annuals.

Further billowing comes in the cloud-like forms of *Ammi majus*, neat puffs of green-white hovering above the pinks and blues, bringing light to the delicate muted tones. In a very subtle manner, the umbels of the ammi also pick up on the golden centres of the cosmos daisies—the friendly welcome of their golden yellow stamens is often overlooked, perhaps even ignored, as it shouldn't work with the petals, especially when they are, as in this case, pink.

But it does. And straight away comes to mind the day the chemist Michel-Eugène Chevreul was hastily summoned to the Gobelins royal tapestry workshops where his job title was, rather fabulously, Director of Dyeing. Each square metre of these absorbingly intricate tapestries took one man-year to create, so you can imagine the workers' desperation when the black dye on their current tapestry was absolutely refusing to manifest itself as it had done in the previous tapestry, even though the dye's formula hadn't changed in the slightest. Chevreul made

A

a rather wonderful discovery: "I saw that the want of vigour alleged against the blacks was owing to the colours contiguous to them, and that the matter was involved in the phenomena of *the contrast of colours*." (Emphasis his.)

There was nothing wrong with the dye itself. It was simply that the colours had been placed in a different arrangement. Red against blue looks different to red against yellow—a Eureka moment which led to a fascinating study on how colour contrast theory was applicable not only to textiles but also to painting and printing. Chevreul eventually worked his way through art, architecture, and fashion to horticulture: "Flowers, presenting a disagreeable contrast of hues, may still produce a good effect, when their assortment makes part of an arrangement of contrasts of colours, strongly opposed; in this case being no longer seen isolated, they become in a manner the element of a picture."

There is nothing in this colour arrangement that stands out and shouts at us. It's gently-gently all the way, creating a feeling of nostalgic happiness.

B

C

	NAME	TYPE	HEIGHT	SPREAD	SEASON	LIGHT	MOISTURE	HARDINESS	SOIL PH
A	*Cosmos bipinnatus* 'Antiquity'	annual	0.5-1 metre, 1-4 feet	0.5-1 metre, 2-3 feet	summer / autumn	full sun	moist but well-drained	half hardy, USDA 2-11	acid / alkaline / neutral
B	*Geranium* Rozanne = 'Gerwat'	perennial	0.5-1 metre, 1-1.5 feet	0.5-1 metre, 1-2 feet	summer / autumn	full sun / partial shade	moist but well-drained / well-drained	very hardy, USDA 5-8	acid / alkaline / neutral
C	*Ammi majus*	annual	1-2 metres, 3-6 feet	0.1-0.5 metre, 1-1.5 feet	summer	full sun / partial shade	moist but well-drained	very hardy, USDA 2-11	acid / alkaline / neutral

Girl Pink, Boy Blue

For centuries, children were clothed in white dresses for the sake of practicality—white dresses could be washed in hot water repeatedly with minimal fading, and there were no worries about who wore what. Things began to change in the early twentieth century, however. Pink and blue were increasingly recommended as colours for baby clothing, but the two colours were not promoted as sex-specific until just before World War I—and even then, it took time for popular culture to sort things out. One of the earliest references to an assignment appeared in a 1918 edition of *Earnshaw's* (then *The Infants' Department*): "The generally accepted rule is pink for the boys, and blue for the girls. The reason is that pink, being a more decided and stronger color, is more suitable for the boy, while blue, which is more delicate and dainty, is prettier for the girl." Pink was seen as a variation of red, which, being the shade of soldier's jackets and cardinal's cassocks, was deemed more masculine than blue.

In 1927, *Time* magazine printed a chart showing sex-appropriate colours for girls and boys according to leading U.S. department stores, telling parents to dress boys in pink. Of course, commercial suggestion led to commercial sales and a whole new wardrobe for the fashionably dressed boy and girl. We are not quite sure why, but all this began to change in the 1940s, when clothing manufacturers settled on pink for girls and blue for boys.

- 81 -

Spring Pink and Yellow

Here's one for all those who are worrying that yellow and pink simply won't work. We have been told that these colours are not quite where they should be on the colour wheel in order to be able to work together. They are just "off" from each other, which means that in theory they neither tone nor complement. Nor do they contrast. They clash.

So, in an attempt to demolish this theory, I give you the splendid jewelbox of a woodland walk at Battleston Hill at RHS Wisley. Between March and June, this area provides a riot of colour in a palette I defy anyone to criticise, and there is one spot which I believe exemplifies the beauty of defying colour rules, doing what you like if you think it will work, and being completely rewarded for your daring by an effect that is exquisite. Lemons and pink with hints of fuchsia and a smattering of back-ground orange: the words may shock, but the images do something else.

The soft lemon flowers of *Rhododendron* 'Karen Triplett' announce the pastel theme here. This lemon so often pairs with whites and blues in the garden, but here, the most elegant shade of pink is the perfect partner. *Persicaria bistorta* 'Superba' should really clash but refuses to do so and, with its clear bluish pink pokers, instead creates a neutral carpet that also catches the light and interweaves with the purple-pink of the low-lying *R. yakushimanum*. And then, as if that weren't enough, rowdy *R.* 'Hanger's Flame' in orange just hovers in the background.

I like how this all works together, a clash and a tone in the same spot, allowing us to be both satisfied by the expected tonings of pinks and purples and at the same time surprised by a use of lemon which should really not work at all. But breaking rules isn't the only concept at play here; the brilliant greens of the foliage run through the planting, touching each colour and introducing it to the next. This is the year-round colour that so many of us want.

Design: RHS Wisley

	NAME	TYPE	HEIGHT	SPREAD	SEASON	LIGHT	MOISTURE	HARDINESS	SOIL PH
A	*Rhododendron* 'Karen Triplett'	shrub	1-1.5 metres, to 4 feet	0.5-1 metre, 3 feet	summer	partial shade	moist but well-drained	very hardy, USDA 7-8	acid
B	*Rhododendron yakushimanum*	shrub	1-1.5 metres, 2-3 feet	0.5-1 metre, 2-3 feet	summer	partial shade	moist but well-drained	very hardy, USDA 4-8	acid
C	*Persicaria bistorta* 'Superba'	perennial	to 1 metre, 2 feet	0.5-1 metre, 2 feet	summer / autumn	full sun / partial shade	moist but well-drained / poorly drained	very hardy, USDA 4-7	acid / alkaline / neutral

Inspiration from RHS Garden Hyde Hall

Curator Robert Brett describes interesting mixed spring planting in the Hilltop Garden:

1 Birch catkins

The island beds are filled with choice plants, many of which are impressive in spring. As with most *Betula* species at this time of year, this un-named birch is strung with dangling catkins that shiver in the breeze, making a most arresting sight.

2 Showy magnolia

Seen through the birch catkins, the beautiful purple goblets of *Magnolia* 'Judy' inject colour and elegance to the planting. The tree's lower stems are masked by an evergreen shrub, the scented, white-flowered *Osmanthus delavayi*.

3 Emerging shoots abound

Never underestimate the impact of verdant young growth in spring, be it the bright green fresh foliage of roses waking from dormancy or the lush upright shoots of miscanthus and other ornamental grasses.

- 82 -

Stealthy Pink and Orange

Some plants are more dramatic than others: *Echinacea purpurea* 'Rubinstern' is one that takes drama to the extreme. Its particular pink, which can fade in shade and often looks merely tasteful against silver, when sandwiched between oncoming bright light and the light clay colour of *Stipa tenuissima* behind, becomes flamboyant, daring, breathtaking in its simplicity.

It's the central orange cone within the flower that is responsible for the dazzling: pinks and oranges, not to be placed together harmoniously if you're following the Colour Police's rules, here work in unison to create a clash in one plant, a melding-together of two colours, which tricks the light into settling over a field that has something of the annual about its character. Hints of blue in the pink further confuse us—how *can* this work? But it does. Perhaps it's something to do with the "burntness" of the orange, with hints of saffron and amber continuing the grip on our gaze.

Reminiscent of the prairie, where the echinacea is so at home, this massed display benefits from the simple yet clever inclusion of silky *Stipa tenuissima*, planted so as to catch the light along with a smattering of *Echinacea purpurea* 'White Swan'. In a less exposed spot this grass can become a depressing tuft of green nothingness, but here it is planted to do the job ornamental grasses are so very good at: basking in the light and relishing every minute of it. Creams become the very best light without being white; here the grass's brown tints show off behind the cones and display simplicity at its very best.

A sea of one plant can create the feeling of a sea behind; here you feel as if you want to take a dip in whatever lies beyond, while in the background, green grass is seductively full of the foreground's sense of gentle movement.

We see it elsewhere in this book, the fact that pink and orange are an uplift rather than a crime against colour harmony.

Opposite | Design: RHS Hyde Hall

	NAME	TYPE	HEIGHT	SPREAD	SEASON	LIGHT	MOISTURE	HARDINESS	SOIL PH
A	*Echinacea purpurea* 'Rubinstern'	perennial	0.5-1 metre, 2-3 feet	0.5-1 metre, 2-3 feet	summer / autumn	full sun / partial shade	well-drained	hardy, USDA 3-8	acid / alkaline / neutral
B	*Echinacea purpurea* 'White Swan'	perennial	0.5-1 metre, 2-3 feet	0.1-0.5 metre, 1-2 feet	summer / autumn	full sun / partial shade	well-drained	hardy, USDA 3-8	acid / alkaline / neutral

- 83 -

Wild Side 1

Keith Wiley, the creator of one of the most beautiful gardens in the world, seeks to work in harmony with nature, allowing plants to thrive much as they would in the wild. He describes what he does as "looking at the treasure trove of gardening ideas to be found in nature, from under our noses to far-flung corners of the globe." He goes on: "By allowing our observations of natural landscapes to inform our plantings, I believe that we can loosen the strait-jacket that long-established horticultural practices impose, allowing the enormous creative potential, latent within most of us, the freedom to express itself."

Here, a flat three-acre field of nothing but grass was sculpted (with tenacity, vision, and a dumper truck to shift 110,000 tonnes of soil) into notional places. Keith has brought these places to life with planting palettes that hover between wild and tamed; every transition is successful, and the results are without exception enchanting.

In the Lower Garden, an unassuming backdrop of greens and purples forms a screen before which little splashes of colour are scattered in the manner of a paintbrush flick. In the foreground, the grassy foliage and arching flower stems of the diminutive wandflower *Dierama dracomontanum* and its cultivars introduce magenta and softer toning rosy mauves and pinks. The flower bells are held by paper-thin bracts of airy silver, which catch the light and ripple up to the pale silvery *Carex acuta* 'Variegata' glowing softly behind. Linking the two is *Chionochloa rubra* (red tussock grass), its bronze stems and feathery flower stems touching the earth around the dieramas and cleverly linking to the purple-maroons and browns of the Japanese maples behind. Light is created again by the white flower sprays of *Tanacetum niveum* in the middle distance, which Keith uses as an alternative to the world-domination ambitions of *Leucanthemum vulgare* (ox-eye daisy).

A completely wild atmosphere, then, has been created, with just enough colour to remind us that there has been human involvement. The natural greens and relaxing neutral beige earth tones are given glimmers of nostalgic pink and white, creating a dreamy, hazy atmosphere. There's a feeling that this is all mistily surreal.

	NAME	TYPE	HEIGHT	SPREAD	SEASON	LIGHT	MOISTURE	HARDINESS	SOIL PH
A	*Dierama dracomontanum*	perennial	0.5-1 metre, 2.5 feet	0.1-0.5 metre, 2 feet	summer	full sun	well-drained	hardy, USDA 8-9	acid / alkaline / neutral
B	*Tanacetum niveum*	perennial	0.5 metre, 1.5-2.5 feet	0.5 metre, 1.5-2.5 feet	summer	full sun	well-drained	very hardy, USDA 6-10	acid / alkaline / neutral
C	*Carex acuta* 'Variegata'	perennial	0.3-0.5 metre, 0.5-0.75 foot	0.3-0.5 metre, 1.5-2 feet	summer	full sun / partial shade	poorly drained	hardy, USDA 5-9	acid / alkaline / neutral
D	*Chionochloa rubra*	grass	1-1.5 metres, 3 feet	0.5-1 metre, 3 feet	evergreen	full sun	moist but well-drained / well-drained	very hardy, USDA 7-10	acid / alkaline / neutral

Opposite | Design: Keith Wiley

-84 -

Wild Side 2

In the canyons of the Upper Garden at Wildside, the pinks give way to bolder colours, and the dreamlike atmosphere is gently stirred by yellows and reds. This time taller dieramas, *Dierama pulcherrimum* and its cultivars, elegant and romantic, shimmer in the foreground; the silvery paper membrane of their scarious bracts creates a light-bringing veil that never fails to please the eye. The earthy tones continue in the form of *Stipa tenuissima*, its straw-coloured faded flowerheads bringing light, as does the paler, green-white *Eragrostis curvula* behind, which in turn passes to the white-flowered *Persicaria alpina* at the very rear. Can you see how the colours fade gradually? Yet by fading they actually introduce more light and punctuation, more vibrancy and stronger shifts of light, moving the atmosphere to a bolder one, still wild and natural at its heart.

But look what happens next. Gone is the dreamlike haze, and that, I assure you, is down to the fun and joy of those two primaries. Keith introduces them gently. The dark crimson-red daylily in foreground is *Hemerocallis* 'Sammy Russell', its golden yellow throat hinting at further introductions of yellow further up the garden.

Design: Keith Wiley

A

B

	NAME	TYPE	HEIGHT	SPREAD	SEASON	LIGHT	MOISTURE	HARDINESS	SOIL PH
A	*Hemerocallis* 'Azor'	perennial	0.5 metre, 1.5 feet	0.5 metre, 1.5 feet	summer / autumn	full sun / partial shade	moist but well-drained	hardy, USDA 3-10	acid / alkaline / neutral
B	*Crocosmia masoniorum* 'Rowallane Yellow'	perennial	1-1.5 metre, 3-4 feet	0.1-0.5 metre, 1.5 feet	summer	partial shade	moist but well-drained	hardy, USDA 5-9	acid / alkaline / neutral

This deep red paves the way for the brighter, bolder, scarlet *Crocosmia* 'Emberglow' in the distance. Red can definitely be tricky in a wilder scheme, and the gentle gradation in tone here demonstrates the perfect way to introduce a colour, without shoving it down our throats.

The same happens with the pool of yellow from *Crocosmia masoniorum* 'Rowallane Yellow'. Again, it is prefaced, this time with *Hemerocallis* 'Azor'.

Keith could so easily have gone for swathes and bands of crocosmia here—he's the first to confess that when he sees a stock bed full of crocosmia, he wants a mass planting of it. But he has held back, steered clear of the hot border, and instead splattered the paint in the most controlled of ways to create the most uncontrived of schemes. This planting will never date.

	NAME	TYPE	HEIGHT	SPREAD	SEASON	LIGHT	MOISTURE	HARDINESS	SOIL PH
C	*Hemerocallis* 'Sammy Russell'	perennial	0.5-1 metre, 2.5 feet	0.5-1 metre, 2.5 feet	summer	full sun / partial shade	moist but well-drained	hardy, USDA 3-9	acid / alkaline / neutral
D	*Crocosmia* 'Emberglow'	perennial	0.5-1 metre, 2-3 feet	0.1 metre, 0.5-1 foot	summer	full sun / partial shade	moist but well-drained	hardy, USDA 5-9	acid / alkaline / neutral
E	*Persicaria alpina*	perennial	2 metres, 3-5 feet	1.5 metres, 3-4 feet	summer	full sun / partial shade	well-drained	hardy, USDA 4-9	acid / alkaline / neutral
F	*Eragrostis curvula*	grass	1-1.5 metres, 3-4 feet	0.5-1 metre, 3 feet	summer	full sun	moist but well-drained / well-drained	half hardy, USDA 6-9	acid / alkaline / neutral

– 85 –

When You Say Winter Colour . . .

Figuring out winter colour is something we should do a lot more of: year-round colour is a frequent request, and those requesting it are often told by the well-meaning plantsperson that there is no such thing. But of course there is a sense in which year-round colour does exist: simply because the colours hover around the orange and buff areas doesn't mean that they don't count. We just need to think and to look a bit harder.

Back at RHS Hyde Hall, this area of the Winter Garden stands out for pops of colour at a time when colour is in short supply. *Salix alba* var. *vitellina* 'Yelverton' deservedly takes a lot of the credit here as its red-orange stems positively glow, a reminder that however pleasing the willows might be when in leaf, they save their best party trick for a time when nothing can beat them for sheer fabulousness. This tree is often grown as it appears here, as a multi-stemmed shrub. Naked in snow, it creates a fiery glow. A stand of this salix is astounding in winter.

The light catches the salix and the new red stems of the cornus, creating a triangle of structural orange and red. The more we think about this, the more extraordinary

Design: RHS Hyde Hall

it is, as these oranges and red are not present during the summer months. We're provided with two completely different effects, green background in the summer, and a complete colour extravaganza in winter.

There's an even cleverer bit now. Good green foliage of *Molinia caerulea* subsp. *caerulea* 'Edith Dudszus' has given way to lovely autumn shades; the dark purple flower stems have faded to brown, and the flowers are straw in the light. This buff-straw fades into the paler fountains of *Calamagrostis brachytricha*, and the mid-ground between the two—we could call it tan, pale brown, or gold—comes from the chunky heads of *Hylotelephium* Herbstfreude Group, while *Anaphalis triplinervis* 'Sommerschnee' wiggles through all, unifying nicely.

It seems strange to be enthusing so much about brown, a colour which the colour psychologists say can lead to feelings of heaviness. The converse is that it brings with it the idea of cosiness: I'd say it's the feeling of being enveloped in a warm winter coat, reliable every year for keeping out what winter wants to throw at me. In the winter garden, these buffs, beiges, tans—all shades and variations on the theme of brown—are indeed colours. So maybe there is such a thing as year-round colour; we just need to shift our perception of what constitutes a colour.

	NAME	TYPE	HEIGHT	SPREAD	SEASON	LIGHT	MOISTURE	HARDINESS	SOIL PH
A	*Anaphalis triplinervis* 'Sommerschnee'	perennial	0.1-0.5 metre, 1.5-2 feet	0.1-0.5 metre, 0.75-1.5 feet	summer	full sun / partial shade	moist but well-drained	very hardy, USDA 3-9	acid / alkaline / neutral
B	*Hylotelephium* Herbstfreude Group	succulent perennial	0.5-1 metre, 1.5-2 feet	0.5-1 metre, 1.5-2 feet	summer / autumn	full sun	well-drained	very hardy, USDA 3-9	alkaline / neutral
C	*Calamagrostis brachytricha*	grass	1-1.5 metres, 3-4 feet	0.5-1 metre, 2-3 feet	summer / autumn	full sun / partial shade	moist but well-drained / well-drained	very hardy, USDA 4-9	acid / alkaline / neutral
D	*Molinia caerulea* subsp. *caerulea* 'Edith Dudszus'	grass	0.1-0.5 metre, 2-2.5 feet	0.1-0.5 metre, 2-2.5 feet	summer / autumn	full sun / partial shade	moist but well-drained / well-drained	very hardy, USDA 4-8	acid / neutral
E	*Salix alba* var. *vitellina* 'Yelverton'	tree	> 12 metres, to 70 feet	> 8 metres, to 50 feet	spring / winter	full sun / partial shade	moist but well-drained / well-drained	very hardy, USDA 2-9	acid / alkaline / neutral

-86-

Brown Light

In *Colour in Turner*, John Gage explains how the artist drew on literary, poetic, and other cultural themes in his work. One of Turner's sources, Edward Hussey Delaval, suggested that the production of colours in plants was analogous to the procedure of the watercolourist: it functioned "by the transmission of light from a white ground through a transparent coloured medium." By focusing on mixing red, yellow, and blue, Turner—who believed that all the colours of the natural world could be subsumed under these three primaries—"resisted the conclusion that colour is simply a function of the action of light on surfaces."

Right | Design: RHS Hyde Hall
Below | Joseph Mallord William Turner, *Light and Colour (Goethe's Theory)—the Morning after the Deluge—Moses Writing the Book of Genesis*, exhibited 1843

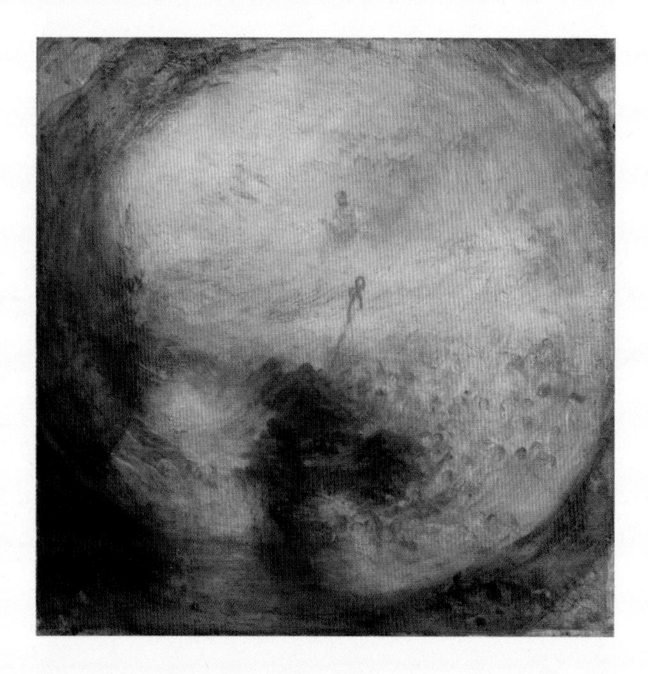

	NAME	TYPE	HEIGHT	SPREAD	SEASON	LIGHT	MOISTURE	HARDINESS	SOIL PH
A	*Viburnum ×burkwoodii* 'Park Farm Hybrid'	shrub	1.5-2.5 metres, 8-10 feet	1.5-2.5 metres, 6-7 feet	spring / autumn	full sun / partial shade / full shade	moist but well-drained / well-drained	very hardy, USDA 4-8	acid / alkaline / neutral
B	*Miscanthus sinensis* 'Graziella'	grass	1.-1.5 metres, 5-6 feet	1-1.5 metres, 3-4 feet	autumn / winter	full sun / partial shade	moist but well-drained / well-drained	hardy, USDA 5-9	acid / alkaline / neutral
C	*Miscanthus ×giganteus*	grass	3-4 metres, 10-12 feet	1 metre, 3 feet	autumn / winter	full sun	moist but well-drained / well-drained	hardy, USDA 4-9	acid / alkaline / neutral
D	*Malus tschonoskii*	tree	8-12 metres, to 40 feet	4-8 metres, 12-15 feet	spring / autumn	full sun / partial shade	moist but well-drained / well-drained	very hardy, USDA 6-8	acid / alkaline / neutral

Why this long preamble? It's all to do with brown, a shade rather than a hue, certainly not contained within the prismatic colours, nor in Newton's handy seven colours of the spectrum. It's the colour of death and decay, of earth and worse, with all the cultural connotations which come with that. And so for some, the idea of leaving plants to decline and die, above expanses of bare soil, might just be a step too far.

In defence of brown I present Clover Hill at RHS Hyde Hall in the December light. The ghostly winter silhouettes show the skeleton of this planting clearly, and its many considered components make it a colourist's dream. Buff-straw *Stipa tenuissima* is pale against the orange-brown bands of *Miscanthus sinensis* 'Graziella' and *M.* ×*giganteus*; dark brown comes from the trunks of leafless ghostly *Platanus* ×*hispanica* and *Malus tschonoskii* with *Viburnum* ×*burkwoodii* 'Park Farm Hybrid' beneath. There is actually a vast range of colours here; it's all too easy to dismiss them as brown.

Standing for a while, we realise that the palette is filled with shades and tones of yellow, brown, red, black. Imagine these colours in a summer planting: the combination of multiple flower forms with a saturation of colours would create a very different effect, with more to tempt the eye and attention in different directions. In this winter garden, there's no real distraction. The forms are nearly all vertical, the saturation is low—and so it is the light, shining both onto and through the plants, that creates perceived colours and shadows in a season supposedly devoid of colour interest.

- 87 -

Fade to Grey

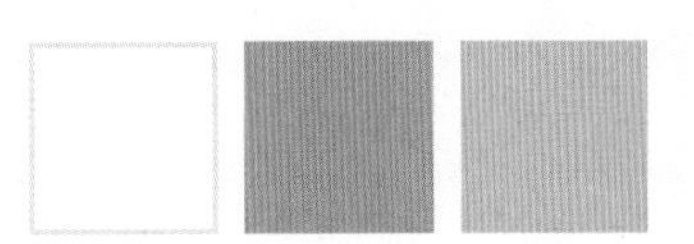

There are plenty of words for brown: tan, camel, ash, coffee, toffee, chestnut, chocolate, taupe, clay, wenge, umber, liver. All are incredibly effective in the winter garden. While more and more plants are being bred for fashionably brown flowers, it's in a planting's decline that this range of colours can play a starring role.

Careful planning and good maintenance are a must here, as dead plants by their very nature will break or flop in winter wind and sogginess. Here at Hyde Hall, the RHS gardeners give this border the very best tender loving care, creating a winter display which is a celebration of neutrals, weaving through beige and cream and brown. Tasteful and wistful at the same time, the tans and browns more than tolerate each other, giving a suggestion of past summer glory yet continuing to hang on to optimism.

Achillea 'Terracotta' is a negative of colour here; its grey-tinged brown would disappear were it not for its umbels catching the light. The orange of the flowers has gone, yet the grey-brown seems a good enough substitute—I would far rather have this grey suggestion of a plant past than nothing at all. Bold swathes of *Sesleria autumnalis*, bright green-yellow earlier on, form tufty straw-coloured bands, merging into *Anaphalis triplinervis* 'Sommerschnee', which still hangs on to its papery, ghostly white flowers. This palette of subdued hues, created by time, is evocative of Georges Braque's ochres and umbers; the dark spaces bring to mind the dark tones he used to throw his subject into the foreground—Mother Nature's chiaroscuro.

To get the best winter interest from a planting of ornamental grasses, it's a question of location, location, location. The skeletons of the leaves and flowers need to be able to catch the light in order for them to have any impact, to create the golds and the browns, the colours of decline, that are displayed here so simply and effectively.

	NAME	TYPE	HEIGHT	SPREAD	SEASON	LIGHT	MOISTURE	HARDINESS	SOIL PH
A	*Anaphalis triplinervis* 'Sommerschnee'	perennial	0.1-0.5 metre, 1.5-2 feet	0.1-0.5 metre, 0.75-1.5 feet	summer	full sun / partial shade	moist but well-drained	very hardy, USDA 3-9	acid / alkaline / neutral
B	*Achillea* 'Terracotta'	perennial	1-1.5 metres, 2.5-3 feet	0.1-0.5 metre, 2-2.5 feet	summer / autumn	full sun	moist but well-drained / well-drained	very hardy, USDA 3-8	acid / alkaline / neutral
C	*Sesleria autumnalis*	grass	0.1-0.5 metre, 0.75-1 foot	0.1-0.5 metre, 0.5-1 foot	summer	full sun / partial shade	moist but well-drained / well-drained	very hardy, USDA 5-8	alkaline / neutral

Opposite | Design: RHS Hyde Hall

– 88 –

What a Difference a Day Makes

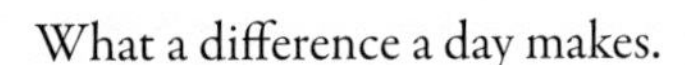

What a difference a day makes.

If you've ever taken a walk just after the skies have dumped a massive load of snow, you'll know how your landmarks vanish. That dip further along the road? Gone. The house with the clay tile roof? No longer visible. As well as wiping away man-made black roads and uneven lawns in various shades of murky green and winter brown, snow blurs shadows, and its whiteness renders all uniform. Anything vertical is somehow drained of the range of its day-to-day colour, all hues magically becoming tightly knit and monochromatic.

You have to be startling to stand out in snow. It's the reason why Father Christmas looks so good in scarlet, I reckon. He just wouldn't have had the same effect in navy blue. Here in the Winter Walk at RHS Hyde Hall, *Cornus sanguinea* 'Midwinter Fire' flickers orange and red, already looking properly campfire-y on a winter's day, but when the snow falls—well, the transformation is complete. All mundane elements are erased: the path and the bare brown soil disappear, as do the surrounding masses of surface green. All are blanketed in white, and we're left with only verticals to show us the way.

This is the job that a massed planting of cornus was born to do. Unexciting when in leaf, boy do dogwoods justify their existence in any garden come wintertime. The monochromes of nearby trees fade and crack black and brown, while oranges, reds, and the merest suggestion of lime all come through the dogwoods' stems, standing out against the absence of colour which would, without these sparks, appear eerie. No ghostliness here, though. Just *oohs* and *aahs* at the winter magic.

Opposite | Design: RHS Hyde Hall

	NAME	TYPE	HEIGHT	SPREAD	SEASON	LIGHT	MOISTURE	HARDINESS	SOIL PH
A	*Cornus sanguinea* 'Midwinter Fire'	shrub	1.5-2.5 metres, 5-6 feet	1.5-2.5 metres, 5-6 feet	autumn / winter	full sun / partial shade	moist but well-drained / well-drained	very hardy, USDA 5-7	acid / alkaline / neutral

Inspiration from RHS Partner Garden Bodnant, Conwy

The Winter Garden at Bodnant sparkles with colour provided by some great plants easily grown at home:

1 Structural conifers

In this view there are three key conifers: *Taxus baccata* 'Fastigiata' forms a bold green column in the centre; beneath is gold-tinged *Pinus mugo* 'Winter Gold'. A mature *Chamaecyparis lawsoniana* dominates the top left of the scene.

2 Fiery stems aglow

A central group of *Cornus sanguinea* 'Midwinter Fire' sizzles beside purple evergreen *Pittosporum tenuifolium* 'Tom Thumb'. In the foreground, red-stemmed *Cornus alba* 'Sibirica' adds further colour and drama.

3 Clumps of miscanthus

Repeated through the garden and contrasting in colour and form with the surrounding planting, the standing stems and seedheads of *Miscanthus sinensis* 'Sarabande' continue to provide interest into the new year.

- 89 -

Beauty

Less is more, and as far as colour goes, nowhere is this maxim more evident, to my mind, than in this exquisite arrangement of colours by Arne Maynard at Allt y bela, his home in Monmouthshire, South Wales. The house dates to the sixteenth century; its garden is a masterclass in how nuances of history, memory, and romance can all be tapped on the shoulder and be present in the atmosphere as well as the reality.

There are only three species here. Yet how many shades and tones do you see? The imprimatura is the peachy coral of the house walls: the paint colour creates a base layer, which allows the colours to register in a way that differs from how we might normally perceive them. I look at this and see textures and patterns of rich fabrics: if we were to squint and imagine instead that the walls were of white paint, or red brick, the effect would be completely different.

There's a skeleton to this planting, a structural base against the coral, in a hundred shades of green into black: we know that the topiary domes and towers of *Buxus sempervirens* are green because as we learn, we codify: we know that buxus is a foliage plant and that its leaves are green, and so whenever we view it, whatever the light, this evergreen is ever green to us, even if the light and shadows

Design: Arne Maynard

A

B

C

	NAME	TYPE	HEIGHT	SPREAD	SEASON	LIGHT	MOISTURE	HARDINESS	SOIL PH
A	*Digitalis parviflora*	perennial	0.5-1 metre, 3 feet	0.1-0.5 metre, 2 feet	summer	full sun / partial shade / full shade	moist but well-drained / poorly drained	half hardy, USDA 4-8	acid / alkaline / neutral
B	*Rosa* 'Cardinal de Richelieu'	shrub	0.5-1 metre, 1-3 feet	1-2 metres, 3-6 feet	summer	full sun	moist but well-drained / well-drained	very hardy, USDA 3-9	acid / alkaline / neutral
C	*Buxus sempervirens*	shrub	2.5-4 metres, 5-15 feet	4-8 metres, 5-15 feet	evergreen	partial shade / full shade	well-drained	very hardy, USDA 5-8	acid / neutral

suggest other colours. The overlooked blacks of empty space between the leaves are equally vital here in creating the ripples of colour and the sense of texture and depth.

The smallest amount of blue in the domes of rose foliage is just enough blue for the downy leaves of *Digitalis parviflora* to make a vertical contrast of form yet only the slightest gradation in colour. The tightly packed copper-chocolate flowers appear to give out some red when viewed in proximity to the rose; stand back and we can see how, against the walls, their orange pushes through.

Looking again and again at these colours, I find that purple isn't a satisfactory enough term for me to log the rose colour, and after days of going down metaphorical rabbit holes, I find myself in a glossary of sixteenth-century paint colours. I'm happy to stop somewhere between hiacintho (jacinth), which related to purple, and deep red-murrey for the velvety flowers of *Rosa* 'Cardinal de Richelieu', which here embroider hazel domes. The romance of the word gives a backstory to the colour.

– 90 –

Gentle

The palettes in the gardens we've seen thus far range from bright to muted, light to dark, monochromatic to packed full of colour. In a book about creating harmonious schemes in the garden, I couldn't not include this image of a wilder area at Arne Maynard's Allt y bela. It displays colour in its simplest form: the light shines through and influences our mood. It's a spot under trees illuminated by the open meadow beyond; the greens are darker in shadow and yellow in the background, and it is this yellow I want to focus on here.

We've already looked at colours being colours by dint of the words we assign them, and again here, grass, though we "know" it to be green, isn't actually very green in an important chunk of this image. It lies gamboge and straw yellow in the light, and this light is the cue for the subtleties that come in the foreground.

Fading narcissi have handed the lead over to little puffs of pale sunlit oxlips, which create small patches of light in preparation for the golden flushes at the base of the petals of *Tulipa orphanidea* (Whittallii Group) 'Major'. This tulip is invariably described in terms of its main colour—orange—but it is the blood-red base that makes the impact here. Appearing a deeper red in the shadows, this rare yet easy little tulip is more copper-orange depending on the amount of light upon it.

Just the lightest scattering of red and yellow against green is all it takes to create an atmosphere that is simultaneously gentle and uplifting. The calmness of the green is more than sufficient as a base for the intervention, here and there, of the reds and yellows—so much more effective than filling the space with a huge scoop of wildflowers in a rainbow of shades.

Design: Arne Maynard

	NAME	TYPE	HEIGHT	SPREAD	SEASON	LIGHT	MOISTURE	HARDINESS	SOIL PH
A	*Tulipa orphanidea* (Whittallii Group) 'Major'	bulb	0.1-0.5 metre, 1 foot	to 0.1 metre, 0.25 foot	spring	full sun	well-drained	very hardy, USDA 5-8	acid / alkaline / neutral
B	*Primula elatior*	perennial	0.1-0.5 metre, 0.75-1 foot	0.1-0.5 metre, 1-1.5 feet	spring	full sun / partial shade	moist but well-drained	very hardy, USDA 4-8	acid / alkaline / neutral

- 91 -

Lemon Drops

Defining colour is never an easy task and, according to historian Michel Pastoureau, defining yellow is even harder. The history of yellow is the history of gold. The bold primary brings with it associations of wealth, riches, brashness, and brave statements. Yet throw some white into the yellow, and you make instead a delicious butter, the softest hue—cheerful, gentle, and generally pleasant, with none of the intensity of its sometimes garish parent.

Optimism and happiness sunshine out of these two palettes, both of which are at Brookergarden, in the Netherlands. The bright tones in the twisty petals of *Tulipa* 'West Point' say all there is to say about yellow in its unaltered form: it is yellow and that's all there is to it.

But look how gentle this palette is: the soft creams of the double-flowered *Tulipa* 'Verona' and the ivory of *T.* 'City of Vancouver' are annexed by the buttercup yellow flames of *T.* 'Flaming Coquette'. Any garishness completely disappears, and we have a feeling of white, whatever white may be, although the shades are all softer than a bright white. If you look closely, you'll see there is no white at all, apart from the petal tips of *T.* 'Flaming Coquette'. *Narcissus* 'Dutch Lemon Drops' does exactly this, scattering drops of citrus through the freshness.

Moving further along (and not overlooking the importance of the foliage providing a neutral, which is darker in our memory than in actuality), all becomes even calmer, and bright yellow gives way to butter. *Tulipa* 'Verona' continues as the link, with *T.* 'Françoise', a taller version of the same ivory, alongside *T.* 'Ivory Floradale'. *Tulipa* 'Maja' supplies the yellow here, butter and primrose in the petals reminding us of *T.* 'West Point', but in a very subtle way. Bells of another flower again provide a contrast: this time it's *Fritillaria persica* 'Ivory Bells', its green and cream bells taking on the job of sprinkling lime green amongst the ivories and yellows. Artist Liane Collot d'Herbois describes this progression, this greening of light, in a way that I cannot beat, writing of the "light piercing the yellow-green, forming a long rhythm of small veils, a loose mosaic continually being stilled."

It's clear here that this was no random collection from the tulip catalogues: careful gradation creates two slightly different atmospheres, one with a hint of energy, the other moving to calm spring renewal.

Design: Loek and Anne-Marie Gubbels

	NAME	TYPE	HEIGHT	SPREAD	SEASON	LIGHT	MOISTURE	HARDINESS	SOIL PH
A	*Narcissus* 'Dutch Lemon Drops'	bulb	0.1-0.5 metre, 0.75-1 foot	0.1 metre, 0.5-0.75 foot	spring	full sun / partial shade	moist but well-drained / well-drained	very hardy, USDA 4-8	acid / alkaline / neutral
B	*Fritillaria persica* 'Ivory Bells'	bulb	0.5-1 metre, 2-3 feet	0.1 metre, 0.5 foot	spring	full sun	well-drained	hardy, USDA 4-7	acid / alkaline / neutral
C	*Tulipa* 'West Point'	bulb	0.1-0.5 metre, 1-2 feet	0.1 metre, 0.25 foot	spring	full sun	well-drained	very hardy, USDA 3-8	acid / alkaline / neutral

	NAME	TYPE	HEIGHT	SPREAD	SEASON	LIGHT	MOISTURE	HARDINESS	SOIL PH
D	*Tulipa* 'Verona'	bulb	0.1-0.5 metre, 0.75-1 foot	0.1 metre, 0.25 foot	spring	full sun	well-drained	very hardy, USDA 3-8	acid / alkaline / neutral
E	*Tulipa* 'City of Vancouver'	bulb	0.5-0.6 metre, 1.5-2 feet	0.1 metre, 0.5 foot	spring	full sun	well-drained	very hardy, USDA 3-8	acid / alkaline / neutral
F	*Tulipa* 'Flaming Coquette'	bulb	0.3-0.4 metre, 1-1.5 feet	0.1 metre, 0.25 foot	spring	full sun	well-drained	very hardy, USDA 3-8	acid / alkaline / neutral
G	*Tulipa* 'Françoise'	bulb	0.6 metre, 2 feet	0.1 metre, 0.25 foot	spring	full sun	well-drained	very hardy, USDA 3-8	acid / alkaline / neutral
H	*Tulipa* 'Ivory Floradale'	bulb	0.5-1 metre, 1-2 feet	0.1 metre, 0.25 foot	spring	full sun	well-drained	hardy, USDA 3-8	acid / alkaline / neutral
I	*Tulipa* 'Maja'	bulb	0.4 metre, 1.5 feet	0.1 metre, 0.25 foot	spring	full sun / partial shade	well-drained	hardy, USDA 3-8	acid / alkaline / neutral

- 92 -

Let There Be Yellow

How wonderful is this combination from RHS Rosemoor? Yellow reigns gloriously, the sulphur yellow of the red hot pokers shining and illuminating all. A heart-stopping mix of shades of yellow and blue, I almost want to jump into this photograph and let the sunshine envelop me. How could someone say that they don't like yellow? Just as in paintings, the yellow leads our eye and almost calls us in.

While I say we have moved beyond Newton's colour wheel, I am not saying that it doesn't have merit. It may not be the basis for many of my observations in this book, but that doesn't mean I can't see some of its uses. It's more that I worry that it leads to elementary pairings that omit the shades between. Orange and purple are a good example of this: on their own, these two colours "go," they are secondary colours formed from mixing two primaries. On the colour wheel, such complementary colours, as they are known, sit opposite each other. It's often thought that "complementary" signifies that two colours look good together, but the intention was to indicate that each colour intensifies the effect of the other.

Hence a contrast is created, but a contrast which often leaves us with the feeling that it's too basic a pairing,

Design: RHS Rosemoor

A

B

C

	NAME	TYPE	HEIGHT	SPREAD	SEASON	LIGHT	MOISTURE	HARDINESS	SOIL PH
A	*Rudbeckia laciniata* 'Herbstsonne'	perennial	1.2-2.1 metres, 4-7 feet	0.6-0.9 metre, 2-3 feet	summer	full sun	moist but well-drained	hardy, USDA 5-9	acid / alkaline / neutral
B	*Rudbeckia fulgida* var. *sullivantii* 'Goldsturm'	perennial	0.5-1 metre, 2-3 feet	0.1-0.5 metre, 1-2 feet	summer / autumn	full sun / partial shade	moist but well-drained	hardy, USDA 3-9	acid / alkaline / neutral
C	*Kniphofia* 'Bees' Lemon'	perennial	0.5-1 metre, 2-3 feet	0.5-1 metre, 1.5-2 feet	summer	full sun	moist but well-drained	hardy, USDA 6-9	acid / neutral

creating too much visual vibration when they are at their most saturated. This isn't to say that this is wrong—it just needs more. Something else. A bit of yellow, more tones and shades of orange; take the blue from the purple and investigate violet.

That's what happens here. *Lobelia ×speciosa* 'Hadspen Purple' softens into the lilac-blue of *Monarda didyma* 'Purple Lace' which in turn goes slightly more deeply and pinkly into *Eutrochium maculatum* (Atropurpureum Group) 'Purple Bush'. Selections of *Crocosmia ×crocosmiiflora* ('Columbus', 'Star of the East', and 'Polo') dabble shades of orange and move the whole scheme beyond a collection of the complementary, making the garden shine in the perfection of plant partnerships. Van Gogh was right: certain colours "complete each other like man and wife."

Inspiration from RHS Garden Hyde Hall

Curator Robert Brett describes impressive autumn planting in Essex as it looks in October:

1 Pokers are still hot

Enjoying the open, sunny, and freely draining conditions on Clover Hill, clumps of *Kniphofia rooperi* with their rounded heads of orange and yellow tubular flowers prolong summer's floral heat, backed partially by the shimmering autumn awns of *Stipa gigantea*.

2 Ribbon of red

Drought resistant, easy to grow, and loved by pollinators, *Hylotelephium* (Herbstfreude Group) 'Herbstfreude' is also one of the best late-flowering perennials; its seedheads last well into winter if allowed to stand.

3 Woody backdrop

Coppiced *Salix alba* var. *vitellina* forms a dome of green foliage and, after leaf fall, its yellow stems will shine and sparkle through winter. Behind it stands lofty *Fraxinus excelsior* 'Aurea', its golden leaves catching the autumn sun.

– 93 –

A Mystical Arrangement of Red and Yellow

Some people can be a tiny bit frightened at the prospect of choosing plants to create a hot planting; although they love the effect, it might just be a step too far in their own garden. But deconstruct this fiery planting, take elements from it, and we can still create a planting with eye-catching colours, just perhaps not quite so many of them.

In the Herb Garden at RHS Rosemoor, the extraordinary flowerheads of *Monarda* 'Gardenview Scarlet' seem to burst and pop, their straggly starry shape somehow enhancing this fizz of colour. We might see red, but look again, look closely, and the red is anything but red, certainly not Rosso Corsa or even that scarlet of Mary Queen of Scots' undergown on the day of her execution. This is a strong red but with a dash of something that might be yellow, just a touch, enough to bring the effect down to something just below dazzling, a shade which allows the eye to stop, to pause for a while and enjoy this extremely satsifying colour.

Design: RHS Rosemoor

	NAME	TYPE	HEIGHT	SPREAD	SEASON	LIGHT	MOISTURE	HARDINESS	SOIL PH
A	*Achillea ptarmica* (The Pearl Group) 'The Pearl'	perennial	0.5-1 metre, 1.5-2 feet	0.5-1 metre, 1.5-2 feet	summer	partial shade	moist but well-drained	very hardy, USDA 3-9	acid / alkaline / neutral
B	*Achillea filipendulina* 'Gold Plate'	perennial	1-1.5 metres, 4-5 feet	0.5-1 metre, 2.5-3 feet	summer / autumn	full sun	moist but well-drained / well-drained	very hardy, USDA 3-8	acid / alkaline / neutral
C	*Monarda* 'Gardenview Scarlet'	perennial	0.5-1 metre, 2-3 feet	0.1-0.5 metre, 1-2 feet	summer / autumn	full sun / partial shade	moist but well-drained	very hardy, USDA 4-9	acid / alkaline / neutral

It's this dash of yellow that makes *Achillea filipendulina* 'Gold Plate' such a successful companion to the monarda. The flat plates of the achillea's flowers are, of course, an excellent contrast in form, but there's a hint of mustard in their yellow, which moves it along from eye-popping yellow to the steadier golden end of the yellow range.

We have yellow and we have red, and green is the complementary colour here, a maximal contrast of red and green reminiscent of religious art in various traditions. Soft red and gold and green, the prime complementaries, contrast strongly and fit neatly in handy colour wheels.

But there is a quiet presence here—let us turn to the shy blue. By now we know that we pick the colour and then select a shade more muted in the same range. Here the just-perceptible blue of the agastache is so dainty and so perfect. Imagine in its place the much more obvious blue of the delphinium visible in the distance and you realise it would be too much; it would demand attention and take away the monarda's glory—we wouldn't want that. Instead, the pale purple-blue against fresh green foliage and the splatters of pure white—courtesy of the loose double flowers of *Achillea ptarmica* (The Pearl Group) 'The Pearl'—are exactly what we need.

– 94 –

Zing

Exuberance and restraint in one garden. This may sound like a contradiction, but you really can create a happy, jolly atmosphere while at the same time exercising an element of control. I designed this garden for a children's hospice—after talking to those who were going to use the garden and listening to what they wanted in terms of colour. The children asked for happy yellows, bright oranges and reds and blues, a mix that had a clear underlying sense of lightness and brightness. The key is to give these colours a bright-enough green to stand against and to fold the flowering plants into a manageable tapestry, so that the playful atmosphere inspires but never overwhelms. The fluorescent backdrop here, formed by the textured foliage of *Foeniculum vulgare* and *Tanacetum vulgare* 'Isla Gold', is the feature which allowed the children's wishlist to work. The yellow in their acid green foliage is highlighted by *Mathiasella bupleuroides* 'Green Dream'.

In line with the requested bright colours, going along the track of primary colours but just shifting the tone along a little, the deep red *Paeonia* 'Buckeye Belle' and rich blue *Iris* 'Titan's Glory' give us our notion of primaries. *Geum* 'Totally Tangerine', a brilliantly acceptable orange for those who find bright orange a bit too much, snuggles into the foliage, creating muted highlights. The dusky pinks of *Verbascum* 'Cherry Helen' add something a little different, its own tones picked up by the raspberry pinks of the aquilegias in the foreground.

There's a zing and a fizz to these colours that could dash around all over the place—and this is where the element of control comes in. The darkness of the stems of *Salvia nemorosa* 'Caradonna' is a calming element, providing a vertical contrast, its shadowy black lines slicing up the lime green fluffiness. Dark purple-black irises take up the darkness but also shine out their blues—how these flowers project the two sensations is extraordinary. Magical light from nowhere and everywhere.

Design: Jo Thompson

	NAME	TYPE	HEIGHT	SPREAD	SEASON	LIGHT	MOISTURE	HARDINESS	SOIL PH
A	*Verbascum* 'Cherry Helen'	perennial	1-1.5 metres, 3-4.5 feet	0.1-0.5 metre, 1-1.5 feet	summer	full sun	well-drained	very hardy, USDA 5-9	alkaline / neutral
B	*Paeonia* 'Buckeye Belle'	perennial	0.5-1 metre, 1.5-2 feet	0.5-1 metre, 2-3 feet	spring / summer	full sun / partial shade	moist but well-drained	very hardy, USDA 4-8	acid / alkaline / neutral
C	*Iris* 'Titan's Glory'	perennial	0.5-1 metre, 3 feet	0.1-0.5 metre, 2 feet	summer	full sun	well-drained	very hardy, USDA 4-9	acid / neutral
D	*Geum* 'Totally Tangerine'	perennial	0.5-1 metre, 1-2.5 feet	0.1-0.5 metre, 0.75-1.5 feet	spring / summer / autumn	full sun	moist but well-drained / well-drained	very hardy, USDA 5-7	acid / alkaline / neutral
E	*Foeniculum vulgare*	biennial or short-lived perennial	1.5-2.5 metres, 3-5 feet	0.5-1 metre, 2-3 feet	spring / summer	full sun / partial shade	moist but well-drained	very hardy, USDA 4-9	acid / alkaline / neutral

- 95 -

Divisionism—in Horticultural Terms

There's something inherently pleasing about this colour scheme, which brings to my mind the divisionist paintings of Paul Signac, who banished all "earthy" colours from his work. Good light helps, of course: here from behind it captures the white flowers of *Phlox maculata* 'Natascha', which means that the flowers' starry lavender-pink centres are what reach us first.

This clear pink with a touch of blue has very definite romantic connotations. There's something about this colour which makes us downright happy. The first pink roses that bloom, the first little geranium flowers that pop out: why are they all so pleasing? We want more, more and more—who knows, if I'd planted this border, I might have carried on with another band of this phlox, and another, and another. It's a good thing, then, that I wasn't left in charge of it. Here, less is very definitely more. Too much pink would have been too romantic, too fragile.

It's time again for some variegation love. I've said it once and I'll say it again: don't dismiss variegated anythings,

Design: Elke Borkowski

unless there's a good reason for it. A leaf with a green-light combination brings exactly that, light, to dark or otherwise boring, unimportant spots. Here, light is brought by the plants themselves: it arrives and is held by *Cornus florida* 'Daybreak' and the papery-white flowers and cream-splotched, fading-to-green leaves of *Astrantia major* 'Sunningdale Variegated'.

Obvious combinations have been avoided; no blues or lilacs here. Instead, there's the sturdy neutral *Acanthus mollis* (Latifolius Group) 'Rue Ledan', the tones of its silver-green stems and white flowers consumed and muted by its architectural form. At the foot of the phlox is the unlikeliest of planting partners: *Hylotelephium* 'Matrona'. Somehow this sedum works here: again, the purple-red tints of its leaves and its pink flowers blur into a neutral, the perfect understorey for the masterstroke in this palette.

This masterstroke is the use of *Hemerocallis* 'Lavender Deal'. What a beauty. The lavender-blue flowers with throats of chartreuse are stunning. No further exaltation necessary—just look at the effect in the photo. Look at the flower by itself, now close your eyes. Open your eyes and look at it in conjunction with the pink; close your eyes again and try to describe that colour. Something very strange is going on. Placed next to pink, the daylily's lavender tones shift to purple, mauve, pink.

Signac realised that to capture the violets, the colours of light and air, the focus needed to be on creating, not portraying, light. By what he called "a methodical divisionism," by eliminating all "muddy mixtures," he believed that he and other Neo-Impressionists could finally achieve what had never yet been obtained: "a maximum of luminosity." Which is just what this garden has, horticulturally speaking.

	NAME	TYPE	HEIGHT	SPREAD	SEASON	LIGHT	MOISTURE	HARDINESS	SOIL PH
A	*Cornus florida* 'Daybreak'	tree	4.5-9 metres, 15-30 feet	4.5-9 metres, 15-30 feet	spring	full sun / partial shade	moist but well-drained	half hardy, USDA 5-9	acid / neutral
B	*Acanthus mollis* (Latifolius Group) 'Rue Ledan'	perennial	1.5 metres, 3-4 feet	0.9 metre, 2-2.5 feet	summer	full sun / partial shade	well-drained	very hardy, USDA 7-10	acid / alkaline / neutral
C	*Astrantia major* 'Sunningdale Variegated'	perennial	0.5-1 metre, 1-2 feet	0.1-0.5 metre, 0.75-1.5 feet	summer	full sun	moist but well-drained / poorly drained	very hardy, USDA 4-7	acid / alkaline / neutral
D	*Hemerocallis* 'Lavender Deal'	perennial	0.5-0.6 metre, 1.5-2 feet	0.5-0.6 metre, 1.5-2 feet	summer	full sun / partial shade	moist but well-drained	very hardy, USDA 3-9	acid / alkaline / neutral
E	*Phlox maculata* 'Natascha'	perennial	0.5-1 metre, 1.5-2 feet	0.1-0.5 metre, 1-1.5 feet	summer	full sun / partial shade	moist but well-drained	very hardy, USDA 3-8	acid / alkaline / neutral
F	*Hylotelephium* 'Matrona'	succulent perennial	0.5-1 metre, 2-2.5 feet	0.1-0.5 metre, 1.5-2 feet	summer / autumn	full sun	well-drained	very hardy, USDA 3-9	alkaline / neutral

- 96 -

Romance

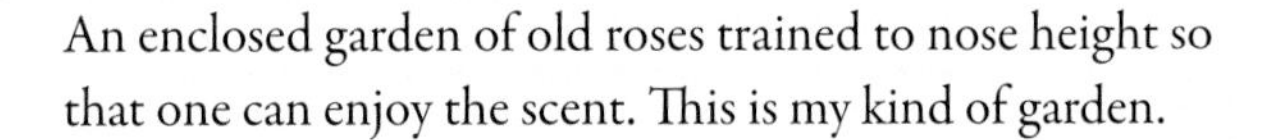

An enclosed garden of old roses trained to nose height so that one can enjoy the scent. This is my kind of garden.

As we walk through an arbour covered in white roses, we are greeted by the sound of a William Pye water feature. The sound of the water mingles with the scent of the roses, all known in the eighteenth and nineteenth centuries, all with romantic names, all with glorious, fragrant blooms.

White grabs the attention: when we work with this, we get the best results. A clever way of using white is to keep it high—white height, in fact. Here at Clinton Lodge, the fading-to-white flowers of *Rosa* 'The Garland' start off cream-blush, a neat link to the pink old roses in the borders. As they get paler, the flowers shift their linking power to the sky: all is pale above, with dark shadows of yew spanning out in perspective lines on either side.

Here's what we expect of a rose garden, with the blush of the roses matched gently by the lime of the inflorescences of *Alchemilla mollis* and the blue-violets of *Nepeta racemosa* 'Walker's Low'. The air colours of the nepeta are another link to that all-important sky above, while the pale green of the lady's mantle connects to the fresh, almost spring green of the summer grass beneath our feet.

Design: Clinton Lodge Gardens

So simple yet so clever and so effective. Remember this one and do it at home. Just because it's simple doesn't mean you need to try to better this palette. The soft pastels are so pleasing and easy on the eye; you want to stay in this secret garden forever and ever. You can almost touch the atmosphere of nostalgia; the senses are totally absorbed by the associations and connotations of this most familiar of colour schemes.

It would be easy to want more here, to shake up the colour a bit and introduce some contrasts. Tulip games would be fun, each year changing the scheme and indulging in some wild colour before the soft-to-bright pink of *Rosa* 'Impératrice Joséphine' and the rich warm pink of *R.* 'Madame Boll' (one of the better old garden roses, according to Peter Beales) have even suggested their arrival. Before *R.* ×*centifolia* 'Cristata' has started putting on its pure pink flowers, before the mid-pink scent-stuffed flowers of *R.* 'Ispahan' start to bloom. I'd love to know if these roses were chosen purely for the colours and scent, or whether their names also had a little something to do with it.

D

E

	NAME	TYPE	HEIGHT	SPREAD	SEASON	LIGHT	MOISTURE	HARDINESS	SOIL PH
A	*Rosa* 'Impératrice Joséphine'	perennial	1.2-1.5 metres, 4-5 feet	1.2-1.5 metres, 4-5 feet	spring / summer	full sun	moist but well-drained	very hardy, USDA 4-8	acid / alkaline / neutral
B	*Rosa* 'Madame Boll'	perennial	1.2-1.5 metres, 4-6 feet	1.2-1.5 metres, 4-6 feet	summer / autumn	full sun	moist but well-drained	very hardy, USDA 4-8	acid / alkaline / neutral
C	*Rosa ×centifolia* 'Cristata'	perennial	1-1.5 metres, 4-6 feet	1-1.5 metres, 4-6 feet	summer	full sun	moist but well-drained / well-drained	very hardy, USDA 4-8	acid / alkaline / neutral
D	*Nepeta racemosa* 'Walker's Low'	perennial	0.1-0.5 metre, 2-2.5 feet	0.1-0.5 metre, 2.5-3 feet	spring / summer	full sun / partial shade / full shade	well-drained	very hardy, USDA 4-8	acid / alkaline / neutral
E	*Alchemilla mollis*	perennial	0.1-0.5 metre, 1-1.5 feet	0.1-0.5 metre, 1.5-2.5 feet	summer / autumn	full sun / partial shade / full shade	moist but well-drained	very hardy, USDA 3-8	acid / alkaline / neutral

- 97 -

Pink

Sometimes a project comes along and you can't quite believe that you've been lucky enough to be entrusted with it. When the owners approached me to help them bring life back to the historic long double borders at their home in Kent, all I could think of was who and what had gone before.

The borders, neglected in previous years in the sense that everything had been allowed to grow and grow, were flanked on either side by specimen shrubs and trees, including *Magnolia campbellii* 'Betty Jessel', named after the wife of the creator of the garden. This truly outstanding yet still relatively little-known magnolia was in full, resplendent flower when I first visited, and on the spot I decided that its wonderful deep crimson to ruby colours would inform any new planting. This approach works in any garden, whatever its size, wherever its location. Whether it's a tree in the garden or a shrub in a neighbouring plot, there are always hints and clues as to what might be effective.

The brief was that the planting should be relevant to a young family but without losing the sense of tradition

Design: Jo Thompson

and history that these borders brought with them. Not wanting to throw the baby out with the bathwater, I undertook a detailed study of existing plants—and decided that not only could a couple of unruly berberis and euonymus stay if clipped into shape, they would in fact play a huge part in the new colour scheme of these sixty-metre-long borders. It was also vital that each border, whether north- or south-facing, should bear some relation to the other, and colour was important in achieving this: pale pinks and deep reds at the beginning of the border walk fade into whites and fresh greens as you make your way to the shaded seating area at the end.

Rosa Mary Rose = 'Ausmary' holds this planting together. Her mid-pink is both classic and fresh, and planted in groups of three, this repeat-blooming rose makes an impact and delivers for a long period over the summer. Palest blue *Geranium pratense* 'Mrs Kendall Clark', pale blue and white *G. p.* 'Summer Skies', and the outstanding violet-blue, white-throated *Campanula lactiflora* 'Prichard's Variety' provide the classic lilac and blue pairing and also successfully carry these contrasting colours over into the shadier borders.

In order to avoid blandness, *Rosa* 'Charles de Mills' makes an appearance at the near end; its extraordinary wine red, with pinkish lilac tones, is then picked up by the dark red thistle knobs of *Cirsium rivulare* 'Atropupureum', which stand as a veil behind. As the borders move from light into shade, the pink of *R.* Mary Rose = 'Ausmary' is echoed by the blush-pink to white *R.* 'Stanwell Perpetual'. A descendant of the native *R. spinosissima*, with the slightly wilder appearance that its provenance suggests, this rose continues to produce flowers all summer long.

Geraniums are these borders' friends. *Geranium phaeum* 'Lily Lovell', with its flared-back purple petals, crosses from side to side and also gives good foliage, as does *Alchemilla mollis*, whose soft green leaves and frothy sprays of lime flowers give repeated zings down along the planting. An overwhelming feeling of casual abundance, of not having to worry if a different colour appears here and there, adds even more length to these borders; the eye enjoys everything it lights upon, rather than experiencing sensory overload, and the planting becomes more and more relaxed as it continues along.

C

D

E

F

	NAME	TYPE	HEIGHT	SPREAD	SEASON	LIGHT	MOISTURE	HARDINESS	SOIL PH
A	*Rosa* Mary Rose = 'Ausmary'	shrub	1-1.5 metres, 4 feet	0.5-1 metre, 4 feet	summer	full sun	moist but well-drained / well-drained	very hardy, USDA 4-11	acid / alkaline / neutral
B	*Rosa* 'Charles de Mills'	shrub	1-1.5 metres, to 5 feet	1-1.5 metres, to 5 feet	summer	full sun	moist but well-drained / well-drained	very hardy, USDA 4-8	acid / alkaline / neutral
C	*Cirsium rivulare* 'Atropurpureum'	perennial	1-1.5 metres, 4 feet	0.1-0.5 metre, 1.5-2 feet	summer	full sun	moist but well-drained	very hardy, USDA 4-8	acid / alkaline / neutral
D	*Campanula lactiflora* 'Prichard's Variety'	perennial	0.5-1 metre, 2-2.5 feet	0.1-0.5 metre, 1.5 feet	summer	full sun / partial shade	moist but well-drained	very hardy, USDA 5-7	acid / alkaline / neutral
E	*Geranium pratense* 'Mrs Kendall Clark'	perennial	0.5-1 metre, 2-3 feet	0.5-1 metre, 2-3 feet	summer	full sun / partial shade	moist but well-drained / well-drained	very hardy, USDA 4-8	acid / alkaline / neutral
F	*Geranium phaeum* 'Lily Lovell'	perennial	0.5-1 metre, 1.5-2.5 feet	0.1-0.5 metre, 1-1.5 feet	spring / summer	full sun / partial shade / full shade	moist but well-drained / well-drained	very hardy, USDA 5-7	acid / alkaline / neutral

- 98 -

What Isn't There

Mostly I "see" potential designs in colour, but I do sometimes like to consider differently textured or shaped plants in black and white, to see if the composition of light and dark works. The first photograph, in colour, appears to show a planting of deep crimsons and reddish purples. But when reduced to black and white, as in the second photograph, it shows itself to be a planting of green, with counterpoints—you can see how the roses here provide dots of contrast against the green, with the salvia doing the same, creating spires against the background.

Background tones are vital if a planting is really and truly to sing: tree bark I count as a colour, of course, and here the pale grey of the multi-stemmed *Carpinus betulus* nicely reflects the surrounding shades of green.

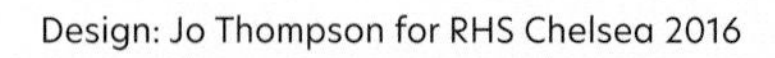

Design: Jo Thompson for RHS Chelsea 2016

A

B

	NAME	TYPE	HEIGHT	SPREAD	SEASON	LIGHT	MOISTURE	HARDINESS	SOIL PH
A	*Rosa* Chianti = 'Auswine'	shrub	1.5-2.5 metres, to 6 feet	1.5-2.5 metres, 5 feet	summer / autumn	full sun	moist but well-drained / well-drained	very hardy, USDA 5-11	acid / alkaline / neutral
B	*Digitalis purpurea* 'Sutton's Apricot'	biennial	1-1.5 metres, 3-4 feet	0.1-0.5 metre, 1-1.5 feet	summer	full sun / partial shade / full shade	moist but well-drained / well-drained	very hardy, USDA 4-8	acid / alkaline / neutral

The cream and green flowerheads of *Angelica archangelica* illuminate what surrounds them, and the placing of these lighter shades of green is really important here: positioned as they are at the top of dark purple stems, which can reach a metre or more in height, the inflorescences create the impression of bursts of lights over the showstopping roses. The lime green of these flowers (together with the leaves, happily in the same tone) needs some anchoring, a smaller-flowered version of the same colour—hence the introduction of the fabulously fresh, lime green cups of *Mathiasella bupleuroides* 'Green Dream'.

But to our showstoppers. *Rosa* Chianti = 'Auswine' is mercurial here—at one point crimson, at another purple, over there maroon. Part of this colour variation is, of course, due to the ageing of the individual blooms; the rest of the colour shifts are the result of light reflected by the surrounding layers of green. The pink tones of this rose are enhanced even more by the use of *R*. 'Louise Odier', her rose-pink petals creating the idea of the purples fading away into the background, where they meet with the voluptuous pinks of *Digitalis purpurea* 'Sutton's Apricot'.

Depending on the individual plant, this foxglove can have flowers of apricot, buttermilk, peach, and pink; what I find fascinating is how these colours can be made to appear stronger or weaker, deeper or paler, depending on where they are positioned. Viewed behind *Rosa* 'Louise Odier', they appear pink; when looked at in front of the yew, the more orange-yellow tones start to show themselves.

All this is taking place in front of a very dark green *Taxus baccata* hedge—the deep shades of the yew retreat into the background, creating depth and allowing the roses to perform their starring role. *Salvia nemorosa* 'Caradonna' plays a similar role at the front of this planting, its dark stems with vivid strong purple-violet flowers working with the redder shades to create a well-known and satisfying colour combination.

	NAME	TYPE	HEIGHT	SPREAD	SEASON	LIGHT	MOISTURE	HARDINESS	SOIL PH
C	*Mathiasella bupleuroides* 'Green Dream'	perennial	0.5-1 metre, to 5 feet	0.5-1 metre, to 5 feet	spring / summer / autumn	full sun / partial shade / full shade	well-drained	half hardy, USDA 5-11	acid / alkaline / neutral
D	*Angelica archangelica*	perennial	1.5-2.5 metres, 3-6 feet	0.5-1.5 metres, 2-4 feet	summer	full sun / partial shade	moist but well-drained / poorly drained	very hardy, USDA 5-7	acid / alkaline / neutral
E	*Salvia nemorosa* 'Caradonna'	perennial	0.1-0.5 metre, 1-2 feet	0.1-0.5 metre, 1-2 feet	summer	full sun / partial shade	moist but well-drained	very hardy, USDA 4-8	acid / alkaline / neutral

– 99 –

Regal Purple to Pink

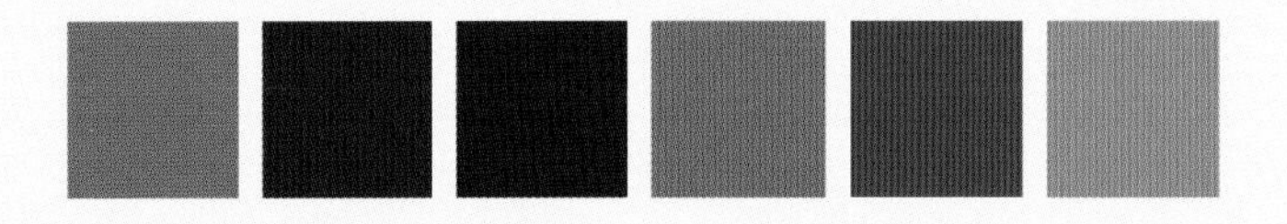

If you want to summon up a bit of richness to your mind's eye, just whisper this Shipping Forecast of colour: claret, orchil, burgundy, rose madder.

Who knows what it is that you see, though? Do we see the colour, or attach the emotion to the shades in this range and then file them accordingly? I look at this astrantia, and I see deep velvet stained with orchil, a purple, but I look again—I strip away the sumptuousness of the effect and then take a steadier look at the colour chart. It appears that what I'm seeing is actually more of a Lee Krasner pink, layers of the deepest and newest pinks worked up over grey-green and emerald.

Hints of red, tints of brown, a drop of blue: looking at what we think of as a wine colour gives a clue as to what will work just perfectly alongside it in this composition. In the first photograph, at Allt y bela, Arne Maynard demonstrates perfectly how to use this irresistible, gently seductive colour. For meadow-freshness, the

Design: Arne Maynard, Clare Coulson

	NAME	TYPE	HEIGHT	SPREAD	SEASON	LIGHT	MOISTURE	HARDINESS	SOIL PH
A	*Digitalis parviflora*	perennial	0.5-1 metre, 3 feet	0.1-0.5 metre, 2 feet	summer	full sun / partial shade / full shade	moist but well-drained / poorly drained	half hardy, USDA 4-8	acid / alkaline / neutral
B	*Knautia macedonica*	perennial	0.5-1 metre, 1.5-2 feet	0.1-0.5 metre, 1.5-2 feet	summer	full sun	well-drained	very hardy, USDA 5-9	alkaline / neutral

backdrop foliage is a palette of grass green. What comes next is interesting: *Digitalis parviflora* and *Echium vulgare*, verticals in silver and the iciest blues, contrast with the buttons of *Astrantia major* 'Claret' and reflect light back to us—a gauze manipulating the light and creating magic.

Later in the year, in her garden, writer Clare Coulson takes a slightly redder claret, this time in the second flush of the pincushions of *Knautia macedonica*. To achieve what comes next, she looks at the blues: scattered in front of glaucous grey-blue foliage of *Euphorbia characias* subsp. *wulfenii*, the knautia's wine-coloured buttons are exquisite, jewellery-box perfection. As the petals fall, the flowerheads glimmer as they catch the autumn light, looking for all the world as if they were born to glimmer up and down alongside the vivid purple stems of *Salvia nemorosa* 'Caradonna', which seems to light up the whole garden as it catches the light; and this too, as it goes over, continues to be one brilliant performer. Look at the contrast with the flowers that have gone over: fuzzy inflorescences of light-reflecting dazzle.

Winifred Nicholson (pseudonym Winifred Dacre) wrote that only great colourists knew how to unleash all the shades of violet—wine, vieux rose, mulberry—"It is a safe indication of their mastery." Nostalgic, regal, sophisticated, mysterious—the use of purple-to-pink is an artist's mastery of colour, low-key yet confident in its creation of an atmosphere.

C

D

E

F

	NAME	TYPE	HEIGHT	SPREAD	SEASON	LIGHT	MOISTURE	HARDINESS	SOIL PH
C	*Astrantia major* 'Claret'	perennial	0.5-1 metre, 1-2 feet	0.1-0.5 metre, 0.75-1.5 feet	summer	full sun / partial shade	moist but well-drained / poorly drained	very hardy, USDA 4-7	acid / alkaline / neutral
D	*Echium vulgare*	perennial	0.5-1 metre, 1-2.5 feet	0.1-0.5 metre, 1-1.5 feet	summer	full sun	well-drained	very hardy, USDA 4-8	acid / alkaline / neutral
E	*Salvia nemorosa* 'Caradonna'	perennial	0.1-0.5 metre, 1-2 feet	0.1-0.5 metre, 1-2 feet	summer	full sun / partial shade	moist but well-drained	very hardy, USDA 4-8	acid / alkaline / neutral
F	*Euphorbia characias* subsp. *wulfenii*	perennial	1-1.5 metres, 2-3 feet	1-1.5 metres, 1.5-2 feet	spring / summer	full sun	well-drained	very hardy, USDA 6-8	acid / alkaline / neutral

– 100 –

Airy Purples

It's the smallest spots of colour that sometimes give the biggest impact.

In the breathtaking gardens at Arundel Castle, allium season is something else. Improbable bobbles of purples and blues right along the range, from the deepest noble Tyrian to the palest shimmering lilac, bounce their way along borders, oozing luxurious elegance and delicate sweetness at the same time. There's something about purple that wavers on the love/hate balance of affairs, sophisticated yet potentially melancholy when light is lacking. The key is most definitely the light: silver foliage and the black-green of the taxus hedges bookending the scene combine to magically turn purples to pink; *Allium* 'Purple Rain' is almost rosy at dawn.

Colour psychologists suggest that violet is an inspirational colour, one that helps us connect with our creative side. This mass of alliums is certainly calming and soothing, but the impact comes from more understated drops of colour. I wouldn't dream of saying that tulips are necessarily understated in themselves, but here their remains are still performing a role. White spots of *Tulipa* 'Mondial' and *T.* 'Spring Green' are the bringers of light, while *T.* 'Passionale' is the rosy forerunner. White can be difficult to use as a tulip, wanting

Design: Arundel Castle

	NAME	TYPE	HEIGHT	SPREAD	SEASON	LIGHT	MOISTURE	HARDINESS	SOIL PH
A	*Tulipa* 'Mondial'	bulb	0.3 metre, 0.5-1 foot	0.1 metre, 0.25 foot	spring	full sun	well-drained	very hardy, USDA 3-8	acid / alkaline / neutral
B	*Tulipa* 'Spring Green'	bulb	0.1-0.5 metre, 1.5-1.75 feet	0.1 metre, 0.25 foot	spring	full sun	well-drained	very hardy, USDA 3-8	acid / alkaline / neutral

all the attention if planted in large groups, but here we have an example of how to harness the light, the tulips, going over, giving just enough of a highlight to provide relief amongst all those shades of purple. They are very definitely white, not the grey of Wittgenstein, who helpfully observed, "Whether I see something as grey or white can depend upon how I see the things around me illumined."

The blues of the purples are picked up in foliage, with alchemilla and santolina bringing varying levels of blue to the scheme. The blues and the greys really do something here: along the length of the borders there's a feeling of a hint of frost, as all the breathy silvers in the foliage add to the general airiness of the colour palette, so neatly compartmentalised by dark slices of yew and greener-green buxus blobs.

	NAME	TYPE	HEIGHT	SPREAD	SEASON	LIGHT	MOISTURE	HARDINESS	SOIL PH
C	*Tulipa* 'Passionale'	bulb	0.5 metre, 1-2 feet	0.15 metre, 0.25 foot	spring	full sun	well-drained	very hardy, USDA 3-8	acid / alkaline / neutral
D	*Allium* 'Purple Rain'	bulb	0.5-1 metre, 3 feet	0.1-0.5 metre, 1-1.5 feet	summer	full sun	well-drained	hardy, USDA 3-8	acid / alkaline / neutral

Acknowledgements

I'd like to thank Chris Young, who invited me to write this book. Also thank you to Stacee Lawrence, for her enthusiastic trust, and to Franni Farrell, for her dedicated checking of absolutely everything. I'm immensely grateful to all the Timber Press team for their support and help.

I'd also like to thank my wonderful studio team at Jo Thompson Landscape & Garden Design, especially Joanna Lowe. All images supplied by me were taken by Katy Donaldson.

I couldn't have written this book without the extraordinary patience and tolerance of my children: thank you George and Cecilia—perhaps now I might even have time to cook supper again. Finally, an enormous and heartfelt thank-you to my mother and father, who instilled my passion for gardens and art and who have always tirelessly, patiently, and enthusiastically supported and believed in me. I'm grateful.

Further Reading

Beales, Peter
A Passion for Roses
Classic Roses

Bennett, Jackie
The Artist's Garden

Chatto, Beth
The Green Tapestry

Christopher, Marina
Late Summer Flowers

Foster, Clare
Painterly Plants

Grigson, Geoffrey
The Englishman's Flora

Jekyll, Gertrude
Colour Schemes for the Flower Garden

Lloyd, Christopher
Christopher Lloyd's Garden Flowers
The Well-Tempered Garden
Colour for Adventurous Gardeners
Christopher Lloyd's Gardening Year

Mabey, Richard
Flora Britannica

Maynard, Arne
The Gardens of Arne Maynard

Mullet, Carolyn
Adventures in Eden

Pope, Nori and Sandra
Planting with Colour

Sneesby, Richard
RHS Colour Companion

St. Clair, Kassia
The Secret Lives of Colour

Stuart Thomas, Graham
The Graham Stuart Thomas Rose Book

Wilson, Andrew
Contemporary Colour in the Garden

Resources

United Kingdom

Arvensis Perennials
perennials
Lower Wraxall
Bradford-on-Avon, Wiltshire
BA15 2RU
01225 867761
arvensisperennials.co.uk

Ashwood Nurseries
hellebores
Ashwood Lower Lane
Kingswinford, West Midlands
DY6 0AE
01384 401996
ashwoodnurseries.com

Beth Chatto's Plants & Gardens
over 2,000 plants
Elmstead Market
Colchester, Essex
CO7 7DB
01206 822007
bethchatto.co.uk

Binny Plants
peonies
Binny Estate
Ecclesmachan Road
Uphall, Scotland
EH52 6NL
binnyplants.com

Bluebell Cottage Gardens and Nursery
flowering perennials
Lodge Lane
Dutton, Cheshire
WA4 4HP
01928 713718
bluebellcottage.co.uk

Bressingham Nursery
agapanthus, perennials
Low Rd
Diss, Norfolk
IP22 2AA
01379 688282
thebressinghamgardens.com

Burncoose Nurseries
azaleas, camellias, hydrangeas, magnolias, rhododendrons
Gwennap
Redruth, Cornwall
TR16 6BJ
burncoose.co.uk

Claire Austin Hardy Plants
perennials, irises, peonies
White Hopton Farm
Wern Lane
Sarn, Newtown
SY16 4EN
01686 670342
claireaustin-hardyplants.co.uk

Crûg Farm Plants
rare plants
Griffith's Crossing
Caernarfon, Gwynedd
LL55 1TU
01248 670232
crug-farm.co.uk

David Austin Roses
roses
Bowling Green Lane
Albrighton, Shropshire
WV7 3HB
0800 1114699
davidaustinroses.co.uk

Duchy of Cornwall Nursery
climate-suited plants for the Southwest, houseplants
Cott Road
Lostwithiel, Cornwall
PL22 0HW
01208 872668
duchyofcornwallnursery.co.uk

Easton Walled Gardens
snowdrops, sweet peas
Easton, Grantham, Lincolnshire
NG33 5AP
01476 530063
visiteaston.co.uk

Edrom Nurseries
rare and unusual plants, Asian specialty
Coldingham, Eyemouth
Berwickshire, Scotland
TD14 5TZ
01890 771386
edrom-nurseries.co.uk

Edulis
rare plants, unusual edibles
1 Flowers Piece
Ashampstead, Reading
RG8 8SG
01635 578113
edulis.co.uk

Fibrex Nurseries
pelargonium, hedera
Honeybourne Road
Pebworth
Stratford-upon-Avon, Warwickshire
CV37 8XP
01789 720788
fibrex.co.uk

Great Dixter
specialty perennials, Great Dixter Seeds
Northiam
Rye, East Sussex
TN31 6PH
greatdixter.co.uk

Hardy's Cottage Garden Plants
herbaceous perennials
Priory Lane Nursery
Freefolk Prior
Whitchurch, Hampshire
RG28 7FA
01256 896533
hardysplants.co.uk

Hayloft Plants
rare plants
The Pack House
Manor Farm Nursery
Pensham, Pershore
WR10 3HB
01386 562999
hayloft.co.uk

Iris of Sissinghurst
irises
Roughlands Farm
Goudhurst Road
Marden, Kent
TN12 9NH
01622 831511
irisofsissinghurst.com

King John's Nursery
specialty perennials
Sheepstreet Lane
Etchingham, East Sussex
TN19 7AZ
01580 819220
kingjohnsnursery.co.uk

Knoll Gardens
ornamental grasses, flowering perennials
Stapehill Road
Hampreston, Wimborne
BH21 7ND
01202 873931
knollgardens.co.uk

Pan-Global Plants
rare plants
The Walled Garden
Frampton Court
Frampton-on-Severn, Gloucestershire
GL2 7EX
01452 741641
panglobalplants.com

Perrie Hale Nursery
trees, specimen trees, specialty fruit trees, hedging
Perrie Hale Nursery Ltd
Northcote Hill, Honiton
EX14 9TH
01404 43344
perriehale.co.uk

Peter Beales Roses
roses
London Road, Attleborough
Norwich, Norfolk
NR17 1AY
01953 454707
classicroses.co.uk

Phoenix Perennial Plants
pollinator perennials, hardy and uncommon perennials
Paice Lane, Medstead
Alton, Hampshire
GU34 5PR
01420 560695
phoenixperennialplants.co.uk

Special Plants Nursery
herbaceous perennials, tender perennials, annuals, biennials, grasses, umbels
Greenways Lane
Cold Ashton
Chippenham, Wiltshire
SN14 8LA
01225 891686
specialplants.net

Taylors Clematis
clematis
Sutton Road, Sutton
Askern, Doncaster
DN6 9JZ
taylorsclematis.co.uk

Thorncroft Clematis Nursery
clematis
Merryfield
North Green, Reymerston
Norwich, Norfolk
NR9 4RD
01953 850407
thorncroftclematis.co.uk

Woottens of Wenhaston
bearded iris, hemerocallis, auriculas, pelargoniums, hardy geraniums
The Iris Field
Hall Road
Wenhaston, Suffolk
IP19 9HF
01502 478258
woottensplants.com

North America

Annie's Annuals and Perennials
annuals, California natives
740 Market Ave.
Richmond, CA 94801
888.266.4370
anniesannuals.com

Arrowhead Alpines
rare and unusual perennials, woodland wildflowers, ferns, alpines, dwarf conifers
Fowlerville, MI 48836
517.223.3581
arrowheadalpines.com

Avant Gardens
dramatic perennials, succulents
710 High Hill Road
Dartmouth, MA 02747
508.998.8819
avantgardensne.com

Bluebird Nursery
mail-order and specialty
519 Bryan Street
Clarkson, NE 68629
800.356.9164
bluebirdnursery.com

Bluestone Perennials
perennials, shrubs, mums, ornamental grasses
7211 Middle Ridge Road
Madison, OH 44057
800.852.5243
bluestoneperennials.com

Botanus
perennials, dahlias, lilies, begonias
Box 3184
Langley, BC V3A 4R5
Canada
604.513.0100
botanus.com

Brent and Becky's Bulbs
bulbs, perennials, seeds
7900 Daffodil Lane
Gloucester, VA 23061
804.693.3966
brentandbeckysbulbs.com

Broken Arrow Nursery
woody plants and perennials
13 Broken Arrow Road
Hamden, CT 06518
203.288.1026
brokenarrownursery.com

Digging Dog Nursery
unusual perennials, ornamental grasses
31101 Middle Ridge Road
Albion, CA 95410
707.937.1130
diggingdog.com

Edelweiss Perennials
mail-order specialty perennials, trumpet gentians
29800 S Barlow Road
Canby, OR 97013
edelweissperennials.com

Far Reaches Farm
mail-order, botanically important rare plants
1818 Hastings Ave.
Port Townsend, WA 98368
360.385.5114
farreachesfarm.com

Flamingo Road Nursery
palms, shade plants, trees, tropicals
1655 S Flamingo Road
Davie, FL 33325
954-476-7878
flamingoroadnursery.com

Fraser's Thimble Farms
native plants, hardy orchids, hepaticas, hellebores
175 Arbutus Road
Salt Spring Island, BC V8K 1A3
Canada
250.537.5788
thimblefarms.com

Gardino Nursery
rare and unusual plants, hoyas, tropicals
Loxahatchee Groves, FL 33470
888.241.1572
gardinonursery.com

Harbour Breezes
daylilies and Japanese iris
10099 Highway #7
Head of Jeddore, NS B0J 1P0
Canada
902.889.3179

Heritage Flower Farm
heirloom flowers
33725 Highway L
Mukwonago, WI 53149
heritageflowerfarm.com

High Country Gardens
water-wise perennials and bulbs
Box 22398
Santa Fe, NM 87502
800.925.9387
highcountrygardens.com

Joy Creek Nursery
mail-order clematis, fuchsia, hosta, hydrangea, penstemon
20300 NW Watson Road
Scappoose, OR 97056
503.543.7474
joycreek.com

Logee's
fruiting, rare, and tropical plants
141 North Street
Danielson, CT 06239
860.774.8038
logees.com

Phoenix Perennial Plants
hellebores, hardy subtropicals, over 4,000 perennials
3380 No. 6 Road
Richmond, BC V6V 1P5
Canada
604.270.4133
phoenixperennials.com

Plant Delights Nursery
mail-order specialty perennials, unusual natives
9241 Sauls Road
Raleigh, NC 27603
919.772.4794
plantdelights.com

Plant Material
California natives, water-wise perennials, succulents
3350 Eagle Rock Blvd
Los Angeles, CA 90065
323.474.6842
plant-material.com

Pleasant Run Nursery
new plants, unusual woody ornamentals,
grasses, perennials, vines
93 Ellisdale Road
Allentown, NJ 08501
609.259.8585
pleasantrunnursery.com

Prairie Moon Nursery
North American natives, grasses
32115 Prairie Lane
Winona, MN 55987
866.417.8156
prairiemoon.com

Richard Lyon's Nursery
rare tropicals, palms, fruit trees
20200 SW 134 Ave.
Miami, FL 33177
305.251.6293
richardlyonsnursery.com

Roseland Nursery
potted roses
247 Main Street
Acushnet, MA 02743
508.995.4212
roselandroses.com

Schreiner's Iris Gardens
iris rhizomes
3625 Quinaby Road NE
Salem, OR 97303
503.393.3232
schreinersgardens.com

White Flower Farm
bulbs, perennials, annuals, vines
Box 50, Route 63
Litchfield, CT 06759
800.503.9624
whiteflowerfarm.com

Wildflower Farm
seed for North American wildflowers and grasses
10195 Hwy 12
Coldwater, ON L0K 1E0
Canada
866.476.9453
wildflowerfarm.com

Xera Plants
low-water plants, West Coast native plants
1114 SE Clay Street
Portland, OR 97214
503.236.8563
xeraplants.com

RHS Hardiness Ratings

RATING	TEMPERATURE RANGES (°C)	CATEGORY	DEFINITION
H1a	>15	Heated greenhouse – tropical	Under glass all year.
H1b	10 - 15	Heated greenhouse – subtropical	Can be grown outside in the summer in hotter, sunny and sheltered locations (such as city centre areas), but generally perform better under glass all year round.
H1c	5 - 10	Heated greenhouse – warm temperate	Can be grown outside in the summer throughout most of the UK while day-time temperatures are high enough to promote growth. (Most bedding plants, tomatoes and cucumbers).
H2	1 - 5	Tender – cool or frost-free greenhouse	Tolerant of low temperatures, but not surviving being frozen. Except in frost-free inner-city areas or coastal extremities requires glasshouse conditions. Can be grown outside once risk of frost is over. (Most succulents, many subtropical plants, annual bedding plants, many spring-sown vegetables).
H3	1 - -5	Half hardy – unheated greenhouse/mild winter	Hardy in coastal and relatively mild parts of the UK except in severe winters and at risk from sudden (early) frosts. May be hardy elsewhere with wall shelter or good microclimate. Likely to be damaged or killed in cold winters, particularly with no snow cover or if pot grown. Can often survive with some artificial protection in winter. (Many Mediterranean-climate plants, spring sown vegetables for later harvesting).
H4	-10 - -5	Hardy – average winter	Hardy though most of the UK apart from inland valleys, at altitude and central/northerly locations. May suffer foliage damage and stem dieback in harsh winters in cold gardens. Some normally hardy plants may not survive long wet winters in heavy or poorly drained soil. Plants in pots are more vulnerable to harsh winters, particularly evergreens and many bulbs. (Many herbaceous and woody plants, winter brassicas, leeks).
H5	-15 - -10	Hardy – cold winter	Hardy in most places throughout the UK even in severe winters. May not withstand open/exposed sites or central/northern locations. Many evergreens will suffer foliage damage, and plants in pots will be at increased risk. (Many herbaceous and woody plants, some brassicas, leeks).
H6	-20 - -15	Hardy – very cold winter	Hardy in all of UK and northern Europe. Many plants grown in containers will be damaged unless given protection. (Herbaceous and woody plants from continental climates).
H7	< -20	Very hardy	Hardy in the severest European continental climates including exposed upland locations in the UK. (Herbaceous and woody plants from continental climates).

Hardiness rating notes:

1. *New hardiness ratings supersede the previous RHS hardiness ratings (H1-H4) which are not the direct equivalents of the new ratings.*
2. *The temperature ranges are intended to be absolute minimum winter temperatures (°C), not the long-term average annual extreme minimum temperature used for the USDA zones.*

Photo and Illustration Credits

Pages 15, 16 (top right, lower left), 18, 19 (lower left, right), 56, 57 (top left), 58–59, 60, 62, 65, 75, 108, 110–111, 114–115, 192–193, 196, 200, 202–203, 204 (left), 205 (lower left), 214, 215 (lower left), 220–221, 346–347, Rachel Warne.

Page 19 (top left), Wikimedia / Derek Ramsey.

Pages 21, 175 (top left), GAP Photos / Richard Bloom.

Page 22 (lower left), iStock / mr_coffee.

Page 22 (lower middle), Wikimedia / Paul Paradis.

Pages 24, 164, Andrew Fisher Tomlin.

Pages 27 (top), 37, 48–49, 148–149, 171, 182–183, 224–225, 298, 300–301, 318–319, 322, 354, Jason Ingram.

Page 27 (bottom), Gift of U. Jannink-Veraguth, Paris. Courtesy of the Rijksmuseum.

Page 28 (top left), Shutterstock / Ctatiana.

Page 28 (top right), Shutterstock / Nancy J. Ondra.

Page 28 (lower left), Alamy / RM Floral.

Page 28 (lower middle), Shutterstock / LariBat.

Page 28 (lower right), Trees and Shrubs Online (treesandshrubsonline.org/articles/itoa/itoa-orientalis/).

Pages 30, 119, GAP Photos.

Pages 31 (top right), 34 (middle), Alan Buckingham.

Pages 32–33, 123, 126, 128–129, 130 (top left), 132–133, 144–145, 153, 350–351, Marianne Majerus.

Page 34 (left), Dreamstime / Agniete.

Pages 35 (left), 127 (top right), 190 (top), 191 (top right, lower middle), 206–207, 210–211, 336, 353 (top), Katy Donaldson.

Page 38 (middle left), Shutterstock / Danny Hummel.

Page 38 (lower left), GAP Photos / Christina Bollen.

Page 38 (lower middle), Shutterstock / blue caterpillar.

Pages 40–41, 79, 96, 99, 136–137, 157, 161, 166–167, 174, 176–177, 186–187, Caitlin Atkinson.

Page 42 (top left), Keir Morse.

Page 42 (top right), Wikimedia / Tangopaso.

Page 42 (lower left), Shutterstock / NilaSito.

Page 43 (middle), Wikimedia / Daderot.

Page 43 (right), Wikimedia / Forest and Kim Starr.

Page 44 (left), National Gallery of Art, Ailsa Mellon Bruce Collection, #1970.17.21.

Pages 44–45, Oehme, van Sweden.

Pages 48–49, 148–149 by kind permission of Jade and Julian Dunkerton.

Pages 54 (bottom), 158 (top right), 264 (top left), 327 (lower right), Shutterstock / Peter Turner Photography.

Pages 68, 89 (top), 180, 268–269, 273, 276–277, 325, 338–339, Elke Borkowski / gardenpicturesock.com.

Page 69 (top), Wikimedia / Chihiro H.

Page 69 (lower right), GAP Photos / Elke Borkowski.

Page 72 (top left), iStock / Juan Francisco Moreno Gamez.

Page 73 (top left), Wikimedia / Xemenendura.

Page 76 (top left), Plant Photo Stock / Matthew Beardsworth.

Page 76 (top right), Alamy / garfotos.

Page 77, Lee Beel.

Page 80 (lower left), iStock / mdurajczyk.

Page 82, GAP Photos / Marcus Harpur.

Page 83 (lower left), Alamy / Steffen Hauser / botanikfoto.

Pages 84–85, Marcus Harpur.

Page 89 (bottom), Alamy / Asar Studios.

Page 90 (left), Shutterstock / Yiyi Huli.

Page 90 (right), Shutterstock / Bryan Neuswanger.

Pages 92–93, Marianne Cartwright-Hignett.

Page 97 (top left), Flickr / UC Davis Arboretum and Public Garden.

Page 97 (top right), Shutterstock / Sachi_g.

Page 100 (top left, lower left), Wikimedia / Stickpen.

Page 104, National Gallery of Art, Collection of Mr. and Mrs. Paul Mellon, #2013.122.1.

Page 112 (top left), Alamy / Antonio Siwiak.

Page 114, University of Michigan Museum of Art, Gift of the Carey Walker Foundation, #1994/1.71.

Pages 121, 143, 155, 185, 237, RHS / Joanna Kossak.

Page 124 (top left), iStock / Nahhan.

Pages 127 (top left), 344 (top right), Wikimedia / Salicyna.

Page 130 (lower left), Wikimedia / TANAKA Juuyoh (田中十洋).

Page 132, Alamy / Martin Thomas Photography.

Page 138 (left), Wikimedia / Stan Shebs.

Page 142 (top left), Shutterstock / simona pavan.

Pages 147 (right), 181 (lower left), 274 (top left), Alamy / Botanic World.

Page 150 (right), Alamy / Tim Gainey.

Page 151 (lower left), Alamy / Mim Friday.

Page 152, National Gallery of Art, Chester Dale Collection, #1963.10.182.

Page 154 (top middle), Wikimedia / Gideon Pisanty (Gidip) יטנזיפ ןועדג.

Page 158 (lower right), Shutterstock / OskarWells.

Page 159 (lower left), Shutterstock / Thomas Trompeter.

Page 160, Met Museum. Bequest of Stephen C. Clark, 1960. #61.101.5.

Page 162 (top left), Wikimedia / C T Johansson.

Page 162 (top right), iStock / igaguri_1.

Page 162 (middle right), Shutterstock / Myimagine.

Page 165 (top right), Alamy / Organica.

Page 168 (top left), iStock / thittaya itthithepphana.

Page 168 (lower right), Shutterstock / Iva Villi.

Page 169 (right), Shutterstock / VojtaMaur.

Page 170, 2021 Georgia O'Keeffe Museum / Artists Rights Society (ARS), New York.

Page 175 (lower middle), Wikimedia / Diego Delso, delso.photo.

Page 181 (top left), GAP Photos / John Glover.

Page 181 (right), Shutterstock / Wiert nieuman.

Page 188 (top left), Shutterstock / MetaCynth.

Page 188 (top right), Shutterstock / Marinodenisenko.

Page 190 (bottom), GAP Photos / Martin Hughes-Jones.

Page 215 (top left), iStock / TonyBaggett.

Pages 218 (lower left), 260, GAP Photos / Jonathan Buckley.

Page 220, National Gallery of Art, Collection of Mr. and Mrs. Paul Mellon, #1973.68.1.

Page 227 (lower left), Alamy / Bailey-Cooper Photography.

Page 227 (lower right), Alamy / Botany vision.

Pages 229, 342–343, 358–359, Mimi Connolly.

Page 230 (lower left), Wikimedia / David J. Stang.

Page 230 (lower middle), Dreamstime / Andersastphoto.

Page 231, The Art Institute of Chicago, Mr. and Mrs. Martin A. Ryerson Collection, #1933.1156.

Pages 232, 235, Marion Brenner.

Page 233 (bottom), iStock / Paulbr.

Page 234, Musée d'Orsay, Dist. RMN-Grand Palais, RF 1947 15. Photo by Patrice Schmidt.

Page 236 (lower right), Shutterstock / Michael G McKinne.

Page 242, Dreamstime / Sergeychernov.

Pages 246, 247–248, 252–253, Stephen Dunn.

Page 247, (top right), Shutterstock / Gonzalo de Miceu.

Page 247 (lower left), Shutterstock / Joe Gough.

Page 247 (lower middle), Alamy / Jeffrey Blackler.

Page 247 (lower right), Shutterstock / Damsea.

Page 250, Shutterstock / Ken Schulze.

Page 251 (top left), Dreamstime / Mollynz.

Page 251 (lower left), Shutterstock / schinkenhuber.

Page 252, Musée d'Orsay, Dist. RMN-Grand Palais. Bequest of Gustave Caillebotte, 1894. RF 2778. Photo by Patrice Schmidt.

Page 255 (left), Shutterstock / Nancy J. Ondra.

Page 255 (top right), Shutterstock / anutr tosirikul.

Page 255 (lower right), Shutterstock / Shahril KHMD.

Page 263 (bottom), The Art Institute of Chicago. With permission of the Renate, Hans & Maria Hofmann Trust / Artists Rights Society (ARS), New York.

Page 265, RHS / Tim Sandall.

Page 270 (right), Shutterstock / Bubushonok.

Page 282 (lower right), Shutterstock / Brian Maudsley.

Page 284 (bottom), National Gallery Prague, Collection of 19th-century Art and Classical Modernism, #18969.

Page 286, The J. Paul Gettty Museum, Object #82. DD.68.

Page 292 (top left), Rhodyman.net / Steve Henning.

Pages 293, 331, RHS / Mark Winwood.

Page 299 (top right), Shutterstock / gianpihada.

Page 299 (lower left), Wikimedia / Agnieszka Kwiecień, Nova.

Page 303 (top left), Dreamstime / Thetinyphotographer.

Page 308, Tate Museum. Accepted by the nation as part of the Turner Bequest 1856, #N00532.

Page 310 (middle), GAP Photos / Christina Bollen.

Pages 313 (right), 341 (top right), GAP Photos / Robert Mabic.

Page 317, Clive Nichols.

Page 320 (left), Shutterstock / Cesar J. Pollo.

Page 327 (top middle and right), Shutterstock / Sergey V Kalyakin.

Page 327 (lower left), Alamy / AY Images.

Page 330 (right), Shutterstock / Gardens by Design.

Page 340 (left), GAP Photos / John Swithinbank.

Page 340 (right), GAP Photos / Fiona McLeod.

Page 341 (top left), Shutterstock / InfoFlowersPlants.

Page 344 (left), Wikimedia / A. Barra.

Page 344 (top right), Wikimedia / Salicyna.

Page 355, Clare Coulson.

Page 360 (left), Shutterstock / AlZayakina.

Page 361 (top), Dreamstime / Werner39.

All other photos are courtesy of the author or the RHS.

Index